Introduction to Operating Systems

A Survey Course

Mary S. Gorman
Tri-State Business Institute

S. Todd Stubbs
Brigham Young University

South-Western
Computer Education
an imprint of Course Technology
Thomson Learning™

Australia • Canada • Mexico • Singapore • Spain • United Kingdom • United States

Publishing Team Leader:	Carol Volz
Project Manager:	Cheryl Beck
Production Coordinator:	Angela McDonald
Art/Design Coordinator:	Mike Broussard
Marketing Manager:	Kimberly Woods
Cover Design:	Grannan Graphic Design
Production Services:	GEX Publishing Services

ISBN: 0-538-72405-6 (perfect bound, soft cover)

1 2 3 4 5 6 7 8 9 10 BM 08 07 06 05 04 03 02 01

Printed in the United States of America

Course Technology is a division of Thomson Learning.

For permission to use material from this text or product, contact us by

- web: www.thomsonrights.com
- Phone: 1-800-730-2214
- Fax: 1-800-730-2215

Introducing our new survey course on Operating Systems

Introduction to Operating Systems
- Student Text (soft cover, perfect bound) — 0-538-72405-6
- Electronic Instructor Package (CD-ROM) — 0-538-72406-4
- Course Test Manager — 0-538-72407-2

A new feature is the *Electronic Instructor*, a CD-ROM which includes lesson plans, SCANS correlations, scheduling charts, and much more!

Other available books include the following:

Microsoft Windows Millennium Edition Comprehensive Course
- Student Text (hard cover, spiral bound) — 0-538-72400-5
- Student Text/Data CD-ROM Package (soft cover, perfect bound) — 0-538-72401-3
- Electronic Instructor Package (CD-ROM) — 0-538-72402-1
- Testing Package — 0-538-72403-X

Microsoft Windows Millennium Edition Beginning Course
- Student Text/Data CD-ROM Package (soft cover, perfect bound) — 0-538-72418-8
- Electronic Instructor Package (Manual and CD-ROM) — 0-538-72419-6

Microsoft Windows 2000 Professional
- Textbook (perfect bound, soft cover) — 0-538-68910-2
- Study Guide — 0-538-68911-0
- Electronic Instructor Package — 0-538-68912-9

Microsoft Windows 2000 Server
- Textbook (perfect bound, soft cover) — 0-538-68900-5
- Study Guide — 0-538-68901-3
- Electronic Instructor Package — 0-538-68902-1

Microsoft Windows Networking Essentials
- Text (perfect bound, soft cover) — 0-538-68477-1
- Study Guide (perfect bound, soft cover) — 0-538-68479-8
- Electronic Instructor CD-ROM — 0-538-68705-3
- NT Curriculum Guide — 0-538-69313-4
- NT Testing Package — 0-538-68592-1

For more information about these South-Western products and others:
**Join Us On the Internet at
www.course.com/swep**

**South-Western
Computer Education**
an imprint of Course Technology
Thomson Learning™

How to Use This Book

What makes a good computer instructional text? Sound pedagogy and the most current, complete materials. That is what you will find in *Introduction to Operating Systems*. Not only will you find an inviting layout but also many features to enhance learning.

Objectives—
Objectives are listed at the beginning of each chapter, along with a suggested time for completion of the chapter. This allows you to look ahead to what you will be learning and to pace your work.

SCANS—(Secretary's Commission on Achieving Necessary Skills) The U.S. Department of Labor has identified the school-to-careers competencies. The eight workplace competencies and foundation skills are identified in the exercises where they apply. More information on SCANS can be found on the *Electronic Instructor*.

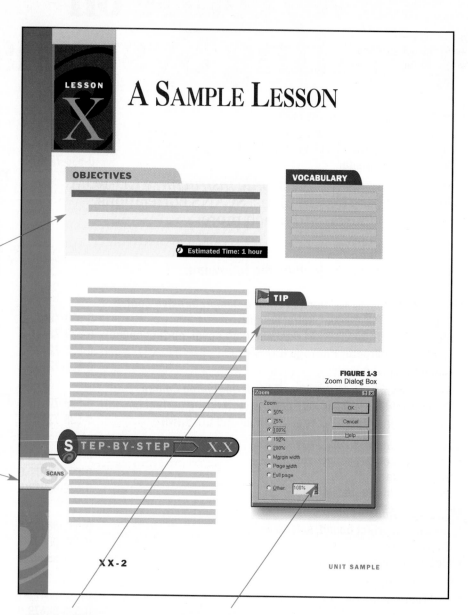

Marginal Boxes—
These boxes provide additional information for Hot Tips, fun facts (Did You Know?), Computer Concepts, Internet Web sites, Extra Challenges activities, and Teamwork ideas.

Enhanced Screen Shots—Screen shots now come to life on each page with color and depth.

How to Use This Book

Summary—At the end of each chapter you will find a summary to prepare you to complete the end-of-chapter activities.

Vocabulary Review—Review of important terms defined in each chapter reinforce the concepts learned.

Review Questions—Review material at the end of each chapter and each unit enables you to prepare for assessment of the content presented.

Lesson Projects—End-of-chapter hands-on application of what has been learned in the chapter allows you to actually apply the techniques covered.

Critical Thinking Activities—Each chapter gives you an opportunity to apply creative analysis and use the Help system to solve problems.

Command Summary—At the end of each unit, a command summary is provided for quick reference.

End-of-Unit Projects—End-of-unit hands-on application of concepts learned in the unit provides opportunity for a comprehensive review.

On-the-Job Simulation—A realistic simulation at the end of each unit reinforces the material covered in the unit.

Appendix—Appendix covers computer concepts.

Summary

VOCABULARY REVIEW

LESSON X REVIEW QUESTIONS

LESSON X PROJECT

CRITICAL THINKING

COMMAND SUMMARY

REVIEW QUESTIONS

PROJECTS

SIMULATION

XX-3

Lesson X Sample Lesson

PREFACE

You will find much helpful material in this introductory section. The *How to Use This Book* pages give you a visual summary of the information you will find in the text. Be sure to review the *Guide for Using This Book* to learn about the terminology and conventions used in preparing the pages and to find out what supporting materials are available for use with this book.

An Ideal Book for Anyone

Because computers are such an important subject for all learners, instructors need the support of a well-designed, educationally sound textbook that is supported by strong ancillary materials. *Introduction to Operating Systems* is just such a book.

The textbook includes features that *make learning easy and enjoyable*, yet challenging, for learners. It is also designed with many features that *make teaching easy and enjoyable*, for you. Comprehensive, yet flexible. *Introduction to Operating Systems* is adaptable for a wide variety of class-time schedules.

The text includes a wide range of learning experiences, from activities with one or two commands to projects that sharpen and challenge learners' problem-solving skills. This book is ideal for computer courses with learners who have varying abilities and previous computer experiences.

The chapters in this course contain the following features designed to promote learning:

- Objectives that specify goals students should achieve by the end of each chapter.
- Concept text that explores each new feature in detail.
- Screen captures that help illustrate the concept text.
- Step-by-Step exercises that allow students to practice using the features just introduced.
- Summaries that review the concepts in the chapter.
- Review Questions that test students on the concepts covered in the chapter.
- Projects that provide an opportunity for students to apply the concepts they have learned in the chapter.
- Critical Thinking activities that encourage students to use the knowledge gained in the chapter to solve specific problems.

Acknowledgements

The authors of this book would like to make the following acknowledgments and dedications:

Mary S. Gorman would like to thank her family for all their support. She would also like to thank her colleagues and students for all they have taught her over the past few years. This book is dedicated to her family and especially her father, Bruce M. Gorman: Thank you for always being there for me.

S. Todd Stubbs would like to thank his wonderful family for their long suffering and patience. This book is dedicated to his family: Joy, Sarah, Marc, Matthew, Manda, Sam, Abby, and to his father Stanford Stubbs.

Both authors would like to thank Cheryl Beck, the manager of this product, for all of her help and patience with this book; Joeth Barlas, copyeditor, Karla Russell and GEX Publishing Services, for turning the book from plain text into the wonderful layout you have before you now, and the Course Technology Sales Representatives for making educationally sound presentations about our book. We would also like to thank AutoGraph International, Inc. (*www.augrin.com*) for their EasyCopy and EasyConvert products which made the Linux screen captures and file conversion easy, fast and high quality.

About the Authors

Mary S. Gorman has a bachelor's degree from Edinboro University in Business Administration and Marketing and is currently working on her master's degree in Public Administration. She teaches at Tri-State Business Institute in the Computer Science department.

S. Todd Stubbs has worked with microcomputers for over 18 years as an educator, programmer, writer, editor and instructional technologist in higher education. His bachelor's degree from Brigham Young University is in English and he currently holds a master's degree in Instructional Technology from Utah State University. He is presently an instructional designer at Brigham Young University's Center for Instructional Design. He and his wife, Joy, are the proud parents of five children.

TABLE OF CONTENTS

INTRODUCTION TO OPERATING SYSTEMS

What Is an Operating System?

Without software, a computer is just a pile of electronics that gives off heat. If the hardware is the heart of a computer, then the software is its soul. An *operating system* (OS) is a collection of system programs that allow the user to run program software (software that allows you to perform a task, such as play a game or write a letter). An operating system manages hardware and other programs; it provides very specific resources to the programs it manages. In the most basic terms, the operating system provides an intermediate interface between the hardware and the user(s). In a more general sense, it provides software and hardware management. For software, it loads, executes, and directs input to the program; displays output; and saves and unloads programs. For hardware, it boots the machine when turned on, provides a connection between the CPU and other hardware, manages memory, and allows for upgrades.

How an Operating System Works

The operating system software provides the look and feel of the system known as the *environment*. Most PCs can run one or more operating systems—and each one can have a very different look and feel. Most operating systems are made up of a number of functionally separate pieces that, together, comprise the operating system. The most basic and fundamental part is the kernel.

The *kernel* is responsible for managing all the other system programs; it can be thought of as upper management, which oversees the whole process of operating the computer system. The process involves the integration of the hardware and the software, so users can operate the machine effectively and efficiently to attain their goals.

In order to start understanding how an operating system works, let's look at a simple example. Consider what happens when you type the following command on a DOS machine:

C:\>*dir*

The command here is the directory command, which is used to display a list of files in a directory, the result is a listing of files on the hard drive in the current directory. See Figure 1-1.

See Figure 1-1.

FIGURE 1-1
Result of the dir command

The *shell* is an environment designed to allow a user to manipulate the system. The shell also supplies cues so users know where they are and what is happening. C:\> is a prompt that the operating system shell displays. This prompt means that the system is waiting for the user to type some command. The keyboard driver enables the system to recognize what characters have been typed.

The keyboard driver passes the command to the shell, which processes it by looking for an executable command of the same name. It finds an appropriate match for the command, and the kernel reads the file containing instructions on how to perform that command. The dir command tells the file subsystem of the kernel to find out what files are available. The file system might make use of the file system information or use the disk device driver to read this information from the disk. The dir command then writes that information out and the video driver displays it on the screen. (It is not important that you understand the whole process just listed; just be aware that many things have to operate in concert in order for it to work.)

TIP

A *driver* is a small program used by the operating system that accepts commands from a program and then translates them into commands the hardware can understand. For example, when you choose Print in Microsoft Word, the printer driver translates the print command into commands the printer understands, so it can output the document.

Although this may seem rather complicated, it shows that even simple commands reveal that an operating system is a cooperating set of functions that work together to give you, the user, a coherent view of the system. Don't lose sight of the fact that the hardware is working in the background as well. Each program is responsible for managing a specific piece of hardware. The video card has a video driver, the keyboard has a keyboard driver, the hard drive has its own driver. The drivers can be thought of as middle management. Each driver controls a different part of the system. The kernel is still upper management, overseeing the whole process. The analogy can be extended further: If one of the managers is not doing its job correctly, it affects the whole system. When the drivers are correctly written, everything works perfectly.

Types of Operating Systems

Operating systems have both an inside and an outside—both a body and an engine. Because the instructions are built to work with the machine, human beings can barely read them. Therefore, the operating system must provide a way for humans to communicate with the machine. This part of an operating system (and all other programs) is called the *human-computer interface* (HCI) or, more often, the *user interface* (UI).

Because the UI is the part of the operating system that we see, we tend to categorize the operating system according to its user interface. User interfaces generally fall into one of three types: command-line, menu-based, and graphical.

COMMAND-LINE USER INTERFACES

Command-line user interfaces use the keyboard to communicate with the operating system and the computer. In the command-line UI, the user types in commands and the computer responds to them. The problem is that, because computers must receive their instructions in very precise ways, the user is required to type the commands in a very specific format (called *syntax*). Because this is true, a command-line UI requires the user to either remember a number of arcane commands, or have a book handy that reminds them what to type. Both Unix and DOS are command-line user interfaces. See Figure 1-2.

FIGURE 1-2
A command-line user interface

```
C:\APPROACH>dir

 Volume in drive C has no label
 Volume Serial Number is 1103-0776
 Directory of C:\APPROACH

            <DIR>        06-25-95   7:42p
            <DIR>        06-25-95   7:42p
EXAMPLES    <DIR>        06-25-95   7:42p
TMPLATES    <DIR>        06-25-95   7:42p
ICONS       <DIR>        06-25-95   7:44p
IMGBMP   DIL       7,088 08-18-93  12:00a
IMGTGA   DIL       9,376 08-18-93  12:00a
IMGGIF   DIL       9,888 08-18-93  12:00a
README   WRI       9,984 08-18-93  12:00a
IMGPCX   DIL      15,920 08-18-93  12:00a
IMGEPSF  DIL      20,784 08-18-93  12:00a
IMGTIFF  DIL      38,496 08-18-93  12:00a
APPROACH HLP     215,152 08-18-93  12:00a
APPROACH EXE   1,205,504 08-18-93  12:00a
APPROACH VZ1           3 08-18-93  12:00a
       15 file(s)    1,532,195 bytes
                   139,026,432 bytes free

C:\APPROACH>
```

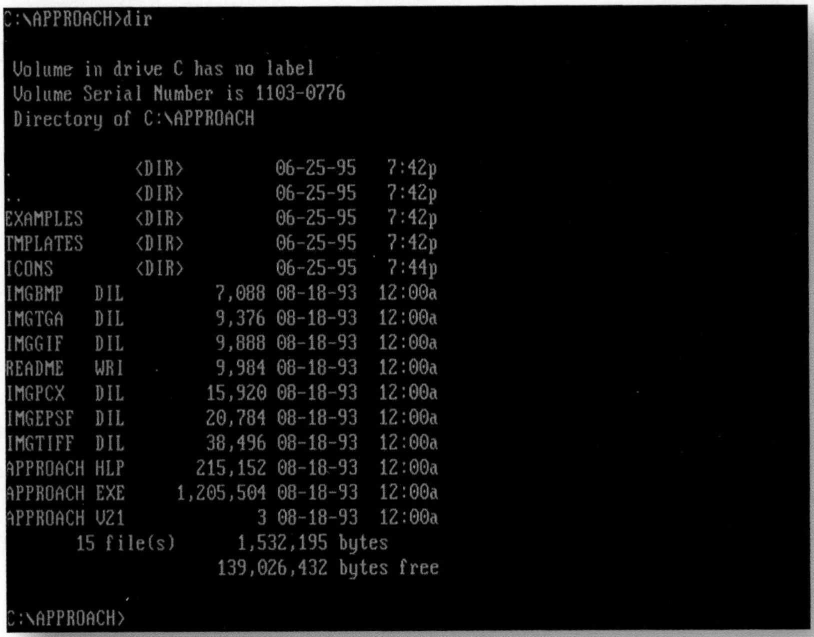

MENU-BASED INTERFACES

Generally speaking, *menu-based user interfaces* are not common in operating systems. However, menus can simplify the use of a command-line UI by providing a list of commands from which to choose. The user selects the menu item by typing an identifier (a number or letter) or by clicking with a mouse, then the menu-based UI types the complete and correct syntax for the user. This makes it much easier for people with few computer skills to interact with a command-line UI.

GRAPHICAL USER INTERFACES

The *graphical user interface* (GUI, pronounced "gooey") is really a very sophisticated form of menu-based interface. However, instead of listing the commands, it represents them as a number of small pictures called *icons*. Windows and MacOS, two of the most popular GUIs, use icons to represent frequently-issued commands. By manipulating these graphic elements with a mouse, the user can open, close, move, and delete files.

Both menu-based interfaces and GUIs are simply *facades* for the command-line interface, which is hidden from the user. Early versions of Windows used this system, as do several of the GUIs for Unix. See Figure 1-3.

FIGURE 1-3
A graphical user interface

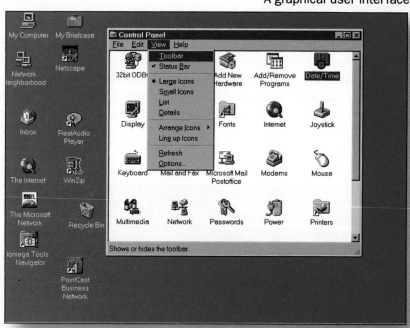

FUTURE USER INTERFACES

User interfaces will inevitably improve. One of the first changes will probably be the introduction of a voice-operated UI, which uses voice commands in lieu of either typed or clicked commands. Another may be the adoption of a three-dimensional look for user interfaces. Connection to worldwide resources will also have an impact on the look and structure of future operating systems.

Hardware

Now that you have some idea of how the computer works, let's take a small tour of its hardware. The following hardware items are physical components you can find in almost any modern computer:

- **CPU**—the *central processing unit*, which is the brain of the computer. Basically it is a microchip that just adds two numbers. From an engineering point of view, division, subtraction, and multiplication are human activities that must be converted into machine terms. For example, machines can't subtract (or divide and multiply). When called upon to subtract, they take a number, convert it into its negative value and add it to another number. To divide, the machine subtracts a number several times and keeps track of how many times it performs the subtraction. To multiply, it simply adds a number several times while keeping a running total: 5×6 = 5+5+5+5+5+5=30. Over the years, many improvements have been added to provide greater functionality and ease of use. Some of these additions allow the CPU to manipulate the data in a more efficient manner.

- **RAM**—random access memory, which functions as the principal workspace of the computer. You change the contents of RAM as you work. However, because RAM chips require power to maintain their content, you must save your data to a disk before you turn off the computer.

- **ROM**—read-only memory, which is programmed once at the factory. You cannot change the contents of ROM. This type of memory is used to store specific control routines, such as the BIOS process described below. ROM instructions are non-volatile; that is, they retain information when you turn off the computer.

- **BIOS**—basic input-output system. This is a ROM chip that has been programmed with the instructions needed to begin the boot process. It contains the necessary code to enable the CPU to talk to the other hardware in the system.

- **Motherboard**—the main circuit board in the computer. On it reside the CPU, RAM, BIOS, and all the other chips your machine needs to run. It also contains empty "expansion" slots where upgrades or expansion cards can be added.

- **Keyboard**—the device used to input information for the computer's programs. It can also be used to manipulate the computer system through keyboard shortcuts that replace using the mouse to communicate with the operating system. For example, when using the Microsoft Word program, the user can click the Save icon on the toolbar with the mouse or press Ctrl + S on the keyboard to save.

- **Mouse**—a generic term for a pointing device, which is used primarily with graphical interfaces. When the user moves the mouse across a surface (say, a table top), a mouse pointer (often in the form of an arrowhead) moves across the screen in a relative motion that corresponds to the motion of the mouse. A mouse has two or more buttons. By placing the pointer at different locations on the screen and then pressing the buttons (clicking), the user can run programs, use menus, and manipulate the system interface.

Classifications of Hardware Components

The hardware components attached to your computer fall into two categories: *input* and *output*. Input components allow the user to communicate information to the computer. The output components allow the communication of information back to the user.

INPUT: KEYBOARD, MOUSE, SCANNER, AND VOICE DEVICES

Input devices such as the keyboard, mouse, scanner, and microphone devices are used to input different kinds of information. Each of these devices has an associated driver that oversees its operation. The driver takes the incoming data, translates it into a common form if needed, and directs it to the appropriate destination. Most input devices include some kind of feedback from an output device (usually the monitor) to let you know whether or not your efforts are working. In the case of the keyboard, your cursor shows you where you are on the screen, while the letters that you type appear on the screen. Other devices may provide feedback in a dialog box that pops up on the screen, or as a change in color or the shape of a symbol.

> **TIP**
>
> QWERTY is the name of the keyboard layout. It is named QWERTY for the first six letters in the left corner of the first alphabetic row.

The *keyboard* is the most common input device. A keyboard is just a collection of spring-loaded switches— one for each letter of the alphabet, number, or symbol. Most keyboards are laid out in a traditional QWERTY pattern that must be learned. Once learned, however, a keyboard allows you to enter text very quickly and efficiently. Special keys on the keyboard, such as Backspace and Delete, allow you to make corrections. Others, such as the Alt or Option keys, can be used in combination with letter keys to display unusual characters. Still others (such as the Control or Command keys) can be used, in combination with letters, to send commands to the program.

As mentioned earlier, the *mouse* is a screen pointing device that helps you move quickly to a certain location on the screen. When you reach the location where you want to work, you use the mouse buttons to make something happen. For example, you might press the mouse button once and let it go; this is called *clicking*. Clicking twice in rapid succession is called *double-clicking*. When you hold the mouse button down as you move the pointer, it's called *dragging*. Each of these gestures produces an action by the computer. These will be discussed in detail for each of the operating systems that use the mouse. Drawing tablets, trackballs, lightpens, and touch-sensitive screens are all variations on the mouse idea. They perform the same function and their names are sometimes used interchangeably.

Another important input device is the *scanner*, which is a close relative of the digital (still) camera and digital movie camera. These devices allow you to capture pictures or other graphics and move them to the computer. Because the input process can be very complex, special programs with buttons and dialog boxes are used to interact with the device and let you know if it's working.

The ability of computers to understand and act on spoken commands was only a dream for many years, but it has recently become a reality. Analyzing human speech is an enormously complex process. As a human being, you perform speech recognition without even thinking about it—it's a tribute to the power of your human brain. Speech recognition requires several devices to work in cooperation: the soundcard, a voice-recognition program, a powerful CPU, and the operating system. Only recently have computers become powerful enough to perform this task. The math involved is extremely complex and the process is time-consuming. To provide feedback, the computer may "type" your message on the screen, as it would with the keyboard. Other indicators, such as an animated icon, may also let you know that you are getting through.

OUTPUT: MONITOR AND PRINTER DEVICES

Computers would be of no value if they could not report back to their human users. The devices for doing so are called *output devices*. The two most common are monitors and printers.

A *monitor* is little more than a fancy television set. However, most monitors lack a tuner for capturing transmitted programs; instead, they take their information directly from the computer. Circuitry inside the computer organizes the electronic signals so that they display properly. Some computers have the circuitry for more than one monitor, and can display more than one screen at a time. Though this configuration is used mostly by professional designers, it gives them the ability to view twice as much information. Monitors that use technology other than the traditional *cathode ray tube* (CRT) displays

6

are becoming more common, with *liquid crystal displays* (LCD) such as those used in digital watches and laptop monitors, and *plasma displays* also becoming popular. The popularity of LCDs and plasma displays lies in the fact that they are flatter (meaning they are only three to five inches from front to back, instead of the usual 15+ inches). They also consume less electricity and con-

A pixel is a term for a picture element. Each dot is a point in an electronic image.

sequently run cooler. The downside is that they have a shorter lifespan than CRTs. Computer monitors traditionally have the same 4:3 aspect ratio as conventional television. This means that if you divide the number of pixels horizontally by 4 and the number of pixels vertically by 3, you get the same number. (For a small monitor, 640 × 480, the common denominator is 160.) Monitors range upward in size from 640 × 480. Some monitors are now appearing in other aspect ratios as well. The operating system (or its extensions) must know the size and type of monitor in order to transmit the correct signals to the monitor.

Early *printers* used actual metal type to print text onto paper. Modern printers use tiny dots of toner or ink to get the same effect and a whole lot more. Modern laser printers (which use lasers to sensitize paper and toner to form the ink) and ink jet printers (which spray tiny droplets of ink on the paper) can be used to print pictures as well as text. With either type of printer, the computer must have the ability to translate the desired output into a form that the printers can understand. Some printers require raw information—that is, information about what dot of ink goes where on the paper. Others can be sent more intelligent information, which then translates into print. Clearly the operating system must be able to speak the printer's language, or printing cannot take place.

Just as computers can receive and act on voice commands, they are able to speak as well. The computer's speakers can be used to play words as well as music and other sounds. Some sounds are used for feedback, others for effect. Most modern computers can even speak instructions to the user from text.

Basic Functionalities of the Operating System

Resource Management

STARTING UP

Turning on a computer is much more complicated than turning on a light bulb or motor. Imagine the processes that are required to turn on a toaster, for example. After you put a piece of bread into the slot and press the lever, at least two other processes must begin: A switch must turn on power to the heating element so the bread can be toasted, and a timing mechanism must keep track of the time elapsed, automatically turn off the heating element at the correct time, and trigger a mechanism to eject the toast.

A computer, by contrast, runs a *program,* a set of detailed instructions on how to do something. The CPU can't load instructions until it knows how and from where to load them. And since nothing has been loaded, it doesn't know where to begin. The computer must find a way to start itself—or, to use the old phrase, "lift itself by its own bootstraps." (In fact, this is where the term *booting* a computer comes from.) To enable a computer to boot itself, designers decided to hard code a standard starting place into every computer. When the computer is turned on, it is set to look at the starting address for the *basic input-output system* (**BIOS**). It then reads the BIOS, the list of all the instructions it needs to get going. The last instruction in the BIOS is to start reading the operating system—first from the diskette drive, or if that is not available, from the hard drive. That way, if the hard drive ever fails, you can use a boot disk to start the computer. The computer just continues to read and execute programs off of the hard drive.

Remember that an operating system is nothing more than a program running on the computer. However, it is unique in that it must oversee all the other programs running on the computer. Part of its job is to make sure that all the parts of the computer are available to the programs that will run on top of the operating system. Modern computers can take considerable time (from five seconds to many minutes) to boot because of the many configurations and connections that must be made to allow for all the various parts of the computer to operate.

SHUTTING DOWN

When you drive a car, you don't drive to the general vicinity of the place you're going and just turn the key off and leave it in the middle of the road. A good driver finds a place to park where the car will be out of harm's way. As the driver, you set the car in a parking gear or set the parking brake, turn off the lights, and so forth. When everything is set, you turn off the key, unbuckle your seat belt, and get out. There is a well-defined procedure people go through to make sure no problems will occur.

A computer has the same needs. There are several processes that need to be finished before power is removed: Data needs to be put away, settings (such as dates and file sizes) need to be calculated and stored, connections with devices and the network need to be terminated, and so forth. The shutdown process accomplishes all of these. It's like putting your tools away after work so you know where they are the next time you want to use them.

If you forget to shut down your computer before turning it off, don't panic. Most operating systems provide for accidents by doing some of these things as you use the computer. If something is damaged by suddenly losing power, tools have been developed to help minimize the damage. If the computer is shut down without going through the entire shutdown cycle, it will take a little time to start up again, and you may notice that you have lost some of your settings when you restart. In most cases settings can be easily restored to their former values.

MULTITASKING AND ALLOCATING CPU CYCLES

Like minicomputers and mainframes, microcomputers have become powerful, complex machines. Unlike their larger cousins, PCs do not always have multiple users using them at the same time; however, they do have to accommodate several programs running simultaneously, as mentioned earlier. In many ways this is the same thing. For example, as I write this paragraph, I am typing into a word processing program while listening to music that is playing from the computer's CD-ROM drive. My computer allows me to type and play music at the same time. Many people add email and an Internet browser, and run other programs all at the same time. Each of these programs requires a part of the microprocessor's attention. The less time the CPU can spend working on a program, the more its performance suffers.

John Von Neumann, a computer scientist of many years ago, noted that computer processors can only do one thing at a time. Even though the machine editing this book has many things running—music, word processor, Internet connection, and network services—only one of the programs is running at any instance in time. In order for the brain of a computer, the microprocessor, to appear

 Did You Know?

In the early years, a CPU was capable of performing one instruction for every CPU cycle. As technology has progressed, this is no longer true because different devices operate at different speeds. For instance, your diskette drive is only capable of moving information at a rate of 300 KB/sec. That is about 1 bit every .0000033 seconds. The RAM on an average machine is capable of moving 64 bits in .0000001 seconds. Obviously RAM is much faster and must sit idle on the diskette drive to supply it with requested information (this is a huge waste of resources). Still, for a quick rule of thumb, comparing CPU speeds is sufficient. A 400 megahertz CPU is faster than a 200 megahertz CPU.

to do more than one thing at a time, it must share its attention in small portions among all the active tasks. This is called *multitasking*. The CPU counts the number of programs running and divides that number into one second; i.e., if ten programs are running, the computer spends 1/10 of a second on each program. Once all the programs have been serviced, it starts at the top of the list and begins again. This is how modern operating systems work.

Of course, it all happens faster than the eye can see. Think of it as watching a movie. The film on which the movie is recorded is composed of individual frames. Each frame is slightly different from the one before it. When all the frames are shown in rapid order, they appear to move. The computer does the same to your programs. It updates every program very quickly—so quickly that you don't notice the tiny pauses.

For example, neither the typing that I am doing nor the CD I am playing require much work by the CPU, so it can accommodate both activities at the same time, with CPU cycles to spare. No matter how fast I type, the music never skips.

However, if in addition to typing and listening to music I were running a complex mathematical formula that required several minutes to compute, the operating system might decide that the math program required more attention, and it might borrow cycles from my word processing program or CD player, or both. In that case, I might notice that letters don't reach the screen as fast as I type them, or the music might start skipping while the CPU was paying attention to the math program. It is usually the operating system's job to manage this.

CHANGING THE WAY IT WORKS: EXTENSIONS

Speaking of CD players, my computer was never intended to be a CD player. So how come it works as one? It's simple, really.

When CD-ROM drives first began appearing in computers to allow large programs to be run, computer designers understood that the mechanism was virtually identical to those used to play music CDs. They extended the operating system to make it possible for the operating system to use the CD-ROM drive to play music. This was accomplished by adding an *extension* that added capability to the operating system, making it able to do something it was never intended to do originally.

There are numerous extensions to operating systems. Some allow computers to recognize each other's file formats; some allow computers to recognize new devices attached to the computer. Others make the operating system itself look or act differently. Still others allow the computer to connect to a network. When you talk about an operating system, you are generally referring to the operating system and all of its extensions. In some cases, the combination of all the extensions to the operating system may be larger than the original operating system.

Memory Management

Once the computer is up and running, the next job of the operating system is to allocate and manage memory. Early microcomputers did not have enough memory to run more than one program at a time, so memory management was easy. Modern PCs, however, are capable of running several programs at the same time. Some *RAM* (random access memory) resources are used by the operating system, some by each of the programs running, and some are shared by two or more of the programs. It is the operating system's job to make sure all of these processes run in harmony without conflicting with each other.

Because computer processes can be so memory-intensive, the computer sometimes runs out of available RAM to run a process. The operating system can handle this in one of two ways: it can simply report to the user that it doesn't have enough memory and stop the process, or it can compensate. One of the ways that computers compensate is through a little trick called *virtual memory*. Virtual memory moves blocks of memory from the RAM to the computer's hard disk so that the process will have room to continue. The difference in speed between the two can be as much as 1000:1. This is why it is so important to have all the RAM your programs expect. This is why it is so important to keep all of the program in RAM so you don't waste time swapping chunks of code to the hard drive. Otherwise, the programs perform poorly and slow the computer down considerably.

File Management

Operating systems arose when it became necessary to connect to storage devices such as the disk drive. It is not enough to tell the computer to put a file away. The computer must know whether there is enough room for storage, must know precisely where the user wants to store the file, and must store the file in such a way that it can be retrieved later. Files sometimes need to be moved, duplicated, and have their names and other information changed. In addition, the operating system must provide a way to discard files that are no longer needed. These are all management functions the operating system performs for file storage.

STORAGE TYPES: TAPES, DISKS, AND HARD DISKS

The computer needs to be able to write data for safekeeping and also have a storage place for programs. *Storage devices* come in many shapes, sizes, formats, and speeds. One of the earliest devices was the *diskette drive*. On most systems today this is a 3.5-inch diskette that holds 1.44 million bytes (a byte is usually equal to one character; a million bytes is called a *megabyte*) of information. *Hard drives* are an advanced form of diskette drive. They hold much more (billions of bytes—*gigabytes*—instead of just over a megabyte), are 100 times faster, and are about the same physical size. The hard drive is a fixed storage device in the computer. It consists of several disks, called *platters*, that store data electronically. Saving data to the hard drive is like writing it down on a piece of paper. It won't change until you physically erase it.

On all IBM-compatible machines the first diskette drive is called A:\ and the second is called B:\. While it is possible to have more diskette drives, it almost never happens. If it did, the third diskette drive wouldn't be C:\, because this letter is reserved for the first hard drive on the system. A computer's hard drives start at C:\ and continue down the alphabet. CD-ROM drives start anywhere from drive letter D:\ and continue down the alphabet. On the machine editing this document there are seven hard drives, ranging from C:\ to I:\. There are also 11 CD-ROM drives, starting at drive letter M:\ and continuing to W:\. You will notice there is a gap between I:\ and M:\. This is because you often leave some letters free, so you can assign future drives to fit your needs.

There are several formats for storage media, each with their own advantages and disadvantages. Different types include *tapes*, *CD-ROMs*, and *magnetic disks* (hard drives, diskettes, and zip drives). The advantage of tape is that it is potentially capable of holding large amounts of information; its disadvantage is that it is relatively slow. Disks, on the other hand, offer much faster storage and retrieval; however, their space is somewhat limited. Once a disk is full, you either have to add another drive or replace it. With tape you can just remove the full cartridge and insert a blank one. One solution is to make the disk removable (like diskettes) so that you can place a new disk in the machine when the old one is full. Removable disks cannot be designed to hold as much information as fixed hard disks, which are hermetically sealed inside the computer. CD-ROMs, which are removable, are a compromise between the two. They are faster than tape but slower than hard drives.

FILE TYPES: PROGRAMS, DOCUMENTS, AND CONTAINERS

Regardless of the storage medium, the operating system usually distinguishes at least three types of files. They are *programs*, *documents*, and *containers*.

Programs, sometimes known as *applications*, are executable files. That is, they contain instructions to have the computer perform some tasks. Common types of programs include word processing programs, spreadsheets, Internet browsers, database programs, financial and tax programs, and many others.

Documents, on the other hand, generally contain human-intelligible information such as text, pictures, sounds, or movies. Most programs play and create documents.

Finally, there are *containers*. Strictly speaking, containers aren't files. They are really just a way to organize all the other files. In some operating systems they are called *folders*, in some *directories*. Basically they exist to organize the stored data into smaller groups of files.

IDENTIFYING FILES AND TYPES

Two principal methods are used to identify the file type. The simplest method, used by DOS and by some versions of Unix, is the addition of an *extension* to the filename. In DOS, for example, a rule known as the 8.3 convention specifies that filenames can only be eight characters long, followed by a period, then by a three-character extension to the name. This extension tells the operating system what kind of file it is. For example, a DOS file ending in .exe is an executable file—usually a program of some sort. A .txt ending indicates a text file.

Some files are identified by information that is hidden from the user, but which is used by the operating system to identify the file. The Mac operating system uses this method by attaching two four-letter codes to every file. The first tells what type of file it is (TEXT, PICT, etc.). The second tells what program created the file. In this way, when you open a document, the Macintosh is aware of what program was used to create that document and opens the appropriate program to deal with that document.

NAVIGATING AND LOCATING FILES

When filing systems consisted of only one layer, navigating to locate files was pretty straight-forward. As numbers of files grew, and as containers were used to classify and hold these numerous files, the situation grew more complicated.

Simply speaking, *navigating* is the ability to recognize a container and open it to see what is inside. Since containers can contain containers, and so forth, this can be very time-consuming if files are stored randomly. For this reason, people usually group files together into logical bunches. On my home computer, for example, there are three folders (containers) on the hard disk. One is for programs (it's called Applications), one is for documents (called Documents), and one is for the operating system (it's called System Folder). Inside the Documents folder are folders for each member of my family. Within each of those, each member of my family has created their own structure to keep track of their files. In this way, if I'm looking for my daughter's English paper, I can narrow down the search pretty quickly, unless it has been misfiled.

Occasionally files get misplaced. When this happens, the operating system provides a way to search for the file by name. The trick is you have to remember the name of the missing file. More sophisticated operating system searches will even search the content of the documents, so you can look for an unusual word or phrase.

COPYING AND MOVING FILES

One of the great strengths of operating systems is their ability to make copies of files and move them. To understand the need for this, imagine that you are taking an English course for which you know there will be two major papers required. You start out believing that, with only two files to keep track of, you do not need to separate these files. You keep them in a container called Homework. As the course begins, you realize that in each case the teacher requires a rough draft, a proof draft, and the final paper. You realize that it might be a good idea to keep a copy of the early drafts of papers just in case you want to locate something you wrote earlier, or in case the teacher loses your paper. Your two files have just multiplied to six, with four of them based on the other two.

Then you find out the English teacher is going to require a bibliography for each of these papers. You need a place to write down every source in rough order so you can clean it up later. There are at least two more files. How will you keep them all straight? Easy. Inside your Homework container, you create a new container called English. All the files associated with your English course will be moved into that container, where you will be able to find them easily.

Because documents are created by programs, the operating system must not only provide a way to find files directly through the operating system, it must also provide the program with a way to store and find files as well.

REMOVING FILES

After the labor of creating those files, you may not think you will ever want to part with them. But as the semester ends, you may realize that if you don't do some housecleaning, you will run out of space on your hard disk. You may choose to back them up onto removable media (like a diskette) to keep them, or you may simply remove them from your hard disk. Either way, the operating system must have the ability to discard files that the user specifies.

Evolution of Computing

What is the earliest computer you can think of? If you watch movies, you might think of mainframes. These were huge computing devices that filled whole buildings. See Figure 1-4. The only resemblance they bear to today's computers is that, given the same problem, they would produce the same answer. Before digital computers, there were analog computers—hardwired circuits that did not use a microprocessor of any sort. Or, more correctly, the whole circuit could be thought of as a custom-built microprocessor.

FIGURE 1-4
Mainframe computer

Some Early Computers

Charles Babbage was an English mathematician and inventor, often referred to as the father of computing. See Figure 1-5. His work in mathematics led him to design a differential calculating machine that contained many of the processes still used today, including an arithmetic unit, a memory for storing numbers, and sequential control techniques.

FIGURE 1-5
Portrait of Charles Babbage

At approximately the same time (1810), the Jacquard weaving loom—an automated weaving loom controlled by a series of punched cards—was developed in France. See Figure 1-6. The punched cards contained a grid of rows and columns. Each column corresponded to the shuttle, a thread on the loom that does the actual weaving. Each row corresponded to one pass of the weaving thread. There were also a series of pins on the loom. As the cards passed across the pins, a pin would poke up through any square that was punched out, and hold up a thread for the next pass of the shuttle. The pattern formed by the holes in the card would thus be woven into the fabric. The great thing about this was that anyone could weave the exact same pattern in a very short time without years of training or without having to count all the threads. It was all handled automatically. This process was so efficient it wasn't abandoned until the 1970s.

These two devices paved the way for the modern computer. Think of the differential engine as a computing engine, i.e., a CPU. The punch cards on the weaving loom are a sort of storage device—a hard drive. Put them together and you have a computer.

Once people realized that these strange machines could save time and effort, computer development was limited only by existing technology. Until World War II, computing machines were so simple that the operating system wasn't part of the design. The user, who controlled how the machine reacted, was the operating system. With the outbreak of World War II, the U.S. War Department (now known as the Department of Defense) needed to know how to accurately place bombs in enemy territory during bombing raids. This is not something that can be done just by looking. It is a complex mathematical calculation that takes into account many factors: wind speed, difference in height between target and launcher, size/shape of the bomb, etc. A small error can mean the difference between a hit and a miss—a very expensive mistake. To calculate all these numbers, the DOD employed hundreds of women who ran through the pertinent calculations for most of the war. Their work was periodically updated in a series of tables used by bombardiers and gunnery crews. The difficulty of a problem was gauged by how many woman-hours it took to solve it. (Remember that even calculators hadn't been invented yet. Everything was done by hand.)

Even with many people working long and hard, the answers could not be produced fast enough for special problems. The answer came from an unlikely source: cryptography, or the art of breaking codes. Code breakers had a similar calculating problem. How do you break a code composed of millions of variations without a key? It was never a question of *whether* it could be done, just *how fast*. People were working as fast as possible, but they needed a machine that could do the job faster. So work started on a machine that was based on differential gears similar to those used by Babbage. It was called project ULTRA (which referred to the intercepted message intelligence), and it could translate a coded message in a day,

FIGURE 1-6
Jacquard weaving loom

JACQUARD LOOM CARDS

TIP

A modern computer is just a collection of circuits, with electronics that make the calculation process faster than it used to be. But a computer can be defined as any device that accepts a valid input, rejects invalid input, and produces output. According to this definition, a soda machine is a type of computer. It accepts coins inserted into a slot, sorts the coins, and delivers a soda. If you insert the wrong coin, the machine won't work until you supply the correct coin.

instead of the month it took to do it by hand. During the war, the Germans had invented a code machine named ENIGMA, which was stolen by the Poles, who gave a copy of it to the British. The device used rotor wheels to mechanically encode a message. Once the British were able to obtain the correct rotor wheels and the key codes, they could use the device to read German messages. The result was victory in the Battle of the Atlantic, which proved the value of computers beyond a doubt.

Although this was the first computer recognizable by today's standards, it still didn't have an operating system. It was completely run by a human administrator. Still, the machine had been a great success: It saved thousands of lives and helped shorten the war. This fact was not lost on the government, which immediately began to develop others that would be faster and solve more complex problems. The more complex the problem, the bigger the machines needed to solve it—and the harder it was to control the machine. Then someone came up with the idea of letting the machine control itself. All the user had to do was set certain operating parameters and the machine configured itself. This helped the situation, but there still wasn't an operating system.

Mainframes and Minicomputers

By the beginning of the silicon age in the1960s, computers had became so large and complex that it was no longer possible for a human to control them. This was the birth of mainframes—giant computers designed solely to solve complex math problems. Think about it:If a machine has two million switches that need to be checked in order for a program to run correctly, even one switch out of order would prevent it from working. There are simply too many connections and switches to monitor. Some method had to be implemented to make the machine easier to use. This is the origin of the operating system.

 Did You Know?

It is interesting to note that the term "debug" literally means to remove the insects from a program. In modern times it means to remove the programming mistakes from the computer code. The first credited use of the term is attributed to USN Rear Admiral Grace Hopper. A program was not working and the technicians were called in to check the switches and relays. The problem was found: A small white moth had lodged itself between the contacts of a relay. This small problem caused the whole program not to work. The technician who found the problem wrote in the maintenance logbook "Debugged program." It should also be noted that Grace is generally credited with starting the Y2K issue as well.

The earliest general-purpose electronic computers had only the barest of operating systems. Each machine was a unique creation, completely customized to the buyer's needs. Basically, the programmers wrote code directly to the computer hardware, so an operating system was unnecessary. As computers caught on, there began to be more than just one copy of a specific brand and model of computer in the world. Each one cost millions of dollars and had a large crew of PhDs who tended to its every need. Programs for these machines took years—and millions of dollars—to develop. Companies realized that they could cut their development cost/time by selling copies of their software to other companies. This worked wonderfully. One company could trade a copy of their program for others and suddenly their machine could do lots of new tricks. And so a brand new technology/market was born.

As the machines grew in sophistication there was a need for better software. Companies also needed a way to make the computers more economically viable. One way was to eliminate the teams of people needed to run them. As more software became available, there had to be some way of loading the code without having teams of engineers to oversee it. The operating system was devised to help handle this. Slowly it was extended to help with other tasks like writing programs. Shortly thereafter someone designed the first computer game. It is not recorded what that game was, but chances are it was tic-tac-toe.

Mainframe computers were so named because they were built on a frame or chassis—initially by hand. With the invention of the transistor, and later the microchip, computers became smaller in size and started to be manufactured rather than custom-built. These smaller, manufactured computers were known as *minicomputers*. They were still big by today's standards. The CPU alone was the size of a large refrigerator. A 16 KB RAM device was about the same size. When you add in all the hard drives, cooling, and communication equipment, the machines still took up a large conference room—instead of a football coliseum. See Figure 1-7.

FIGURE 1-7
Analog computers

The smaller size and lower cost meant larger production runs of a model. The greater numbers of computers being built led to standardization and an assembly line production, which meant that software no longer needed to be unique to a given installation. Now general-purpose software could be created and sold separately from the computer and its support. Because different computers of the same model could exchange software, the need for an operating system became more apparent.

The operating system was responsible for starting up all the components of the computer and for managing the storage and communication devices connected to the computer. Most early operating systems were proprietary, meaning that they would only run on a certain brand and model of machine. Even today, operating systems will only run on certain hardware. For instance, you can't run Macintosh software on a PC.

One of the earliest operating systems was developed not for computers, but to solve phone switching problems. Like most milestones in computing, big solutions often come from unexpected places. During the 50's and 60's the phone company experienced huge growth. The problem was not to physically connect all the customers, but to make sure there were lines available for them all to use. One workaround involved the hassle of party lines. So AT&T commissioned a mathematical model of the phone system to be built. This enabled them to quickly test various solutions without investing heavily in hardware. The model was so complex a computer was needed to solve it. Also a new operating system was needed to handle the very complex model. Here again, the answer came from an unlikely source. The operating system designed for the first multiuser game, called SKY, was adopted and modified. The result is the most powerful and flexible operating system ever invented, called Unix. Unix became a popular operating system with engineers because of all it would do. The downside was that it was so expensive to buy the program and all the hardware it required, only governments or the top 20 companies in the world could afford it. It was also hard to learn.

For 25 years this one thing—cost—held back computer development more than anything else. There were also other issues. For example, how do you talk to a machine so it understands what you are saying, and how do you know what it is saying? In the early days people communicated with the computer by typing on a kind of typewriter that punched holes in cards. A stack of these cards was then fed into a special machine to be read by the computer. The results were printed on paper. Later, users could communicate directly with the computer by typing into a device called a *dumb terminal*. The first terminals used a printer to show the computer's response. Later computers used a television-like screen.

Because of the costs associated with computers, they were built to be multiuser systems. A multiuser system means that there is one computer and lots of people using it at the same time. This spread out the cost and made it cheaper per user. Each of the users was connected to the computer by a terminal. The operating system had to keep track of what everyone was doing, so computer operating systems became very adept at multitasking, that is, doing more than one thing at a time.

Early Microcomputers

While minicomputers were considerably less expensive than their big, mainframe cousins, they were still more than most individuals could afford. In the early and mid-70's there was a movement to bring less expensive computers to the masses. The advent of the microchip made it possible to create computers that individuals could afford. Most of the small computers of this period were experimental machines built by electronics hobbyists. Like their early mainframe cousins, these computers were so simple they hardly needed an operating system. They were usually built by hand and had few useful features.

The device credited with being the first mainstream microcomputer, the Altair 8800, was based on an early microprocessor (the Intel 4004). Its relationship to modern microcomputers is hard to see: It was a metal box with several switches and lights on the front; it had no keyboard, no monitor, only 256 bytes of RAM, and it was operated (programmed, really) by clicking the switches and watching the lights flicker. Still, a million of them were sold. Keyboards, monitors, and more memory were soon added to make the machine useful. When designers added a flexible, removable disk storage device (floppy disk drive), they needed a way to control and manage it. This was the reason for the invention of CP/M—the first really usable microcomputer operating system. CP/M looked a lot like Unix.

One group of electronics hobbyists, the Home Brew Computer Club on the San Francisco peninsula, had a number of members—later to become famous—who were especially interested in building and showing off these new microcomputers. The idea of making prebuilt microcomputers that were genuinely useful (as opposed to a kit for hobbyists) belongs to two members of this club. Steve Wozniak, with his friend Steve Jobs, came up with the concept of a fully functional personal computer, which included a keyboard for input and a television screen for output. They called it the Apple II. Wozniak and Jobs sold enough Apple I computers (a hobbyist kit) to finance the Apple II. See Figure 1-8.

FIGURE 1-8
Wozniak and Jobs

Storage for the original Apple II used a connection to an audio cassette tape recorder. Later, when floppy disks became available, Apple added the ability to store programs and data on these 5¼-inch disks (like the Altair's). A program was needed to call and work with the contents of this disk drive, and that program was the real beginning of Apple's operating system.

When computer giant IBM saw the microcomputer concept taking hold, they decided to create a system of their own. IBM created its microcomputer from mostly generic parts. In a marketing coup, they called it the IBM Personal Computer—and the term PC was born. One of the parts they purchased for this computer was the operating system, which IBM licensed from a small startup called Microsoft, headed by a man named Bill Gates. The operating system was called MS-DOS, which stands for Microsoft Disk Operating System. This operating system had many similarities to Unix.

Because the new IBM PC was built with mostly commonly-available parts, and since IBM's arrangement with Microsoft was not exclusive, there was an opening for someone to create PCs without the IBM brand name on them. A critical part of the system called the BIOS (basic input-output system), which is the intermediary between the operating system and hardware, was the hardest part to replicate. But once it had been done, clones came into existence, and computers began to be common in businesses and homes. The open-ended design also encouraged other software companies—such as word-processing vendors like WordStar and WordPerfect, and financial software developers such as Lotus Development Corporation, whose 1-2-3 spreadsheet program was an early bestseller—to develop a wide range of programs for the PC.

As microcomputers became commonly available, MS-DOS (shortened to DOS) became the prevalent PC operating system, and slowly emerged as the standard system for businesses. Meanwhile, Apple II (and its successors) became dominant in schools.

Steve Jobs recognized the need to create a system to compete with IBM. While looking for ideas for a new computer, he visited Xerox's Palo Alto Research Center (PARC). A computer scientist named Doug Englebart had begun to experiment with a different kind of operating system, which used visual symbols and metaphors on the screen. They were manipulated using a screen pointing device called a *mouse*, which replaced the hard-to-remember file commands of DOS and the Apple II operating system. Englebart's idea was that computers should be easy to use.

Jobs brought the concept back to Apple and used it to create a computer called the Lisa. Lisa was an engineering and user interface marvel, but at over $15,000 each, nobody was buying them. Jobs and Apple worked to package the system in a more cost-conscious model, and the Macintosh was born. See Figure 1-9.

From the beginning, the Macintosh was recognized as something distinctly different from an IBM PC. Software for the machine was scarce. Because it was so easy to use, thanks to its graphical user interface (GUI), it seemed more

FIGURE 1-9
The first Macintosh design

like a toy to many people than a serious computer. But even Microsoft took notice and began working to replicate its ease of use and functionality.

Their first attempts, Windows 1.0 and 2.0, were considered imitations of the Macintosh. This had as much to do with the relative power of the microprocessors in the two machines as it did with the operating systems themselves. Finally by the time Windows 3.0 and 3.1 were introduced, the PC microprocessor had become powerful enough to handle the complex graphics required. It brought the magic of a GUI to millions of PC users, and due to the open IBM PC-style computers (whose hardware and software could be produced by virtually anyone) rather than a closed system (like the single-vendor Macintosh), it was an immediate success.

Since that time, microprocessors have become ever more powerful, and both Microsoft and Apple have added capability and features to their operating systems. During a brief flirtation with open systems Apple called their operating system MacOS. But by then the equivalent version of Windows, called Windows 95, was more or less on par with MacOS in terms of features.

During the same time frame, users realized that having their own computer was great, but they were isolated from each other. Large computing mainframes were still very desirable despite their price tag because users could share their data and ideas across multiple computers also referred to as a network. A small computer company called Novell, in Provo, Utah, headed by their new president, Ray Noorda, decided to create a way to connect multiple computers together to share printers and hard disks. Novell created another kind of operating system, a *network operating system* called Netware. The network operating system allowed for the connection of two or more computers, which can share files and services (such as a printer) between them. Microsoft followed along years later and created their own version of the network operating system, called Windows NT.

Unix, the multiuser operating system for larger, more expensive minicomputers, had not been idle all this time. It had been gradually moving toward desktop computers that used a GUI. One of those moves was made by Stephen Jobs who, after he left Apple, created a Unix-based GUI operating system called Nextstep. Apple later acquired Jobs' company, Next, and Nextstep became the foundation of Apple's MacOS X.

Another, even more important, movement of Unix toward the desktop in recent years was the development of a version of Unix by a Finnish student named Linus Torvald. He lent the new Unix his name—Linux (pronounced Len-ix). One of Linux's most interesting features is that, unlike Windows and MacOS, it is free and open and legally situated to stay that way. In many ways, Linux has an advantage over other operating systems because it has millions of average, everyday computer users developing programs versus a few hundred for Apple or IBM PCs. The disadvantage of Linux is that it is much harder to learn initially.

You will continue to learn about operating systems throughout this book. Subsequent chapters will describe the various operating systems mentioned in this introduction. Each chapter will give a brief overview of the operating system, and describe its evolution into its present form. You will then walk through a typical installation and setup of the operating system. From there, the discussion will focus on the basic functionalities of the operating system—including resource management, memory management, and file management. Finally, the unique features of the operating system will be explained.

Summary

In this chapter, you learned:

- An operating system is a collection of system programs that allow the user to run program software (software that you allows you to perform a task, such as edit a document or play a game). An operating system manages hardware and other programs.

- There are three basic types of user interfaces (UI). Command-line user interfaces use the keyboard to communicate with the operating system and the computer. In a command-line user interface, the user types in commands and the computer responds to them. Menu-based user interfaces are often used to simplify the use of a command-line UI by giving the user a list of commands from which to choose. The graphical user interface (GUI) is a sophisticated form of menu-based interface. Instead of listing the commands, the GUI presents them as a series of small pictures called icons.

- Hardware includes the physical components of your machine. All modern computers have the following components: **CPU**—the central processing unit, at the heart of the computer. **RAM**—random access memory, the main memory of the computer, which is updated as you work, and which requires power to maintain information. **ROM**—read-only memory, which is programmed once at the factory and cannot be changed. **BIOS**—the basic input-output system, a ROM whose program contains the bare essentials to get the machine up and running. **Motherboard**—the main circuit board in the computer. **Keyboard**—a device used to input information to the computer's programs. **Mouse**—a generic term applied to any pointing device.

- An operating system manages resources in many ways. Its main functions are starting up, shutting down, multitasking and allocating CPU cycles, and changing the way it works by using extensions and managing memory.

- An operating system also manages files in many different ways. Its main functions are utilizing the different storage devices available, recognizing and using the different file types (programs, documents, and containers), navigating and finding files, and copying and moving files as needed.

- The evolution of the modern personal computer and its operating system has occurred over the past half-century and will continue into the future.

VOCABULARY REVIEW

Define the following terms.

basic input-output system (BIOS)	central processing unit (CPU)	network
	graphical user interface (GUI)	operating system (OS)
command-line user interface	menu-based user interface	

CHAPTER 1 REVIEW QUESTIONS

TRUE/FALSE

Circle T if the statement is true or F if it is false.

T F 1. Admiral Grace Hopper is responsible for Y2K.

T F 2. The term debugging historically meant to remove insects from a computer.

T F 3. Computers are the result of dedicated work by engineers and scientists over the past 40 years.

T F 4. A computer is only an electronic device that computes numbers.

T F 5. A computer is a collection of devices working together for a common goal.

MULTIPLE CHOICE

Select the best response for the following statements.

1. Most keyboards are of this style:
    A. ANSI
    B. QWERTY
    C. American Typist Standard
    D. None of the above.

2. Which is an example of a pointing device?
    A. Mouse
    B. Tablet
    C. Touchpad
    D. None of the above.

3. Which is an example of a storage device?
    A. Printer
    B. Hard drive
    C. Scanner
    D. Modem

4. Which is an example of an input device?
    A. Scanner
    B. Tape drive
    C. Printer
    D. Sound card

5. Operating systems can be of these types. Circle all that apply:
    A. GUI
    B. Command-line
    C. Menu-driven
    D. Portable

WRITTEN QUESTIONS

Write a brief answer to the following questions.

1. Why did different operating systems evolve rather than having one OS that just got bigger and better?

2. Describe how programs, data, and operating systems work together.

3. Where does the term *booting* come from and what does it mean?

4. What is the difference between an input and an output device? Can the same device be both?

5. What is an operating system?

MATCHING

Match the following terms with the correct definition.

____ 1. OS   **A.** Graphical user interface

____ 2. BIOS   **B.** Operating system

____ 3. CPU   **C.** Basic input-output system

____ 4. RAM   **D.** Central processing unit

____ 5. GUI   **E.** Random access memory

CRITICAL THINKING

1. Given what you know about computers and the operating systems that control them, discuss what new problems will have to be solved as more and more of the world becomes connected.

2. How much should computers be allowed into our lives? Should restrictions be imposed on how far technology should go? Give reasons and examples.

3. Discuss the implications of allowing computers to invade your daily life and privacy. What restrictions should be imposed, if any? Who gets to decide what is private and what isn't? How much information do you think is freely available about you?

DISK OPERATING SYSTEM: DOS

OBJECTIVES

Upon completion of this lesson you will be able to:

- Understand why DOS is still prevalent and important in today's personal computers.

- Prepare the hard disk drive for installation of DOS.

- Install DOS correctly on your personal computer.

- Create and use directories for file management.

- Create, view, print, copy, move, delete and rename files in DOS using the text editor.

- Recognize common error messages in DOS.

🕐 **Estimated Time: 14+ hours**

VOCABULARY

CD

COPY

DEL

DIR

FDISK

Format

MD

REN

Introduction

In this chapter, we will be discussing **DOS** (*disk operating system*). DOS was the first widely installed operating system in personal computers. The first version of DOS, called PC-DOS, was developed for IBM by Bill Gates of Microsoft Corporation. He retained the right to market a Microsoft version, called MS-DOS. PC-DOS and MS-DOS are almost identical, and most users have referred to either of them as just "DOS." DOS is a command-line operating system, with a relatively simple user interface. It uses verbal commands, the user keys them at the command prompt. A prompt to enter a command looks like this:

C:\>

DOS was once a major operating system and the underlying layer of Windows products. It is still useful, and some development continues even today. DOS is still prevalent in today's computers, but usually in a behind-the-scenes way. You say, "But I never see DOS." Well, you look at it every time your Windows computer starts up. It's the black-and-white screen that says, "Starting Windows 9x…" . You may say "Why would I use DOS? Windows is so much easier." Well, what happens when Windows doesn't start correctly and you find yourself staring at a black-and-white screen, looking at the C:\> prompt and thinking, "What am I supposed to do with that?"

There are a variety of reasons why you need DOS.

1. DOS controls the flow of information between you and the computer (the translator).

2. DOS allows you to store information on your computer.

3. DOS allows you to retrieve information stored on your computer.

4. DOS interprets and translates the software you have on your computer.

5. DOS gives you access to all its functions, such as saving, copying, and printing files.

6. DOS allows you to fix your system when Windows cannot load properly.

The beauty of DOS from a user's standpoint is that it is fast and easy to use. From a developer's standpoint, it allows the developer to easily control the entire PC hardware and virtually all of its timing capabilities.

You don't need many commands to use DOS effectively, but you do need to learn how to get "syntax" help. Syntax means proper spacing and word order in your commands. There was a catchphrase in the '80s that is still fitting today, GIGO: Garbage In, Garbage Out. In other words, any command with incorrect syntax is garbage. If you key a command incorrectly, the computer will not do what you expect. As a result, it gives you garbage back.

Preparing for Installation

Before you install any operating system, your system must be prepared. That means that your connections should all be secure and any internal components (hard drives, cables, sound card, modem, and so on) should be installed. The machine needs to be set up physically and you must have all the necessary tools available to construct the operating system to correctly operate your hardware. This means you have all the necessary drivers, settings, and documentation you will want to correctly set up your hardware to work with the operating system. Drivers tell DOS how to interact with hardware components such as a mouse. Driver objects can be obtained online from the manufacturer of the specific hardware device.

Preparation of the Hard Disk Drive

Once your hardware has been installed properly, your *hard disk drive (HDD)* needs to be prepared. In DOS, this is accomplished with the help of two external utilities: ***FDISK*** and ***Format***. FDISK is a fixed disk utility; its purpose is to partition a hard disk drive. A *partition* is the structure DOS uses to designate usable space, just as we designate space in a building by giving it a name (room, closet, and so on) Once the hard disk drive is partitioned, it must be formatted (using the format utility) so that it may hold data. A formatted disk accepts and holds data in the same way that we build shelves and drawers to store our belongings. Once the disk is formatted, DOS can be installed.

Think of your hard drive/fixed disk as an empty dirt lot. When you partition the drive, you are pouring the foundation of the operating system. With that in place, you can format the drive and actually build a house to hold everything you need. Setup/Install then places all the finishing touches such as plumbing, wiring, and fixtures. Your house is ready for occupancy and your operating system is ready for use.

You need to begin with a formatted DOS system disk (often called a *boot disk*). This floppy disk contains special files that allow it to start DOS without the hard drive. This is usually Disk 1 of a DOS installation set. Once booted, it prompts you for the date and time. Most computers have an internal clock that will automatically set the date and time for you when you turn on the computer. However, if your computer does not have this feature, you will need to use the following steps to set the date and time.

Setting the System Date and Time

1. At the C: prompt, key the date in this format: **mm-dd-yy**. For example, if today is January 16, 2000, you would key the date as **01-16-00**.

3. At the C: prompt, key the time in this format: **hh:mm**. For example, if the current time is 8:46, you would key it as **8:46**.

2. Press the **Enter** key on the keyboard.

Notice that the C:\> prompt appears.

4. Press **Enter**.

FIGURE 2-1
Setting the System Time

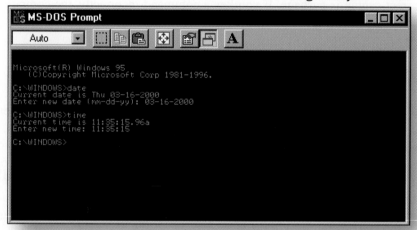

DOS marks the date and time on everything you do. It is important to periodically check the date and time to ensure that the system clock is correct. See Figure 2-1.

Check the Date and Time

DOS lets you check or change the date and time once it has been set. The procedure to check the date and time follows in Step-by-Step 2.2.

Checking the System Date and Time

1. Key **date** and press **Enter**.

2. If the correct date is displayed, simply press **Enter**. If the date is incorrect, key the correct date and press **Enter**.

3. Key **time** and press **Enter**.

4. If the correct time is displayed, simply press **Enter**. If the time is incorrect, key the correct time and press **Enter**.

Using FDISK

Now you'll use the FDISK utility to prepare the hard drive for formatting. To begin, key FDISK and press Enter. You are now presented with a menu. See Figure 2-2.

1. Create DOS partition or Logical DOS Drive

2. Set active partition

3. Delete partition or Logical DOS Drive

4. Display partition information

FIGURE 2-2
Setting the DOS Partition

The first option, Create DOS Partition or Logical DOS Drive, is the most frequently used. You will press 1 and then Enter to create the DOS partition.

A submenu opens to offer three additional options.

TABLE 2-1
Options on FDISK Submenu

Option	Description
Create Primary DOS Partition	Allows you to construct the first and main partition.
Create Extended DOS Partition	Allows you to create additional partitions. This is also how you set any partition that is secondary.
Create Logical DOS Drive(s) in the Extended DOS Partition	The primary partition automatically gets drive C; however, you must assign a drive letter to any other partitions so you can access them).

If you don't want to use the options in the submenu, you can press Escape to return to the main menu. Computers have a pecking order, or hierarchy, that they follow. In the case of FDISK, you must first create a primary partition, then you can create any additional partitions/drives or extensions of the primary partition.

Why not just keep everything in the primary partition and forget about the extended partitions? Until Windows 95 Service Release 2 (SR-2) was developed, the DOS file system's FAT-16 (16-bit File Allocation Tables) could only manage two gigabytes per partition. If your hard drive was larger than this, you had to create multiple partitions and logical drives to be able to use the entire memory space. Once Windows 95 SR-2 was released, FAT-32 (the 32-bit File Allocation Table, which has more capability) offered support for larger hard drives. Many rejoiced when the 2 GB barrier was shattered.

You must create the primary partition by pressing 1 and the Enter key. The DOS boot disk verifies the drive integrity to ensure it can hold the data, then it asks if you wish to use the maximum amount of space and set the partition active.

What is hard drive integrity? A hard drive stores information on a metallic disk that is surrounded by a magnetic field. If the magnetic field has weak spots, those locations may be unstable and unsafe for data. So the boot disk is basically verifying the magnetic field of the hard drive.

If you do not set an active partition, the hard drive cannot boot. To set an active partition, you press Y and Enter. The boot disk partitions the drive and prompts you to press Esc to continue. Now you must restart the computer for the changes to take effect. To do that, press Esc until you are back at the DOS prompt (A:\>), then restart the computer.

 Computer Concepts

Just as the Dewey Decimal System categorizes the library, FATs categorize your hard drive and provide a table of contents so the computer can find the files. FATs are an internal component of the operating system and not viewable. One FAT is used by the operating system, and a second is kept as a back-up copy in case the first is corrupted.

Did You Know?

There are two ways to reboot. You can simply turn off the computer; this is known as a *hard boot*. Alternatively, you can press the Ctrl, Alt, and Del keys on the keyboard simultaneously; this is known as a *soft boot*.

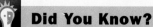 **S** TEP-BY-STEP ⟹ 2.3

Creating the Primary Partition

1. Press **1** and **Enter**. A submenu opens with three additional options.

2. Press **1** to create the primary partition, then press **Enter**.

3. Press **Y** and then **Enter** to use the maximum amount of space and set the partition active.

4. Now press **Esc** to continue.

5. Press **Esc** until you are back at the DOS prompt (A:\>), then restart the computer by pressing **Ctrl+Alt+Del**.

Formatting the Hard Drive

Now the drive is ready for formatting. To start the process, you key Format C: and press Enter. The disk prompts you with a warning that all data will be lost, and asks if you wish to proceed. Press Y and Enter. The boot disk begins to format the drive while displaying the percentage of completion. Once it is completed by reaching 100%, it prompts you for a label, which is the name you choose to assign to that drive. This is optional: You can key a label and press Enter—or simply press Enter.

The drive is now ready for installation of the operating system.

Note

Formatting the C drive is a dangerous activity. It will erase data on the drive. Please use caution whenever executing this command.

Installation of the Operating System

To start the installation process, you key Setup at the A:> prompt and press Enter. The installation menu will scan your system and then appear with a welcome message. This screen explains Setup, prepares MS-DOS to run on your system, and advises you to press F1 if you need additional help. You may also exit the setup program by pressing F3. As the screen indicates, you press Enter to continue the setup process.

Settings

Now you see a menu screen that contains the basic settings the computer will use: DATE/TIME, COUNTRY, KEYBOARD, and INSTALL TO. You can use the arrow keys on your keyboard to move up and down the menu. The DATE/TIME option allows you to set the correct system time. The COUNTRY option lets you enter your COUNTRY settings. The KEYBOARD option sets your keyboard to work with DOS, and the INSTALL TO option allows you to choose where you want to install the DOS operating system.

STEP-BY-STEP ▷ 2.4

Creating the Basic System Settings

1. Highlight **DATE/TIME** and press **Enter**. The menu highlights System Date.2. If the date is incorrect, key the correct date and press **Enter**. System Time now highlights.

2. Key the correct time and press **Enter**. Now you are back at the original settings screen.

3. If you are in a country other than the USA, highlight **COUNTRY** and press **Enter**.

4. From the list of countries supported by DOS, select the appropriate country and press **Enter**. You are now back at the original settings screen.

5. Highlight **KEYBOARD** and press **Enter**.

6. From the list of supported keyboards, select the keyboard used with your system and press **Enter**. You are now back at the original settings screen.

7. Highlight **INSTALL TO** and press **Enter**.

8. Select **Hard Disk** and press **Enter**.

9. If all settings are correct, highlight **'The settings are correct'** and press **Enter**.

Changing the Install Directory

The boot disk now prompts you to verify and change the install directory. The default is C:\DOS. If you want DOS to install to some other location, you may highlight the option to change the install directory and press Enter. This allows you to select a different directory to install to or leave C:\DOS as the default. Choose the option you want, then press Enter.

This screen also gives you an option to Run Shell on Startup. This is set to Yes by default, which means it will launch the MS-DOS shell overlay. This simply offers a fancier environment in which to communicate with the operating system, if you prefer. In this installation you will change that option to No, and then highlight 'The listed options are correct' and press Enter.

The screen now reports that MS-DOS is being set up; you should see a status bar that shows the percentage of completion. The operating system files are now copied to the hard drive from the installation set. If there are multiple disks in the set, you may be prompted to insert the additional disks. Simply remove the current disk, insert the requested disk, and press Enter. Once the files are copied, you are prompted to remove all disks and press Enter. The computer restarts and you are at the DOS Prompt [C:\>]. Installation is now complete.

Basic Functionalities of the Operating System

The Environment

The environment provided by DOS is not a pretty one. Its purpose is to give the user quick and direct access to the basic utility of the computer and little else—a carryover from the days when the abilities/limitations of the computer dictated how the user could interface with it. All tasks are accomplished by typing in commands at a command prompt (described in the following section). This is not to say, however, that a command prompt interface doesn't have its advantages. Once you learn the interface, it can offer advantages such as speed, efficiency, and reliability.

Usually, however, users or network administrators alter their system so that the user does not have to deal with this command-line interface. An example of this is Windows or other graphical user interface overlay programs. However, GUIs can prevent the beginner (or new) user from becoming comfortable with DOS itself.

In DOS and other command-line interfaces, it is easy to become disoriented. Unlike your office, in which you know where you are because of the physical things you see and feel, the computer environment is organized around your work and your files. Therefore, any sense of "where you are" is going to be with respect to the files on your disk.

Note

An argument specifies exactly what a command is going to do. For example, if I wanted to copy the file mine.txt from C to A, the command would be as follows: copy mine.txt a:\.

The filename itself and the directory it is being copied to are examples of arguments. They specify that the copy command should duplicate the file mine.txt to the A drive.

Many commands in the DOS environment follow a certain format. In order to tell DOS to perform a function, at the command prompt, you would key the command followed by *arguments*, which specify what you want DOS to do. You may only use *one* command at time at the command prompt. For example:

C:\>COPY practice.txt a:

"COPY" is the command that you want DOS to perform. "practice.txt a:" is an example of an argument that specifies what will be affected by the command. In this case, DOS will copy the file practice.txt from the C: drive to the A: drive. Commands such as edit, del, and rename require arguments similar to the example listed above. You will see more examples of these arguments throughout this chapter.

The Command Prompt

When you look at the screen of a computer that's running DOS, you are likely to see a blank screen with only a few lines, at least one of which begins with a capital letter followed by a colon, a backslash, and a greater-than symbol (>). See Figure 2-3.

FIGURE 2-3
DOS command prompt

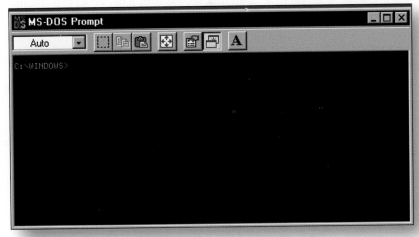

C:\>

Any line in DOS that begins like this is a command prompt. This prompt tells users where they are in DOS. Here is how:

The *C:* tells the user that he/she is working within the file space (disk storage) on the hard drive given the designation C. C is usually reserved for the main internal hard disk of a PC.

The *backslash* (\) represents a level in the hierarchy of the file structure. There is always at least one backslash because the first one represents the *root directory*—the very first level of your hard disk.

C:\DEMO\DOS&WIN\SAMPLES\SAMPLE.TXT

means that the file SAMPLE is on the internal hard disk, four levels deep (inside the directories DEMO, DOS&WIN, AND SAMPLES). The list of directories (\DEMO\DOS&WIN\SAMPLES\) is referred to as a *pathname* (following the path of directories will get you to the file). The name of the file itself (SAMPLE) is referred to as the *filename*. Think of a filing cabinet. If you had a folder called Purchase Orders, inside of which was a folder called Microsoft, and you submitted an order to purchase some new software from Microsoft, the order would be placed in the Microsoft subfolder. Directories work the same way. You have to follow the path of directories to end up eventually at your file.

Directory

If you need more help in orienting yourself, it sometimes helps to look at the files and directories available by using the *DIR* command (short for directory).

C:\>dir

The DIR command is like a table of contents in a book. This directory will list the following information:

- File names

- File extensions

- Size of each file

- Date and time the file was last updated.

This will give you a listing of all the files and directories contained in the current directory in addition to some information about the directory itself. See Figure 2-4. You will see the word "volume" in this information. Volume is simply another word for a disk that the computer has access to. Your hard disk is a volume, your floppy disk is a volume, a server disk (hard disk served over a network) is a volume. Now you know the fancy words for all the parts of the format DOS uses to represent a file.

Volume: C:
Pathname:\DEMO\DOS&WIN\SAMPLES\
File name: SAMPLE

Here are some helpful extensions of the DIR command: (These are often called *switches*, and are just additional options to get more out the command.)

C:\>dir | more

(displays the directory one screen at a time with a < more> prompt. You use Ctrl-C to escape)

C:\>dir /w

(wide: displays the directory in columns across the screen)

C:\>dir /a

(all: displays the directory—including hidden files and directories)

You can print a list of the files in your directory by instructing DOS to send the information to your printer.

FIGURE 2-4
Result of dir command

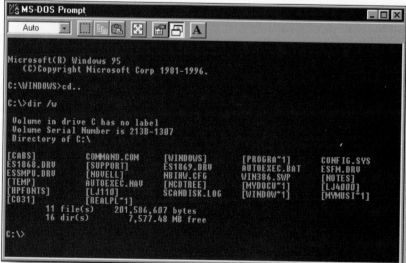

S TEP-BY-STEP ▷ 2.5

Print a Directory Listing

1. Key **dir>prn** and press **Enter**.

The > symbol stands for output. The PRN stands for printer.

Now that you have a grasp of where you are in DOS and how to find out, let's take a look at how to manage the files.

File Management

Understanding how to manage files on your disk is not the same as being able to use them, though it's a start. If you've ever looked inside a folder of a freshly installed commercial package (such as WordPerfect), you'll have seen a large number of files with many different kinds of extensions. It can be rather daunting.

 Note

You can print a wide listing of your files by typing dir/w>prn. LaserJet printers and other sheetfeeder printers will not eject the page after the dir>prn command. You must take the printer offline and press the form-feed button. Remember to press the online button when you are done, in order to continue using the printer.

File Types

However, DOS (like most operating systems), recognizes only two kinds of files: *binary files* and *text files* (ASCII). Text files are quite easy to read or view. Binary files, on the other hand, are not easily viewed. In fact, most binary files are not to be viewed, but to be executed (like a full program such as WordPerfect or simple commands such as Copy). When you try to view these binary files (with a text editor, for example), your screen is filled with garbage and you may even hear beeps.

While there are only two types of files, it is often difficult to know which kind a particular file is, for files can have any extension. Fortunately, there is a small set of extensions that have standard meanings:

Text   Binary
.TXT   .EXE
.BAT   .COM
.DAT

Executing Binary Files in DOS

Binary files ending in .EXE are usually "executed" in DOS by typing the file name as if it were a command. The following command would execute the WordPerfect application, which appears on the disk directory as WP.EXE:

C:\APPS\WP51>WP

Binary files ending in .COM often contain one or more commands for execution either through the command prompt or through some program.

Let's make sure we are at the root directory, the first directory on the hard drive. The root directory is where all the startup files must be located and from where all subdirectories stem.

Make a Directory

Now, let's make a couple of directories so we can put our files away in places that make sense to us. The DOS command for making a directory is **MD** (short for "make directory") and is followed by the name of the directory you want to make.

STEP-BY-STEP ⟹ 2.6

Creating Directories

1. At the C: prompt, key the command **md dosclass**. This creates a directory on C: called dosclass.

2. At the C: prompt, key the command **dir/w**. This will show a directory listing of C: with the new dosclass subdirectory.

3. At the C: prompt, key the command **cd dosclass**. This will move you into the dosclass subdirectory. At the C:\dosclass prompt, key

the command **md samples**. This makes a subdirectory named samples inside of the dosclass directory.

4. At the C:\dosclass prompt, key the command **dir**. This will allow you to view the new directory samples in the dosclass directory.

As soon as you change the directory, (cd dosclass) the prompt changes to represent the new directory. See Figure 2-5.

FIGURE 2-5
Prompt changed to show new directory

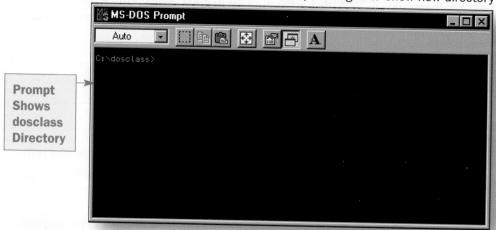

Prompt Shows dosclass Directory

...ber that if you want to get your bearings, you can look at the command prompt or dis-...y list of the current directory (dir).

Change Directory

To move to a different directory, use the command **CD** (for "change directory"), followed by the directory you want to move to. The backslash by itself always represents the root directory.

S TEP-BY-STEP ▷ 2.7

Changing Directories

1. At the command prompt key **cd**. This will return you to the root directory.

2. At the command prompt key **cd dosclass**. This will change the directory from the root to dosclass.

Working with a Text Editor

Before we move on to creating files in DOS, let's take a look at the text editor provided with DOS. It is known simply as Edit. To load the editor, key Edit from a command prompt and press Enter. See Figure 2-6.

FIGURE 2-6
Working with a text editor

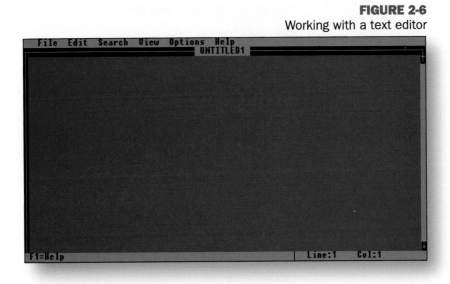

Figure 2-3 shows the screen you see when you open a new Edit window. Across the top are the menu bar and document title. On the right side is the scroll bar and on the bottom is the status bar. If your mouse driver is loaded you will also see a blinking square, which is the mouse cursor. On the menu bar, you have a number of options. You access them by moving the cursor over one of them and clicking, or you can press Alt and the first letter of the menu you want. For example, the key combination Alt-F opens the File menu. The following table displays the keyboard shortcuts used to display the editor's menus.

These tables show the common keyboard shortcuts used in the DOS Editor. See Tables 2-2 and 2-3.

TABLE 2-2

KEYBOARD COMBINATION	DISPLAYS
ALT-F	File menu
ALT-E	Edit menu
ALT-S	Search menu
ALT-V	View menu
ALT-O	Options menu
ALT-H	Help menu

TABLE 2-3

KEYBOARD COMBINATION	FUNCTION LOCATED UNDER
ALT-N	File menu. Creates a new file
ALT-O	File menu. Opens a file
ALT-S	File menu. Saves a file
ALT-A	File menu. Opens the Save As dialog box, which allows you to save the file to a different storage device, different directory, or with a different file name.
ALT-C	File menu. Closes the file
ALT-P	File menu. Prints the contents of the file
ALT_X	File menu. Closes the editor
ALT-X	Edit menu. Cuts (removes) text
ALT-C	Edit menu. Copies text
ALT-V	Edit menu. Pastes (inserts) cut or copied text
DEL	Edit menu. Clears unwanted text

From the File menu you can start a new file, open an existing file, save your file, save your file under a different name, close the current file, or print your file. On the Edit menu, you may cut, copy, paste, and clear text. You can use the Search menu to find a certain set of characters or words, repeat your search, or replace one set of characters or words with a different set using the Replace option. The next menu available in a true DOS version of Edit is Options, where you can change the settings and colors. The final menu is Help. Here you can receive help with the text editor commands or find information about the editor.

Now let's create a file. At this point it is important to mention that DOS requires that file names be no longer than eight characters, with the option of a three-character extension for descriptive purposes. In addition, no spaces or slashes are acceptable.

S TEP-BY-STEP ▷ 2.8

Creating Files

1. First, make sure that you are in the root directory by looking at your C: prompt. If you are not, key **cd** and press **Enter**.

2. At the C:>\ prompt, key **edit practice.txt** and press **Enter**. This opens the editor to a screen where you can key your document.

3. Key your name or some other message.

4. Press the **Alt** key, followed by the **F** key (make sure to keep pressing the Alt key when you press the F key) to display the File menu. (You may also use the mouse.)

5. Press the **S** key to save the file. To exit, press the **Alt** key, the **F** key, and then the **X** key.

If we look at the root directory, the PRACTICE.TXT file will be included. See Figure 2-7.

FIGURE 2-7
Directory listing showing the practice.txt file

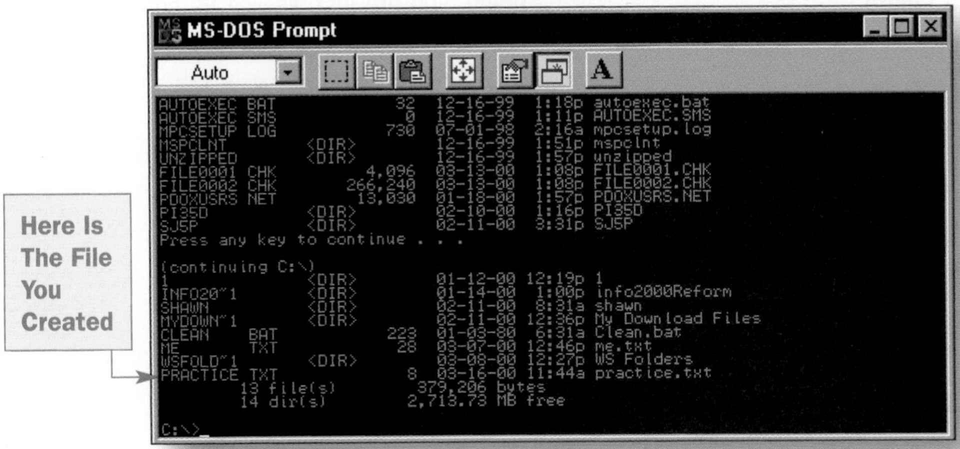

Here Is The File You Created

Viewing Text Files

You can quickly view text files by using the type command. See Figure 2-8.

FIGURE 2-8
Quick view of a file

Viewing a File Quickly

1. At the command prompt key the command **type practice.txt | more**.

2. When you display a file with the type command, you are just viewing its contents and cannot make any changes to it.

Editing Text Files

Alternatively, you can view the file in the DOS text editor (just as you did when you first created practice.txt).

Editing a File

1. First, make sure that you are in the root directory by looking at your C: prompt. If you are not, key **cd ** and press **Enter**.

2. At the C:>\ prompt, key **edit practice.txt** and press **Enter**. This opens the editor to a screen where you can edit your document.

3. Key another line of text into to your practice file.

4. Then press the **Alt** key, followed by the **F** key (make sure to keep pressing the Alt key when you press the F key) to display the File menu. (You may also use the mouse.) Then press the **S** key to save the file.

5. To exit, press the **Alt** key, followed by the **F** key followed by the **X** key. Now quickly view the practice.txt file by typing at the command prompt **view practice.txt | more**.

Printing Text Files

If you want to send a text file to the printer, you can use the print command.

S TEP-BY-STEP ▷ 2.11

Printing a File

1. At the command prompt, key the command **print practice.txt**.

2. When DOS prompts for the name of list device [PRN], key **lpt2**. If you want to print to a networked printer, usually lpt2 is the

correct response. For a local printer (which is physically connected to the computer, as opposed to a network device), the correct response is usually lpt1.

Copying Files

The *COPY* command allows us to make a duplicate of a file. We can create a backup of the practice file created earlier by copying that to the SAMPLES directory which is inside the DOSCLASS directory.

To keep things simple, let's use the cd command to return to the root directory where the practice file is.

**C:\>cd **

Now copy that file to the SAMPLES directory, which is inside the DOSCLASS directory. In order to copy something, you must first issue the command (copy), then identify the file to be copied (source), and then name the directory to which you want to copy the file (destination).

S TEP-BY-STEP ▷ 2.12

Copying Files

1. At the prompt, key the following command: **copy practice.txt dosclass\samples**.

2. This copies the practice file to the samples subdirectory in the dosclass directory.

3. At the command prompt key **CD dosclass\ samples** to change to the samples subdirectory.

4. Check to make sure the practice file was copied to the samples subdirectory by keying in **dir** at the command prompt.

A somewhat unfriendly yet useful diagram of the command format would look something like this (where items in brackets are optional):

Copy [volume+pathname+]file name [volume+path name+]directory

This means you don't have to include the volume and pathname of the source file and the destination directory (we didn't in the first example). DOS assumes that any file name or directory included in the copy command is in the current directory (the one you're currently in.). Because you had moved to the root directory, both PRACTICE.TXT and DOSCLASS were in the current directory.

The command-line interface makes it possible for the user to use one command to copy any file anywhere to any other location; you don't have to be in the directory of the files you want to act on. From any directory (within volume C:), you could have used the following command to copy the same file to the same directory:

C:\DOSCLASS>copy \practice.txt \dosclass\samples

This tells the computer where to find the source file (since it wasn't in the current directory) by placing a backslash in front of the file names (which told the computer that the file was in the root directory). You use the same procedure to copy files between volumes. All you have to do is specify the volume:

Z:\ANYWHERE>copy c:\practice.txt c:\dosclass\samples

Another common and useful example is:

C:\>copy practice.txt a:\backup\dosclass

This command copies the file to a floppy disk in the PC's floppy drive (which already had the directories, BACKUP\DOSCLASS).

Copying a File from the Hard Drive to a Floppy Disk

Sometimes you may need to copy a file from the hard drive onto a floppy disk. This is helpful if you would like to have an extra copy of a certain file as a backup or to transport the copied file to another computer.

STEP-BY-STEP ⟹ 2.13

Copying Files to a Floppy

1. At the command prompt key **copy Practice.txt a:** and press **Enter**.

2. Wait for a few seconds; notice the light on the floppy drive. Never attempt to remove a disk from the disk drive while this light is on.

3. To check to see if the file was copied, key **a:** at the C:\> prompt and press **Enter**.

4. Key **dir** and press **Enter**. If the file was copied correctly you should see listed here the file practice.txt.

Diskcopy Command

Sometimes you may need to copy all the files from one diskette to another. First you will need a blank formatted disk (refer to the section on formatting disks.)

 Note

Most floppy disks you buy today in the store are already formatted, meaning they are prepared to hold data.

STEP-BY-STEP ▷ 2.14

Copying an Entire Disk

1. At the command prompt, key **diskcopy a: a:** and press **Enter**.

2. When asked to insert the source disk, insert the diskette that has the information you want to copy into drive A and press **Enter**.

3. Wait a few seconds. When asked to insert a target disk, remove the diskette from drive A, insert a blank diskette, and then press **Enter**.

4. When the process is complete, you will be asked if you want to write to another duplicate diskette (Y/N). Press **N**.

5. Then you will be asked if you want to copy another disk (Y/N)? Press **N**.

 Note

If your machine has two floppy disk drives, insert the original (source) disk into drive A and the blank (target) disk into drive B. Then key: DISKCOPY A: B:

Moving Files

"Move" means to take a file from one location and place it in a new location. In order to move something, you must first issue the command (move), then identify the file to be moved (source), and then name the directory to which you want to move the file (destination).

STEP-BY-STEP ▷ 2.15

Moving Files

1. First change to the samples subdirectory. At the command prompt key **cd dosclass\ samples**.

2. Insert a floppy disk into the A drive.

3. At the prompt, key **move practice.txt a:**.

4. This moves the practice file from the samples subdirectory to your floppy disk.

5. At the command prompt key **a:** to change to the floppy drive.

6. Check to make sure the practice file was moved by typing **dir** at the command prompt.

Delete

Now you discover you have a slight problem. The PRACTICE.TXT file was copied into the SAMPLES directory, but there is no reason to have two copies of PRACTICE.TXT. To delete a file, use the *DEL* command (short for "delete"), followed by the name of the file.

Deleting Files

1. At the C: prompt key **cd \dosclass\sample** to change to the samples subdirectory.

2. Then key **del practice.txt** to delete the file practice.txt from the samples subdirectory.

Again, you can delete the file from any directory by including the full pathname.
Z:\>del c:\practice.txt

Rename

The **REN** command allows the user to change the name of a file previously created. As with the DOS commands described earlier, you need not be in the same directory as the file you want to rename, provided you include the pathname of the file you wish to change. However, the second argument of this command, the new filename, will not accept a pathname designation. In other words, the second argument should just be a filename (with no pathname):

C:\>ren \dosclass\samples\practice.txt prac.txt

Use caution: if you do not include the extension (.TXT, .BAT, .DOC), some programs may not be able to open the file.

Renaming Files

1. At the command prompt key **cd** to return to the root directory.

2. To rename the file practice.txt to prac.txt the command would be **ren practice.txt prac.txt**.

Unique Features of DOS

There are many commands that are unique to DOS. Earlier in the chapter you were introduced to the most popular commands of the DOS operating system. The following commands are also helpful when working in the DOS environment.

Command Functions

F3

The F3 function key can be a timesaver if you're prone to typographical errors. If you make a mistake when typing in a command and receive an error message, you can have DOS completely rekey the last command by pressing the F3 button. Pressing F1 will do this one character at a time.

Directory Commands

Parentdirectory(..)

If you wish to move up one level in the hierarchy of the file structure (for example, change to the parent directory), DOS provides a shortcut—two consecutive periods ("..").

C:\DOSCLASS\SAMPLES>cd ..

This works in a pathname as well:

C:\DOSCLASS\SAMPLES>ren ..\practice.txt prac.txt

If the file PRACTICE.TXT were in the directory above SAMPLES (the DOSCLASS directory), the above command would change it to PRAC.TXT.

Directory, Delete

Deltree removes the directory and all of its contents (meaning all files and subdirectories).

Key: **DELTREE [directory name]**

RD removes the directory only if it is empty (meaning that it contains no files or subdirectories).

Key: **RD [NAME OF DIRECTORY TO BE REMOVED]**

File Commands

Wildcards (*) and (?)

Another benefit of the command-prompt interface is the ability to use *wildcard characters*—special symbols that stand for other characters. The * wildcard character stands for any combination of characters. For example, dir*.doc means list every file with a .doc extension; dir training.* means list every file named *training*, regardless of its extension. The ? wildcard character is used when you can't recall one letter or if you need files that are similar. For example, to get all copies of the Windows registry, you would enter dir system.da? This would list System.daT and System.da0 (which is the backup copy).

For example, if you want to copy only files with the .txt extension, you would employ a wild-card character, as in the following command: **C:\>copy *.txt a:\backup\txtfiles**. This command would copy all of the files with the .txt extension onto a floppy disk inside the TXTFILES directory that is inside the BACKUP directory. However, to copy all files from the C drive to the A drive, you would enter **C:\>copy *. * A:**.

The wildcard character is also used to retrieve a directory of similarly named files, as in **C:\>dir *.txt**. This command would display all files ending with the .txt extension. To list all files that begin with the letter g, you would key **C:\>dir g*.***.

Additionally, the ? can be used to substitute for individual letters as previously mentioned. If there are many similarly named files that end with the letters GOP but begin with letters A through G, then you can use the **C:\>dir ?gop. *** command to list those files. The following command would list all similar files beginning with the letters REP and ending with A: **C:\>dir rep?a. *** .

Wildcard characters such as * and ? can be useful when you do not know the full name of a file or files and wish to list them separately from the main directory listing.

Batch Files

Batch files are text files that contain a series of DOS commands that will be executed in the order listed in the file. You can create batch files that will perform a variety of commands. These are commonly used for repetitive tasks. For example, if every day when you sit down at your PC, you check the date and time. Why not create a batch file to do this for you, instead of typing in two commands daily? To do this we would use the editor and inside have the commands for date and time. If you name the batch file morning.bat, when you sit at your PC everyday, you would only have to type in the command "morning," and the date and time commands would execute for you. These are time savers.

S TEP-BY-STEP ⟩ 2.18

Create a Simple Batch File

1. Key **edit LS.BAT** and press **Enter**.

2. Key **dir | more**.

3. Then press the **Alt** key, then the **F** key to display the File menu. (You can also use the mouse.)

4. Then press the **S** key to save the file. To exit, press the **Alt** key, then the **F** key, then the **X** key.

5. Now, when you press [**LS**] + [**ENTER**], the operating system will run the LS.BAT batch file, which in turn will provide a page-by-page directory.

Data Protection and Integrity Commands

To Create a Backup Disk

You should always back up data that is important to you. If the information is something that you cannot live without, the following command will create a backup disk for you.

MSBACKUP

Check Disk

This is useful when ScanDisk isn't available. It checks the file structure and informs you of errors. You can add /F to fix any errors that may be there.

CHKDSK [drive]:

Defragment Disk

This command organizes files so the computer can find and read them more easily.

DEFRAG

Diagnostics

This program will take a snapshot of the computer and run a series of diagnostic tests that examine the computer's condition and determine if all is well.

Enter **MSD** to display diagnostic information about your system.

FIGURE 2-9

Display of MSD examining the computer system

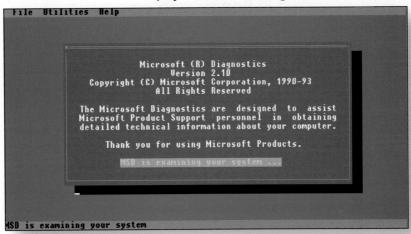

MSD will examine your system and then tell you what is in it. You can click any of the buttons or press a topic highlighted in red that you would like to see more about.

You can also use this handy tool to see a memory map, which graphically shows your memory usage. See Figure 2-10.

FIGURE 2-10(a)

System properties analyzed with MSD

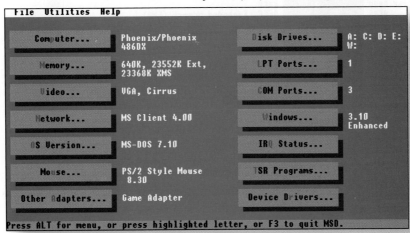

FIGURE 2-10(b)

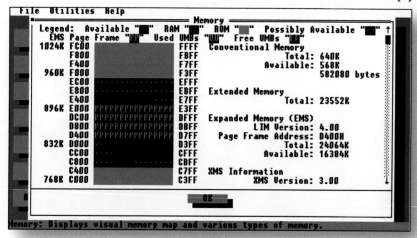

FIGURE 2-10(c)

ScanDisk

Replaces CHKDSK; adds functions such as the ability to do a surface scan of the hard drive to find problem areas of memory and mark them unusable.

SCANDISK

Other Commands

DOS Version

To display the version of DOS
VER

Format Disk

To prepare a disk to hold data, insert the disk in the drive:

FORMAT [drive letter]

 Note

Be careful with this command. It will erase all of the information on the drive. If you accidentally run the FORMAT command on the C drive, it will erase your entire hard drive.

DISK OPERATING SYSTEM: DOS

Format Disk, Bootable

This creates the essential boot disk.

FORMAT [d]: /S

Unformat

Like UNDELETE, this command is available in case you accidentally format a floppy or hard drive and you need to unformat it.

UNFORMAT [drive:]

Help

HELP [command]

FASTHELP gives you a complete list of all DOS commands.

Label Disk

Insert the disk to be labeled in drive [d]: Use this command to give the drive a name. The main purpose of this command is to organize the contents of your drive(s). **LABEL [d]:**

Volume

To display volume label, which was created with the LABEL DISK command:
VOL

Common DOS Error Messages

Here is a listing that explains the DOS messages you may see on your screen.

ABORT, RETRY, FAIL?

The computer cannot read the disk in the drive, or there is no disk in the drive.

ACCESS DENIED

This usually means the file has an attribute on it. An attribute is a file setting that limits the use of the file.

BAD COMMAND OR FILE NAME

You may have miskeyed a command or entered a command DOS does not understand.

BAD OR MISSING COMMAND INTERPRETER

DOS cannot locate COMMAND.COM, an important file that enables the operating system to interpret commands. You will need to recopy it into your root directory. There is also a chance your computer could be infected with a virus.

DRIVE NOT READY ERROR

Disk in the drive is not readable, or there is no disk in the drive.

DUPLICATE FILE NAME OR FILE NOT FOUND

When attempting to rename a file, the computer could not find the file to be renamed, or it has discovered an existing file with the designated name.

FILE CANNOT BE COPIED ONTO ITSELF

An attempt to copy a file could not be completed because the file already exists, or the source and destination are the same.

FILE CREATION ERROR

Directory could be full because DOS limits the number of files allowed in one directory, or the file may already exist, or the file was not copied correctly.

FILE NOT FOUND

The directory you searched does not contain the file named, or there are no files in the directory.

GENERAL FAILURE

This message is displayed when DOS is uncertain of the specific problem. DOS could not read the specified drive. If the problem is a floppy disk, try using another disk. If it's the hard drive, you should try rebooting. Consult a repair person if the problem persists.

INSUFFICIENT DISK SPACE

The disk may be full or the file may be too big to fit on the disk.

INTERNAL STACK OVERFLOW

DOS's internal storage areas are full. You may need to go into your config.sys and increase the STACKS=0,0. For more information about the config.sys file, please refer to your MS-DOS manual. On most Windows systems you should set the increase to STACKS = 9,256.

INVALID DIRECTORY

Directory does not exist or is not accessible from the current directory.

INVALID DRIVE SPECIFICATION

Drive does not exist or cannot be found on the computer.

INVALID FILE NAME OR FILE NOT FOUND

DOS couldn't find the file specified in the current directory or the file has an invalid character in it.

INVALID MEDIA, TRACK 0 BAD OR UNUSABLE

Format command cannot format the specified disk or the disk capacity is invalid, or bad disk.

INVALID NUMBER OF PARAMETERS

The command was miskeyed, a necessary element was omitted, or an extra space was added.

INVALID PARAMETER

The command specified an incorrect parameter, such as format /z.

INVALID SWITCH

The wrong slash was keyed—such as cd/ instead of cd\.

NON-SYSTEM DISK OR DISK ERROR

When booting the computer, this error often occurs when there is an unbootable floppy disk in the external drive slot. If there is no disk in the slot, this could be an indication of an unrecognized hard drive, unformatted hard drive, or a hard drive with missing system files.

NOT READY, READING DRIVE X

Attempted to read a disk that is not readable, or there is no disk in that drive.

WRITE FAULT ERROR

Tried to reroute text to a device that is not connected, not valid, or not hooked up.

WRITE PROTECT

Tried to write to a disk that is write-protected

Summary

In this lesson, you learned:

■ DOS controls the flow of information between you and the computer (translator); allows you to store information on your computer; allows you to retrieve information stored on your computer; interprets and translates the software you have on your computer; gives you access to all its functions (saving, copying, and printing files); and allows you to fix your system when Windows cannot load properly.

■ Your hard disk drive (HDD) needs to be prepared to hold data. You accomplish this in DOS by using two external utilities, FDISK and Format. FDISK, which stands for fixed disk utility, is used to partition a hard disk drive. DOS uses partitions to designate usable space—something like the rooms in a house. Once the hard disk drive is partitioned, it must be formatted (using the Format utility) so that it can hold data. Formatting it prepares it to accept and hold data.

■ How to run through the installation program and follow the screen-by-screen instructions to install DOS correctly on your personal computer.

■ You want to save files in an orderly fashion, organized like the file folders in a filing cabinet. The command MD allows you to create directories for file storage and the command CD allows you to move into these directories and work with the files located there.

■ You can create files in DOS by using the EDIT command. This opens the text editor provided with DOS, where you create your file. To view a file's contents without having to open the text editor, use the VIEW command followed by the file name. You can print files in DOS by using the PRINT command. After you create files in DOS, you may later need to copy, rename, and delete them. The COPY command will create a duplicate of a file in another directory. The MOVE command will take a file from one place to another. The REN command will rename a file and the DEL command will remove a file from the directory when it is no longer needed.

■ There are many commands in DOS that help you do more things with the operating system. You can change the actions of commands themselves, issue data-protection commands to prevent loss of data, and use file and directory commands to make your work more efficient.

■ The ability to recognize common errors in DOS will help when you are working with the operating system. Although errors will happen, your ability to decipher what the operating system is trying to tell you will save you time in the long run.

VOCABULARY REVIEW

Define the following terms.

CD	DIR	MD
COPY	FDISK	REN
DEL	Format	

MULTIPLE CHOICE

Circle the answer that best applies.

1. Which command will display the current directory in a wide column format?
   - **A.** dir/p
   - **B.** dir/q
   - **C.** dir/w
   - **D.** dir|more

2. Which command will create a directory named Reports?
   - **A.** rd reports
   - **B.** md reports
   - **C.** cd reports
   - **D.** mkdir reports

3. Which command will copy the file report.txt from the hard drive to the floppy drive?
   - **A.** copy C:\report.txt A:
   - **B.** copy C:\report.txt B:
   - **C.** All of the above.
   - **D.** None of the above.

4. Which command opens report.txt in the DOS text editor?
   - **A.** Edit C:\report.txt
   - **B.** Open C:\report.txt
   - **C.** Spawn Edit Report
   - **D.** Create C:\report.txt
   - **E.** All of the above.
   - **F.** None of the above.

5. Which command will rename the file myfile.txt to file.txt?
   - **A.** Ren file.txt myfile.txt
   - **B.** Ren myfile.txt file.txt
   - **C.** Ren myfile.txt
   - **D.** Rename myfile.txt file.txt

TRUE/FALSE

Circle T if the statement is true or F if it is false.

T F   1.   cd.. will always return you to the root directory.

T F   2.   Del *.* and Del ????????.??? will perform the same task.

T F   3.   Del homework will delete the homework directory.

T   F   4.   DOS is considered a GUI-type operating system.

T   F   5.   The commands CHKDSK and SCANDISK perform the same function.

WRITTEN QUESTIONS

Write a brief answer to the following questions

1.   Explain the difference between a GUI and command-line operating system.

2.   Explain the difference between an executable file and text file.

3.   Why is a knowledge of DOS important in modern computing?

4.   What does DOS stand for?

5.   Is DOS a dead operating system? Explain.

MATCHING PART 1

In the blank space match the following error messages to the correct explanation of the error.

___ 1.   Write protect

___ 2.   Write fault error

___ 3.   Invalid file name or file not found

___ 4.   Invalid drive specification

___ 5.   Invalid switch

___ 6.   Insufficient disk space

A.   Tried to reroute text to a device that is not connected or is not valid or not hooked up.

B.   Drive does not exist on the computer or cannot be found.

C.   The wrong slash was typed, such as cd/ instead of cd\.

D.   Disk is full or, if you are trying to copy a file to a disk, the file is too big to fit on the disk.

E.   Tried to write to a disk that is write-protected.

F.   DOS couldn't find the file specified in the current directory, or the file has an invalid character in it.

In the blank space, match the command with its function.

   ___ 1. CD   **A.** Copy a file or directory

   ___ 2. RD   **B.** Change directory

   ___ 3. MD   **C.** Executes LS batch file (if created)

   ___ 4. COPY   **D.** Remove directory

   ___ 5. LS   **E.** Make directory

CHAPTER 2 PROJECTS

PROJECT 1

1. Put your disk into the floppy drive.

2. Change to the **A:** prompt.

3. Using the DOS editor, create two text files on drive A. Name one **junk.txt** and the other **garbage.txt**.

4. Create a directory on drive A named the **Schedule**.

5. Create two subdirectories in the **Schedule**, called **Work** and **Play**.

6. Create a subdirectory in the **Work** directory, named **School**.

7. Create two subdirectories in **Play**, named **Workout** and **Walk**.

8. Return to the root directory.

9. Create another directory on the root, named **Clean**.

10. Create two subdirectories in **Clean**, named **Room** and **House**.

11. Create two subdirectories in the **Room** directory, named **Makebed** and **Vacuum**.

12. Create two subdirectories in the **House** directory, named **Living** and **Kitchen**.

13. Return to the root directory.

14. Copy the **junk** file from the root to the **Clean** directory.

15. Copy the **junk** file from the **Clean** directory to the **Work** directory.

16. Rename the **junk** file in the **Work** directory to **myjunk.txt**.

17. Copy the **garbage** file from the root directory to the **Kitchen** directory.

18. Delete the **garbage** file from the root directory.

19. Rename the **garbage** file in the **Kitchen** directory to **mygarb.txt**.

20. Remove the **Living** directory.

21. Remove the entire **Schedule** directory tree.

22. Hand in your disk to your instructor for credit.

PROJECT 2

1. Create a batch file on your disk named **mybatch.bat**.

2. The batch file should perform the following actions:

   ■ Clear the screen.

   ■ Display the version of DOS that is being used.

   ■ Display the current date.

   ■ Display the current time.

   ■ Display a directory listing of A: in the wide format.

CRITICAL THINKING

1. Using the Internet, search the classifieds for jobs requiring DOS. Were there any jobs that require knowledge of this operating system? Were you surprised at the outcome? Why do you think knowledge of DOS is still so important in today's job market?

2. DOS has a COPYDISK command that allows you to duplicate the contents of one disk to another. Software that is copyrighted may not be copied legally, yet this practice of pirating software continues. Do you think that it is ethical to pirate software? What are the penalties for pirating software? How do you think the software companies could better prevent this practice?

CHAPTER 3

MACINTOSH OPERATING SYSTEM

OBJECTIVES

Upon completion of this chapter you should be able to:

- Describe the hardware used on the Macintosh computer.

- Install and correctly set up the Macintosh operating system.

- Identify and be able to use different objects on the desktop.

- Identify and use different objects in windows.

- Move information in the operating system.

- Use features that are unique to the Macintosh operating sytem.

- Perform some general troubleshooting when errors occur.

⏱ **Estimated Time: 12+ hours**

VOCABULARY

Apple menu

close box

Finder

multitasking

resize button

Trash

windowshade

zoom box

Short Introduction to Macintosh

The Macintosh, introduced in 1984, was the first commercially viable computer with a *graphical user interface (GUI)*. One of the main distinctions between the early Macintosh and early PCs was that Windows was in reality a shell over DOS. That meant that there was a command-line user interface under the surface that users could resort to when needed. Until recently that was not true of Macintosh—all the capability of the OS was to be found in the GUI. With the release of MacOS X (pronounced 'MAC oh ess TEN'), that has changed somewhat because parts of the command-line Unix OS underlie MacOS.

Hardware Description

Because the Macintosh is a complete system (hardware and software) from a single vendor, the available hardware configurations are not as varied as they are for other types of operating systems. The advantage to this approach is that the operating system and hardware are much better integrated.

CPU

Another difference between Macintosh computers and Windows-based computers is the central processing unit (CPU) or microprocessor on which the computers are founded. Macintosh computers use a PowerPC chip invented by IBM and manufactured by Motorola. The PowerPC chip architecture uses a form of "reduced instruction set computing" (RISC). This architecture allows the computer to respond to instructions very quickly. The PowerPC chip family is among the most powerful microprocessors in the computing industry.

In addition to the native RISC portions of the chip, newer PowerPC chips contain additional instructions especially built to handle multimedia. This technology has various names, but it was originally called Altavec.

MEMORY

The first Macintosh, like all microcomputers of its time, was only able to execute one program at a time. As memory and capability increased, the operating system was altered to allow multiple programs to run simultaneously. This process is called *multitasking*.

As computers came to be used for multiple tasks, more memory was needed. Generally speaking, adding memory is one of the easiest ways to improve the performance of your Macintosh. The minimum amount of RAM recommended for running the traditional MacOS was 24 MB; 64 MB is suggested for running MacOS X if you want to have room left over for additional programs.

DISK DRIVES

The main storage for the Macintosh is in the form of a permanent hard drive. The hard drive will hold in the range of 6 to 20 gigabytes (GB), though larger hard disks are available. These drives may be connected to the computer via either an IDE interface (short for integrated drive electronics, as in Intel-based PC systems) or SCSI (for small computer system interface, an interface that offers faster drive access). Because the hard drive is the principal storage for the computer, the operating system is most often located on this drive. Your Macintosh may have other hard drives as well.

In addition to the main hard drive, the computer will often have CD-ROM or DVD-ROM drives, as well as removable media drives like the Iomega Zip drive or a SuperDisk, a 120-MB removable drive. See Figure 3-1.

CD-ROMs and DVD-ROMs are shiny read-only memory (ROM) discs, read by lasers, that can contain large amounts of information. Today's DVD-ROM drives usually can read CD-ROMs as well. A CD-ROM is capable of holding over 640 MB

FIGURE 3-1
Typical drive slots

CD-Rom Drive

Zip Drive

of storage, and a DVD-ROM can hold as much as 5, 10, 13, or 18 GB of data, depending on the disc. Often this data is in the form of music or video. Drives that can create CD-ROMs—called CD-R (recordable) and CD-RW (read-write)—are also available.

In a surprise move in 1998, Apple began offering a computer called the iMac without a 3.5-inch diskette drive. Actually, by that time, the traditional diskette did not offer enough storage capacity (approximately 1.4 MB) to be very useful. Still, it is nice to have a removable storage device that can be transported in your pocket, briefcase, or purse. Naturally, diskette drives can still be purchased and still come on some models, but their extinction is in sight.

Instead of a diskette drive, some other form of removable disk for your microcomputer is often added. Examples of removable disks include the Zip and Jaz drives from Iomega, and the SuperDisk from Imation. See Figure 3-2. (The SuperDisk has the advantage of being able to read floppies, as well as its own higher-density disks). These removable disks are very similar to the diskette, but store much more material—on the order of 100 MB to over 2 GB. Many models of Macintosh now come with Zip disk drives built-in.

FIGURE 3-2
Removable media

Operating System

The MacOS and MacOS X

With the introduction of MacOS X, Apple made a major change to the operating system. Earlier versions of MacOS (8.0, 8.1, 8.5, 9.0, and so forth) used cooperative multitasking, which allowed programs to do their own multitasking. (The feature makes the computer appear to do more than one thing at a time.) MacOS X uses true threaded multitasking, in which the operating system carefully controls each application's share of the microprocessor. But the MacOS X has more than improved multitasking. The foundation of MacOS X (called the *kernel*) is built from NextStep, a product developed by a company founded by Steve Jobs (one of Apple's original owners) and purchased by Apple. Because NextStep has a Unix kernel, many of the MacOS X functions are more complete and flexible than they were under previous versions. However, Apple has worked very hard to keep the look and feel of the Macintosh consistent, while changing its underlying structure.

MacOS X will seamlessly run most older programs using internal emulators. These emulators simulate the functions of the older operating system so that most of the original API (application programming interface) calls will work. Newer programs that take advantage of the power of the new operating system are said to be Carbon-compatible. Carbon is Apple's code name for the MacOS X

API. To make older programs Carbon-compatible, the programmers must change a small amount of their code (less than 10%, according to Apple) and recompile the program for use in MacOS X.

Similarities Among Macintosh Programs

Historically, one of the big advantages of the MacOS was that it presented a consistent user interface, both in the operating system and within each of the software programs written for it. (IBM PCs and compatibles finally have this advantage as well, under Windows.) This was accomplished primarily through the API as well as voluntary compliance to a set of programming rules. This made programming much more difficult, but helped make the experience of using a Macintosh computer much more pleasant for users. (Early IBM PC programmers often complained about how difficult Macintosh software was to write, but with Windows 95 and beyond, programmers face very similar difficulties in either platform.)

When the operating system and the individual programs have similar architecture, a lot of your knowledge about one can be transferred to the other. For example, the windows look the same and allow you to perform similar tasks, and mouse actions (click, double-click, and drag) have consistent functions. The first three or four pull-down menus contain related commands, and so on. Many of these features will be discussed in detail in this chapter.

STEP-BY-STEP ▷ 3.1

Start Up a Macintosh

1. Check to make sure that: 1) The power is correctly connected; 2) The monitor is correctly connected (if you have an iMac, don't bother—it is); and 3) The keyboard and mouse are connected to the Macintosh.

2. Press the **On** button on the keyboard. A chime will sound, and then the startup procedure will begin.

3. The Macintosh performs several tasks as it starts up. On a separate sheet of paper, write down each of the changes to the screen, and what parts of the booting process you believe they represent. Check your answers with your instructor. (There are approximately five of these steps, starting with the chime.)

Installation and Setup

Connections

MONITOR CONNECTIONS

Most of the current Macintosh line (the professional portable, the PowerBook; the consumer desktop, the iMac; and the consumer portable, the iBook) comes with a *monitor* already attached. Only the professional desktop series requires a monitor to be added. See Figure 3-3.

The professional desktop series and the PowerBook allow you to add a monitor. You can also add video cards so you can attach multiple monitors. When this situation occurs, the Macintosh automatically allows you to treat both screens together as one large virtual screen or to mirror the contents of one onto the other.

FIGURE 3-3
Connecting the monitor to the computer on a G3

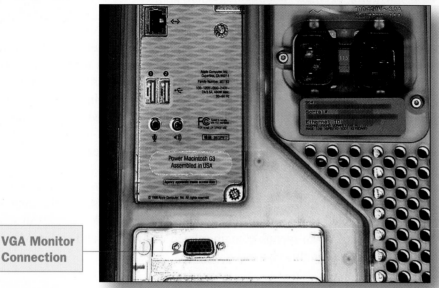

VGA Monitor
Connection

AUDIO IN AND OUT

Unlike early IBM PC-compatibles, all Macintosh models come with built-in sound. Therefore two of the standard *ports* on a Macintosh are for sound; these are stereo mini-phone jacks, like the kind used with Walkman headphones. One will have an icon of a speaker, and the other an icon of a microphone. See Figure 3-4.

FIGURE 3-4
Microphone icon for audio in; speaker icon for audio out

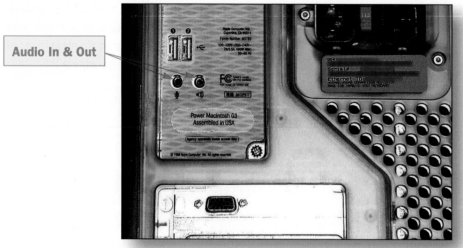

Audio In & Out

For sound input, use only a microphone intended for use with a computer. Others may work, but may accidentally damage the computer's sound input.

For sound output there are two things to remember. The first is that the sound output is *unamplified*. That means that whatever you plug it into must amplify the signal. For example, you could not plug it to the speakers on your home stereo system, but you might be able to plug it into the auxiliary input of your CD player or amplifier. The second thing is that the output is *stereo*. If you plug a mono connector into the jack you will probably get only one channel or the other (not both, and not stereo).

If your Macintosh has a CD-ROM drive in it, with the proper audio connections, your computer can play CDs just like a CD player.

KEYBOARD, MOUSE AND OTHER I/O CONNECTIONS

If you are working on an older Macintosh, the keyboard is connected via a unique port called *ADB*—Apple desktop bus. This bus connection is capable of daisy-chaining up to seven devices and can be used for other input and output devices besides a keyboard or mouse. Graphic tablets and joysticks are also connected in this way.

For certain kinds of software, a hardware key is required to run the software. These hardware keys, called *dongles*, are often connected to the ADB port. In addition to the ADB port, older models of Macintosh had two *serial ports*: one for a modem connection, and one for a printer.

In Macintosh computers since 1999, a *USB* (universal system bus) port has replaced the ADB port. See Figure 3-5. The USB has two advantages: It's considerably *faster*, and it's *compatible* with other hardware besides Macintosh. Because of its increased speed, the USB port can be used for other devices besides a keyboard and mouse, such as printers and disk drives.

Most Macintosh computers come with only one or two USB ports. If you add more than two devices, you will need to get a *USB hub* (USB does not daisy-chain like ADB). Fortunately, if you are adding an Apple monitor, it may have a USB hub built into it, with additional ports.

FIGURE 3-5
Older Macintoshes used ADB; newer Macs use USB

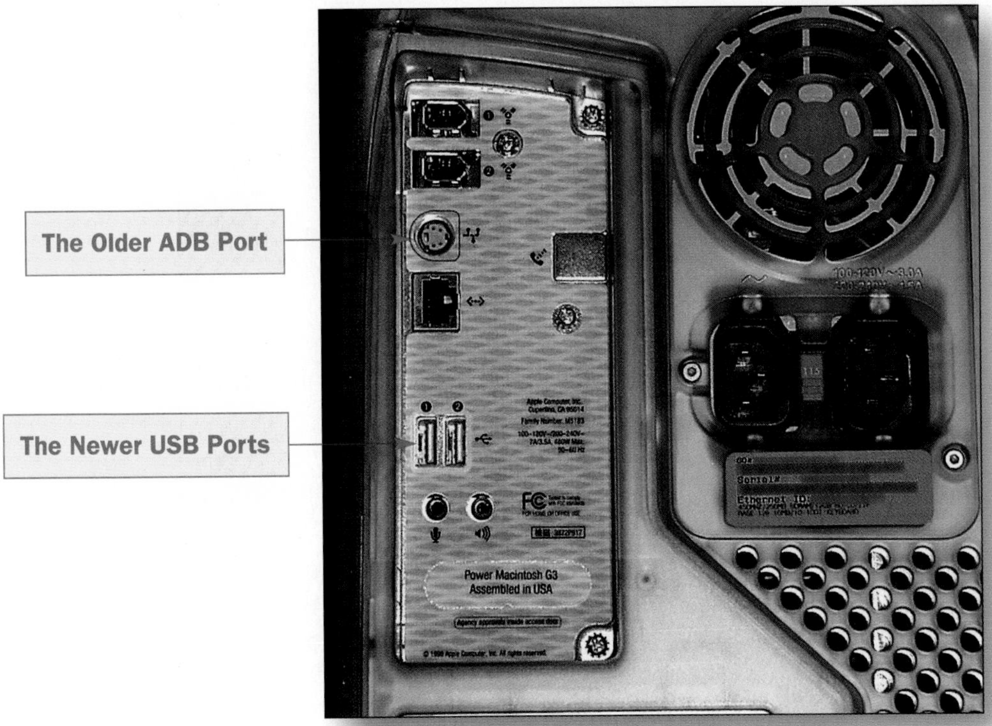

The Older ADB Port

The Newer USB Ports

EXTERNAL DISK AND OTHER HIGH-SPEED CONNECTIONS

For higher-speed connections, there is a parallel port called a SCSI, which used to be standard on all Macintosh models. However, Macintosh computers now use the popular IDE drives. In addition, a new port, called a *FireWire* connection, is now being used for high-speed transfers. Many digital video cameras and other devices are made with FireWire so that their contents can be transferred directly to the computer. FireWire is also fast enough for disk drives, scanners, and other devices. SCSI is also used for fast, reliable disk drives—especially those that need to have fast, redundant data for capturing video and sound.

A Field Trip to the Back of a Macintosh

Small icons printed or impressed into the plastic in the case can identify the ports on a Macintosh. See Figure 3-6(a) and 3-6(b). In this activity you will learn to recognize the ports both by the icons and by the shape of the ports themselves. Cut paper into small squares and draw the icons for the various ports down one column, down another write the port's name, and in another column, its purpose.

FIGURE 3-6(a)
Back of Macintosh G3 showing connections

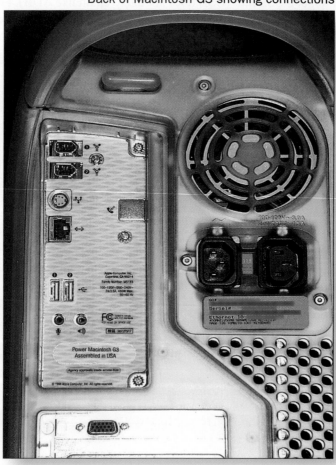

FIGURE 3-6(b)
Side of iMac showing connections

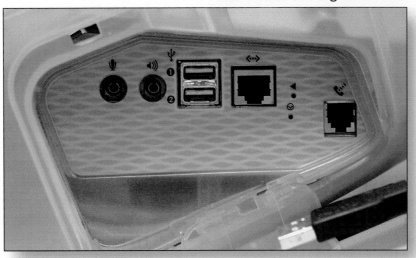

FIGURE 3-6(b)
Side of iMac showing connections

OS Installation—Easy

Apple has worked very hard to make it a pleasant experience to use the computer. To accomplish this, they start with an easy-to-install operating system. In a newly purchased Macintosh, the system is already installed. You would be required to install the operating system only if the system became *corrupted* (broken) for some reason, or if you were *upgrading* the system to the next version. In either case, you would simply insert a CD-ROM disc with the operating system on it, double-click on the install icon, and proceed with the installation by answering the questions (you may be provided with an Easy Install selection to do this).

The install program will analyze your Macintosh to determine memory, storage, and additional resources and begin to install a standard operating system that will function on your machine.

The install program also keeps all your preferences so that any software you have installed on your Macintosh will be maintained. Occasionally this could cause a problem, but most of the time this feature is a significant help to you

After you have installed the system, you may be required to set up some of the attributes of the system again. In particular, your network setup may have been forgotten in the installation.

OS Installation—Customize

Occasionally, an easy install is not enough. On rare occasions, you want to install some unique features, or avoid installing some features that you will never use. When this happens, your configuration has unique attributes that do not fit the easy install paradigm. Choose Customize Install for more control of the installation, if it is available.

The main difference between the standard install and a custom install is that in the latter you are given more options. Generally, these are options of things to leave out, not to add. So a Customize Install is often a smaller installation than the Easy Install.

Another option under Customize Install is to do a *clean install*. In a clean install, no part of the existing OS is used in the install—it's as though the OS were being placed on the computer for the first time. The previous OS files are placed in a separate file. This option is used particularly for installations that are having problems. See Troubleshooting, later in this chapter, for more information about a clean install.

Set up a Macintosh

1. If it is on, turn your Macintosh off, then gently remove all the cables and plugs connected to the Macintosh. This is what you would do if you were going to transport your Macintosh.

2. Look carefully at the connector area of the Macintosh. Examine each of the different kinds of connections. Then, one by one, plug each of the connectors into the Macintosh. If you have a Macintosh User's Manual, follow its instructions for connecting. Otherwise, start with the power cord, then the monitor (if needed), then the keyboard and mouse, and finally other connections (modem, Ethernet, printer, etc.) Do not force these in. Carefully check the shape of the connector to make sure you are placing it correctly.

3. On a piece of paper, sketch each of the connector icons. Next to that, write the connector's name (if you know it), and note what kind of devices are plugged into that connector.

Install the Macintosh System

1. Locate the Macintosh system CD-ROM you want to install. Unless you are having problems with your computer (see Troubleshooting) you will rarely install a previous version of the system. Place the Macintosh System CD-ROM into the CD-ROM drive. If your Macintosh has a DVD-ROM drive instead, place the CD-ROM in that drive.

2. There will usually be an icon in the CD-ROM contents called MacOS Install or something like it. Double-click that icon. (The instructions may ask you to reboot the computer with the CD-ROM as the system disc. If this happens, reboot the computer and hold down the 'C' key as it reboots.)

3. Subsequent screens will show you:
   ■ The installation steps
   ■ Special instructions before beginning
   ■ Apple Computer licensing agrement for this version of the MacOS
   ■ An options screen, showing options you can install
   Not all install programs have all of these screens, and not all operate the same way.

4. After the screens mentioned above, the Continue button becomes an Install button. If you are going to abort installation, this is the time to do so. Otherwise, click **Install**.

5. The computer will proceed to install the system on your Macintosh. Once it is finished, you will be instructed to restart your computer.

Basic Functionality

With your hardware and operating system set up, you can now enjoy your Macintosh. When you first start up a Macintosh, after the operating system is fully loaded and operating, you will see what is known as the Macintosh Desktop, with icons and maybe a window or two. This program, which permits you to navigate and find your files, is known as the ***Finder***. Many times in this document the term *Finder* is used to refer to the MacOS. A phrase such as "return to the Finder," means to bring the Finder (or MacOS) to the front so you can work in it.

A *cursor* is a screen pointer. The Macintosh has two types of cursors. The first follows the mouse around the screen. It appears to float over the screen because it can go anywhere on the screen. Over certain parts of the screen, it may change shape (from a simple arrow to an I-beam, for example) as a signal to the user that it is prepared to perform a certain function.

The second type of cursor indicates your location in the text (that is, if you were to press a key on the keyboard, this cursor indicates where that character would be inserted). It is usually a small, blinking, vertical line in the text. You can use the mouse to place a text cursor by clicking the location where you want to insert the cursor.

Before exploring the Finder, however, let's look at some of the devices connected to the computer which you can control directly.

Using the Mouse

The one thing that made the original Macintosh a Macintosh was the *mouse*. The mouse is a screen pointing device shaped something like a puck with one or more buttons on top.

MOUSE ACTIONS

As you move the mouse around on the table, a cursor (known as the *mouse cursor*) moves around on the screen. The mouse can be used in the MacOS to select files, select options, push buttons, and move things around by dragging them.

CLICK

The basic mouse action is called a *click*. To click the mouse, you move its cursor over something you want to act upon and lightly press and release the mouse button. (If your mouse has more than one button, you normally do this to the left mouse button.) It's called a click because of the sound the mouse makes when you do this.

Clicking is used to select icons on the screen, press buttons in multimedia software, and to point to something.

DOUBLE-CLICK

A second action that is commonly used is called a *double-click*. You do this by pressing and releasing the mouse button (or left mouse button) twice in rapid succession. This must be done fast enough that the cursor does not move between clicks.

Double-clicking is used to open something. For example, clicking an icon once in the operating system selects the icon, but doesn't do anything with it; however, the icon does darken to show it is selected. When you double-click an icon, MacOS attempts to open the program, document, or folder associated with the icon.

DRAG

The third and final mouse action is to *drag*. To drag, you first move the mouse into position, then press and hold down the mouse button (or left mouse button) as you move the mouse to a new position.

Dragging can be used to select multiple objects, or to move objects from one place to another, depending on the starting position of the mouse. For example, if you start over an icon and then drag, you will move the icon to another position in the window or to another container on the screen. If you start in a location where there is no object, dragging will draw a rectangle and select all the items that fall within the rectangle.

MOUSE-KEY COMBINATIONS AND RIGHT CLICK

For maximum flexibility, some keyboard keys can be used in combination with mouse actions. For example, if you click one icon, then, while holding down the Shift key, click another icon, MacOS will select both simultaneously. Generally, mouse-key combinations are used only with the Shift, Control, Option, and Command keys. See Figure 3-7.

Here are a few standard mouse-key combinations:

FIGURE 3-7
Keys that affect the function and other keys

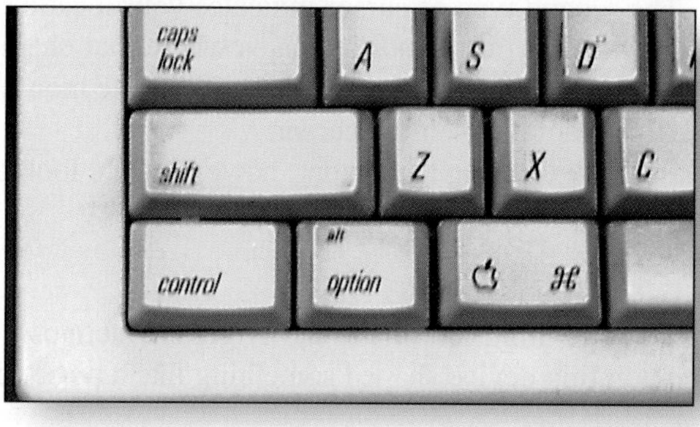

- *Shift-click* allows you to select multiple items.

- *Command-click* lets you select discontinuous items from a list.

- *Control-click* brings up a "context menu" whose *context* is whatever the mouse is pointing at.

When a context menu pops up, it display the options available at that point. For example, if you control-click over an icon, you will see a short menu of options available with that icon, such as opening it, sharing it, or moving it to the Trash.

Sometimes a mouse has more than one button. When that is the case, the left button functions as the mouse button described above, and the right button functions as a Control-click—allowing you to look at context menus. The section on keyboards below details the location of the other keys.

Using the Keyboard

THE ON KEY AND THE REST OF THE KEYBOARD

The keyboard functions pretty much as any keyboard, with letters, numbers, and symbols. However, there are a few unique keys with which you need to be familiar.

On many computers, you turn on the computer using a switch or button located somewhere on the computer. To turn on a Macintosh, you press the On key, located at the upper-right corner of the keyboard. The On key has a left-pointing arrow icon on it, or a circle with a line coming out the top. See Figures 3-8(a) and 3-8(b).

FIGURE 3-8(a)
The On key, Macintosh

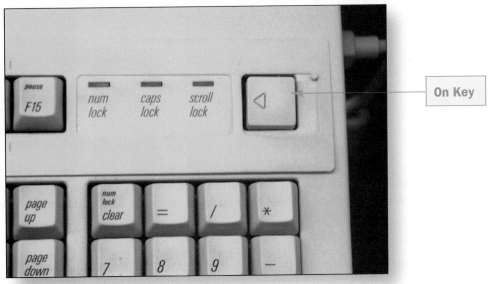

On Key

FIGURE 3-8(b)
The On key, iMac

On Key

OPEN-APPLE AND COMMAND KEY

There are at least two ways to accomplish the most common functions on the Macintosh. One is with the mouse, and the other is with the keyboard. Most of the keyboard functions are performed using the Command key. The Command key on a Macintosh has a propeller figure (⌘) and an open Apple () symbol on it. It is usually found on either side of the space bar. The Command key should not be confused with the Control key—the Macintosh Command key is unique.

A number of Command key combinations are either standard or traditional—meaning they work in most programs, as well as in MacOS:

Control-x   Cut

Control-c   Copy

Control-v	Paste
Control-p	Print
Control-o	Open
Control-w	Close
Control-n	New
Control-s	Save
Control-a	Select All
Control-z	Undo
Control-q	Quit

In addition to these standard Command key combinations, Command keys are used in many non-standard ways. For example, where Command-s means Save on many programs, Shift-Command-s means Save As....

OPTION KEY—ALT KEY

The Command key, which allows the user to perform functions, should not be confused with the Option key. The Option key (similar to the Alt key on an IBM PC-compatible) allows the user to type characters on the screen that are not standard alphanumeric characters. For example, on many fonts Option-c gives you a copyright symbol (©). Option-2 types a trademark symbol (™), Shift-Option-8 gives a degree symbol (°), and so forth. A desk accessory (a small program found under the Apple menu) called Key Caps tells you which Option-key combinations can be used for which characters.

In particular, MacOS has always been able to type diacritical marks of European languages. Here is a short list of most European characters the Macintosh keyboard can type.

ä	a-umlaut	press Option-u, then type a
ë	e-umlaut	press Option-u, then type e
ï	i-umlaut	press Option-u, then type i
ö	o-umlaut	press Option-u, then type o
ü	u-umlaut	press Option-u, then type u again
â	a-caret	press Option-i, then type a
ê	e-caret	press Option-i, then type e
î	i-caret	press Option-i, then type i again
ô	o-caret	press Option-i, then type o
û	u-caret	press Option-i, then type u
á	a-accent	press Option-e, then type a
é	e-accent	press Option-e, then type e again
í	i-accent	press Option-e, then type i
ó	o-accent	press Option-e, then type o
ú	u-accent	press Option-e, then type u
à	a-grave	press Option-`, then type a
è	e-grave	press Option-`, then type e
ì	i-grave	press Option-`, then type i
ò	o-grave	press Option-`, then type o

ù	u-grave	press Option-`, then type u
ñ	enye	press Option-n, then type n again
ã	a-tilde	press Option-n, then type a
õ	o-tilde	press Option-n, then type o
ç	cidilla	press Option-c
ø	crossed-o	press Option-o
å	halo-a	press Option-a

These combinations also work to create capital letters with these special marks.

CONTROL KEY

Technically speaking, when combined with a letter of the alphabet, the Control key generates an actual character that may not be visible on the screen. Some of these combinations represent their literal meaning in ASCII (like Control-m is Return, and Control-i is Tab). Some programs take advantage of these combinations, some do not.

On Macintosh computers with a one-button mouse, holding the Control key can substitute for the second mouse button. To show context menus (the main purpose of the second button on a PC mouse) hold down the Control key while clicking. (See context menus, previously explained in this chapter.)

FUNCTION KEYS

In the history of the Macintosh, there was a point when Apple was trying to promote the Macintosh platform as a serious business machine. It was never a big contender in that market, in spite of the fact that most good business software was available for both platforms and the Macintosh was easier to use. To compete in the business market, a row of *function keys* was added to the top of professional keyboards. Some Macintosh programs use these keys; many do not.

Function keys are particularly useful for programs that need a lot of control buttons, such as video editors. Often when this is the case, a keyboard template overlay is provided to identify which keys perform what function. Similarly, the Escape key on a Macintosh is really superfluous, though it has been used for various things at different times.

OTHER KEYS AND KEY COMBOS

There are a number of other keys that are of special note.

Arrow keys work as expected, moving the text cursor up, down, left, and right. Thanks to Microsoft and the fact that early Macintosh models had no arrow keys, the number pad can also be used for other things (like arrow keys—using 8 for up, 2 for down, 4 for left, and 6 for right). The NumLock key, in the upper-left corner of the number pad, allows you to toggle between these two functions.

Be aware that some programs also distinguish between the Return key (next to the alphabet keys) and the Enter key (on the number pad). For example, Microsoft Excel uses the Return key to enter data and move down a line, while the Enter key enters the data but does not move down a line.

The Desktop

After the computer boots up, you will see the *desktop*—the most familiar part of the MacOS. See Figure 3-9.

The most notable features of the desktop (when there are no windows open) are the *menu bar* across the top, the *icons* of disks or other volumes in the upper-right corner, and the *trash can* in the lower-right corner. The menu bar always appears at the top of the screen (not at the top of individual windows as in the Windows OS). The volumes (such as disks) always appear at the top right. They

FIGURE 3-9
The Macintosh Desktop

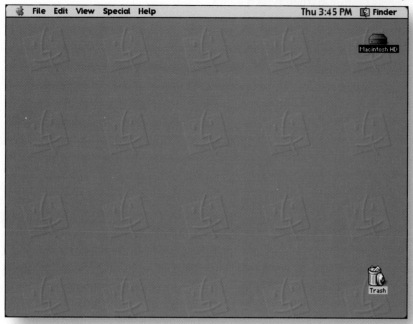

can be moved around the desktop, but when you reboot, they will reappear at the top right. The Trash icon can be moved anywhere and will stay wherever you put it—even after rebooting.

MENU BAR

Across the top of the Macintosh desktop is the menu bar. See Figure 3-10. The menu bar is always across the top of the screen except when some program, like a multimedia program, has turned it off.

FIGURE 3-10
The menu bar

When multiple programs are operating at the same time, the menu bar changes with whichever program is on top (active) at that time. Some programs also change the menus in the menu bar depending on what function is currently running. You can identify the active program by looking at the icon located at right end of the menu bar. Each program has a unique icon, and a small version of the icon is visible in that position if the program is on top. If you still can't identify the active program, click on the icon, and a list of all currently running programs opens, with a checkmark by the one that is currently active.

The first three or four menus in the menu bar are pretty standard in most programs. They are the *Apple menu* (represented by the Apple symbol), the File menu, the Edit menu, and sometimes the View menu. These are discussed in detail below. In fact, even if there are no File or Edit functions (like in some games), the menus are often there anyway, to maintain consistency in the look and feel of the software.

The right side of the menu bar contains a menu that enables you to change the active program, and do some other system-related tasks. Next to that may be a clock and icons for other services provided by the system.

ICONS

Files (and other elements) are represented on the computer screen in MacOS as icons. Icons are simply small pictures that are representative of an actual item. The pictures are 32 × 32 pixels, and can be full-color.

There are three kinds of files in the Macintosh operating system. The first of these is *applications* (also known as *programs*). The second is *documents* (sometimes called *data files* on other systems). The third is a *container*, usually a *folder* or *volume*. These are occasionally called *subdirectories* on other systems. See Figure 3-11.

There is a general rule that will permit you to identify the three types of files according to the appearance of their icons.

Application icons usually contain a square turned 45° with a hand, sometimes holding a pencil or other tool. Document icons look like a piece of paper with the corner turned down, and folder icons look like a file folder. There are many variations of these icons, and some do not follow these rules.

FIGURE 3-11
Three different kinds of icons

VOLUMES (PHYSICAL CONTAINERS)

On the desktop the icon in the upper-right corner, just below the menu bar, is the *startup volume* (a container). This is usually the hard disk, but it may be any other device used to start up the Macintosh. For example, if the Macintosh is started with a CD-ROM, the CD-ROM's icon and name will be there. It may also be a diskette, a Zip or Jaz disk, or even a remote hard disk. See Figure 3-12.

Other hard disks, diskettes, CD-ROMs, DVD-ROMs, Zip and Jaz disks, and other volumes or containers will appear just below the startup volume.

FIGURE 3-12
Volumes on a Macintosh desktop

Double-clicking a volume opens a window that represents the contents of that volume. You can also open the window by clicking the volume once (to select it) then using the File menu's Open command to open the window. Once open, the window will show icons (or a list) of the contents of the disk.

If the volume is removable (like a CD-ROM, diskette, or Zip disk) you can eject the disk by dragging it to the Trash. **Important: Dragging a volume to the Trash ejects it; dragging any other icon to the Trash throws it away!** Removable disks can also be ejected by selecting the disk and choosing Eject from the Special menu, or by pressing Command-e.

When you move a file from one place to another within one volume, it simply moves the file. On the other hand, if you move a file from somewhere in one volume to somewhere in another, it does not move the file, but makes a copy of the file on the new volume. You now have two copies of the file—one on each volume. One way you can tell whether you are moving or copying a file is to watch the mouse cursor: A plus sign appears while dragging if the effect of dropping the file would create a new copy rather than moving the original file.

TRASH

The **Trash icon** acts like any other container. One difference is that when there is anything in it, the icon looks different (the lid is off and you can see items inside). See Figure 3-13. You can retrieve things from the Trash by opening its window (just like any other container—by double-clicking on it) and moving the item out that you want to retrieve.

One nice thing about the trash can on a Macintosh is it never runs out of space.

On the Special menu you can find the Empty Trash command. If you select this menu item, the Trash icon changes to an empty one (with the lid on) and you can no longer retrieve items from the Trash. (Strictly speaking, you can still retrieve things after you empty the Trash, but it's very difficult.) See Figure 3-14.

Unless you have set it not to warn you, emptying the Trash causes a warning dialog box to appear; you must agree before it will empty the Trash. See Figure 3-15. (You can also empty the Trash and do several other things through a context menu that appears if you right-click—or Control-click—the Trash icon.)

FIGURE 3-13
The trash can icon with items inside

FIGURE 3-14
Empty Trash

FIGURE 3-15
The warning dialog box

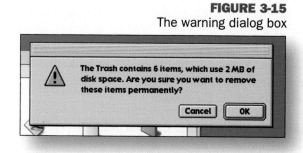

ALIASES

Another kind of file that may appear on the desktop is an *alias*. An alias is a representation of a file that appears elsewhere. In Windows these are called *shortcuts*. An alias is a way to have a file appear in two places at the same time. One of them is the real file; the other is just a pointer to the real file.

Aliases can be distinguished from the real files in two ways. On an alias, the filename appears in italics, and there is a small arrow symbol on the icon itself.

OTHER FILES ON THE DESKTOP

Volumes and trash are not the only types of files that can appear on the desktop. Actually, just about any file can be moved to the desktop. (Technically, they are not really on the desktop, but in a special, invisible folder inside the volume called a Desktop Folder.) They will stay where you put them on the desktop. This is one way to make files easy to find.

We strongly urge you to avoid putting many files on the desktop, even though it is permitted. For one thing, when you have so many files on the desktop, it becomes hard to find anything (just like on your real desktop). Here's another reason.

Each volume (disk) has its own desktop folder and the contents of all of the volumes appear on the desktop at the same time. Suppose you have the Macintosh's hard disk, a CD-ROM, and a Zip disk all mounted and visible on your desktop. You move a file from a folder inside the hard disk to the desktop and it actually moves to the Desktop Folder, which belongs to the hard disk. Now you do the same to a file on the Zip disk. Though the two files appear side-by-side, one is actually in the Desktop Folder that belongs to the hard disk, and the other is in the Desktop Folder that belongs to the Zip disk. When you eject the Zip disk, the second file will disappear (because its Desktop Folder is no longer mounted on the computer).

Now suppose you move a file from the CD-ROM to the desktop. In this case, MacOS is smart enough to know that it cannot move the file to the Desktop Folder of the CD-ROM because that folder cannot be changed (it is on an unwritable CD-ROM). So MacOS automatically puts the file in the hard disk's Desktop Folder. But there is no indication to you, the user, where it actually is storing the file. This kind of confusion makes it a good idea not to place files on the desktop.

Windows

The MacOS uses *windows* to show the contents of files and folders. See Figure 3-16. When you double-click on a folder, a window opens to show you what's inside the folder. When you double-click on a document, a window opens to let you see that document in the program in which it was composed. Though program windows and MacOS windows have a lot in common, they can be different, too. We will focus on what MacOS windows look like. Most of what you learn here can be applied to program windows as well.

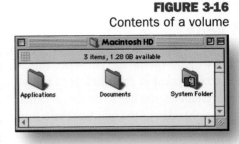
FIGURE 3-16
Contents of a volume

TITLE BAR

The striped or gray bar across the top of a window is known as the *title bar*. See Figure 3-17. The title bar contains buttons that affect the window as well as the title of the window. This title is usually the same as the icon that you double-clicked to open it. The title bar also acts as the main handle of the window. To move a window's position on the screen, drag the title bar. (You can also move most windows by dragging any outside edge.)

FIGURE 3-17
The title bar

CLOSE BOX

Nearly every window in MacOS has a small, empty square in the upper-left corner of the title bar. This square is known as the ***close box***; clicking it closes the window. See Figure 3-18. (You can also close the window from the File menu, and with the Command-w shortcut). The close box is analogous to the X button in the upper-right corner of a window in the Windows OS.

FIGURE 3-18
The close box

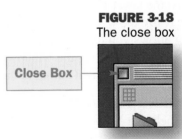

Close Box

ZOOM BOX

Another button found on the title bar is the ***zoom box***, in the upper-right corner of the window. See Figure 3-19. The zoom box looks like a square within a square. Clicking on the zoom box changes the size and shape of the window to its optimum size. Clicking it again will change it back to the original shape.

WINDOWSHADE

The button in the title bar next to the zoom box is the **windowshade**. See Figure 3-19. The windowshade allows you to roll up the window into its title bar, just like an old-fashioned windowshade. When you click on the windowshade button, the window disappears, leaving only the title bar. Click it again and the window reappears. (The window can sometimes be rolled up by double-clicking anywhere in the title bar.)

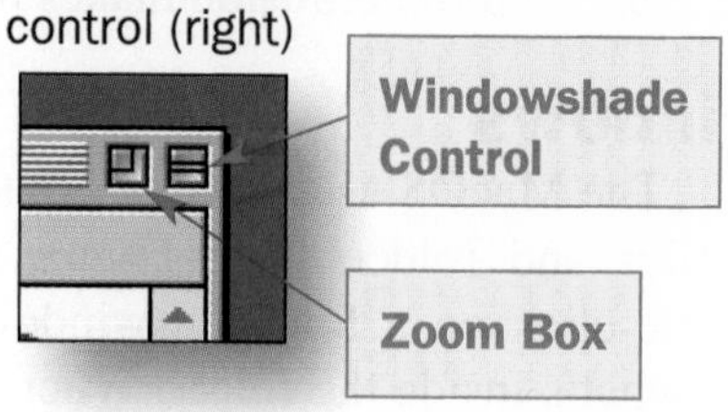

SCROLL BARS

Often the contents of a window do not fit inside the space given for the window on the screen. When this happens you need to be able to scroll around in the window to show the rest of the contents. The mechanism you use to do this is called a *scroll bar*. See Figure 3-20. There is a vertical scroll bar along the right edge of the window and a horizontal scroll bar along the bottom. Each scroll bar consists of four parts: an arrow pointing in one direction (up or left), another arrow pointing in the opposite direction (down or right), a slider (to show where you are), and a gray area in which the slider moves. The relative position of the slider in the gray area tells where you are in the window. For example, if the slider is at the top, there are window contents that are below the window's current view.

You can scroll through a window in three ways: 1) You can press the buttons at either end of the scroll bar. This makes the slider move smoothly through the gray area, and consequently scrolls the window's contents smoothly through the window's opening. 2) The slider itself can be dragged to a new position. The window will scroll as you drag—you can see the contents of the window move through the window opening. 3) Last of all, you can click anywhere in the gray scroll area. When you do this, the slider jumps to a new position, and one whole window's contents move through the window opening.

RESIZING THE WINDOW

At the lower-right corner is a small draggable area that allows you to resize the window. See Figure 3-21. This works very differently from the zoom box: The *resize button* allows you to change the window to nearly any size or shape you want. To resize a window, use the title bar to drag the window's upper-left corner to the position you want, then drag the size button in the lower-right corner to the size and shape you want.

CHANGING THE VIEW

The typical view for a window in MacOS is to show icons lined up in columns and rows. There are other ways in which to view the contents of a window. See Figure 3-22. These include smaller icons (with the labels to the side) and

FIGURE 3-19
The zoom box (left) and windowshade control (right)

Windowshade Control

Zoom Box

FIGURE 3-20
Two kinds of scroll bars

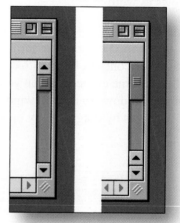

FIGURE 3-21
Resize button

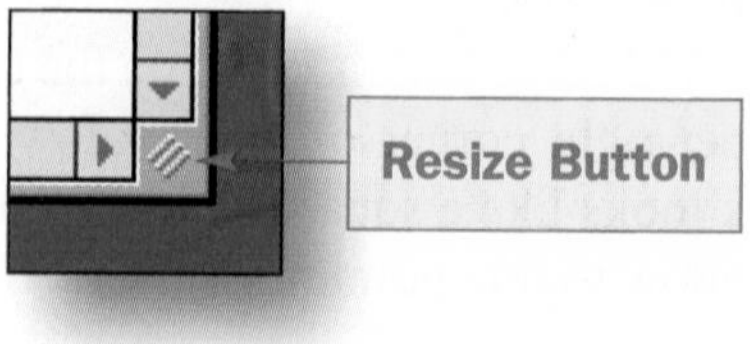

Resize Button

lists. Sometimes it is more convenient to view the contents of a folder in some way other than by icons. For example, you may have a large number of pictures in a folder and need to have them sorted alphabetically by name to find them quickly.

FIGURE 3-22
The View menu

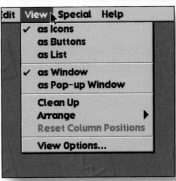

 TEP-BY-STEP ▷ 3.5

Identify the Parts of the Finder

1. Name three mouse actions and tell what each is used for. For example, *clicking* is pushing the mouse button down quickly and releasing it. When you place the mouse over an icon and click, it selects the icon.

2. Identify the two special keys on a Macintosh keyboard and explain how they differ.

3. Pull down the Apple menu and run the desk accessory called Key Caps. From the Key Caps menu select the Helvetica or Times font. In the Key Caps program, find out how to type the following special characters. Write down your solutions and share them with your group. If your partner or members of the group cannot figure this out, teach them how to do it.
- A bullet (•)
- The copyright symbol (©)
- The trademark symbol (™)
- The registered trademark symbol (®)
- Curly quotes, in and out ("and")
- The not equals sign (≠)
- A Spanish, upside-down exclamation mark (¡)

If these are too easy for you, here are some more advanced characters:
- A diamond character (◊)
- A long dash (called an *em dash* by printers) (—)
- A 'plus or minus' symbol (±)

Here are some even more advanced keys:
- The accented 'e' in *résumé* (é)
- The accented 'n' in *el niño* (ñ)

4. With no windows open in the Finder, take turns (with a partner) pointing to various parts of the screen. With each of them, describe a) what the part is called, b) what the part does, and c) how you use it. For example, you might point at the Trash and say, "This icon is called the Trash. It lets you throw stuff away—delete files from the hard disk. To throw something away, you drag its icon to the Trash." You do not need to go into detail about each of the menus unless you want to. Do this for the following desktop items:
- Icons
- Disks (sometimes called volumes)
- The menu bar

73

5. Explore the contents of the system's hard disk. Identify one of each of the following kinds of files. Describe to your partner or group why you think it is the kind of file it is, and explain what it does. Identify at least one of each of these three types:
- An application
- A document
- A folder

6. Open a window on the desktop by double-clicking on a volume or folder. With your partner or group, take turns describing the name, function, and method of using each of the parts of a window, as you did in Step 4. Do this for the following items:
- A title bar
- A scroll bar
- The close box
- The zoom box
- The windowshade button
- Resize button

The Menu Bar

In the early days, you would select a menu item by putting the mouse cursor over a menu and then holding the mouse button down. The selected menu would then drop down. Still holding down the mouse, you would then move the mouse cursor (drag) to the option you wanted and let go. When you let go, the drop-down menu disappeared, and the selected action took place. MacOS will still allow you to work this way, but Apple has also learned a trick from Windows: You can simply click once on the menu, and then click on the menu option. If you do not make the second click within a certain amount of time, the drop-down menu automatically closes.

Menu items that end in **...** indicate that a dialog box will open if you choose that item. A dialog box contains a message or enables you to interact with the program. You must complete the action requested by the dialog box before you can move on. Typical dialog boxes have fields in which you can enter data (such as a filename) and buttons (such as Cancel and OK).

Menus also show the shortcut keys that can be used in lieu of the menu item. If a shortcut combination is available, it is displayed to the right of the menu item. When menu items are active they are in full color (usually black); when they are inactive they are *dimmed out* (light gray in color). Also, active items invert (highlight) when the mouse cursor moves over them to indicate that you can choose them; inactive menu items do not change—they stay gray. Menu items are organized into groups, using horizontal separator lines.

As mentioned previously, the menu bar in MacOS doesn't move. It stays at the top of the screen; however, it does change. Depending on what program is on top (active) some of the menus that appear in the menu bar will change, and the contents of each menu will also change. This is intentional. Although it may seem confusing at first to have all the menus look alike and appear in the same location, it actually makes the screen easier to use in the long run. For example, no matter what program you're using, you will always know where to find the Open and Save functions (under the File menu), where to find the Cut and Paste functions (under the Edit menu), and so forth.

Next we'll discuss each menu separately and describe what each typically contains. Remember that different menus may appear in different programs, and the contents of even the standard menus may be different.

The Apple Menu

The *Apple menu* is visible in every program and does not change much. See Figure 3-23. It contains system-level programs and utilities to help you operate your Macintosh. For example, choosing a printer, changing the attributes of a screen saver, and reconfiguring your system can all be done through utility programs found on the Apple menu. Some of the more important ones are discussed below.

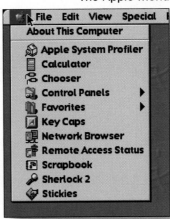

FIGURE 3-23
The Apple menu

CHOOSER

The Chooser allows you to choose services attached to your computer. The most common of these is a printer.

To select a printer you must perform the following steps:

- Open the Chooser by selecting it from the Apple menu. See Figure 3-24.

- Select the driver (or service) by clicking the icon located in the box in the upper-left corner of the Chooser dialog box. If you are choosing a printer, you would select the driver for that printer. As an example, if you are printing to an Apple LaserWriter printer, select the LaserWriter icon in the box.

FIGURE 3-24
Using the Chooser

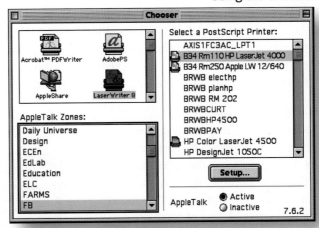

- If you are in a large installation of Macintosh computers, you may also see Macintosh zones listed in a box right below that box. If that is the case, select the zone in which the printer you are looking for is connected.

- A list of printers that can use that driver appears in the list on the right. Select the one to which you want to print by clicking on its name.

- Close the Chooser by clicking its close box.

That's it. You have now selected a printer. Selecting other services (such as access to a file server) is very similar to this process, though it may involve other dialog boxes that require you to enter passwords, and so on.

EXTENSIONS AND THE EXTENSION MANAGER

Extensions are additions to the MacOS that enable it to perform additional tasks. For example, the ability to display movies is an add-on called QuickTime. These files are generally kept in a special folder within the System folder called Extensions. There is another folder called Extensions (unused) for extensions that are not currently in use.

FIGURE 3-25
The Extension Manager

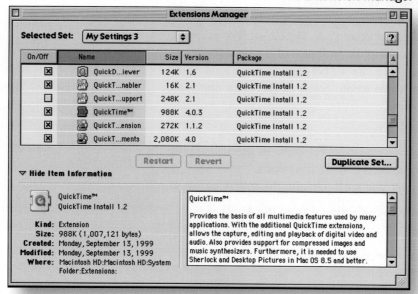

There is a control panel called the Extension Manager that lets you choose which extensions are active. See Figure 3-25. When you click on an extension to deactivate it, MacOS moves the extension to the "Extensions (unused)" folder. The next time you reboot the system, it will boot without that extension. You can also activate extensions to be part of MacOS the next time it boots.

CONTROL PANELS

Control panels are small utility programs that change the way the MacOS operates. See Figure 3-26. You can change the appearance of the screen, the date and time, the way the keyboard or mouse responds, and many other facets of the operating system. A few of these are discussed below.

FIGURE 3-26
Control panels

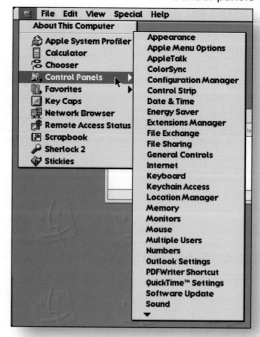

■ *Appearance*: Lets you change how the Macintosh screen looks and operates. Allows you to change colors, sounds, and other screen elements.

■ *Date and Time*: Lets you update the time or date of the system clock on your Macintosh.

■ *General*: This control panel has the functions for modifying some general operations of MacOS.

- *Mouse*: Allows you to adjust how the mouse works—for example, how fast you have to sequentially click for a double-click.

- *Keyboard*: Allows you adjust how the keyboard works, such as how long you hold the key down before it starts to auto-repeat.

- *Memory*: Allows you to change the way the MacOS manages memory.

- *Monitors and Sound*: This set of control panels allow you to manage several things: the volume and balance of sound, the resolution at which your screen will display, and, if you have more than one monitor attached to your Macintosh, their relative location to each other. (Some versions of MacOS have separate control panels for monitors and sound; others merge them.)

File Menu

The File menu contains items related to storing and retrieving files. In a program, it usually contains such options as Open..., Close, Save, Save As..., Page Setup..., Print..., and others. In MacOS it usually includes Open and Close, among others.

GET INFO

Two of the most important menu items found under the File menu are Get Info and Find File. See Figure 3-27. Get Info opens a dialog box about any selected program, document, or folder to give you basic information about that item. In the case of a folder or volume, it tells the size and location of the file. In the case of a program, it provides the memory allocation among other things. In the case of a file, it tells the dates that file was created and last modified.

Of particular note in Get Info is the ability to re-allocate the memory settings for a given program.

- To change the amount of memory required for a program to open, select the program by clicking it once.

- Pull down the File menu to Get Info. This will open the Get Info dialog box for that program. See Figure 3-28.

- Click on the pop-up menu in the middle of the dialog box. Select Memory Setting from that pop-up menu. Three fields appears at the bottom of the dialog box. These are the suggested, minimum, and preferred memory allocations for that program.

- Change the minimum or preferred memory allocations as needed. Never lower either one below the suggested memory allocation. Doing so will cause the program (and sometimes MacOS) to be unstable, or will prevent the program from starting up.

FIGURE 3-27
Use Get Info

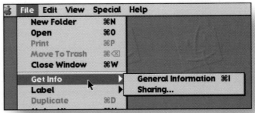

FIGURE 3-28
Changing memory allocation

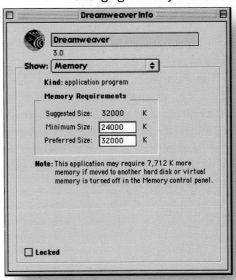

FIND FILE

Another important function found under the File menu is Find File. This option helps you find a file by identifying part of its name. You can also limit your search by looking for other attributes of the file, such as size, last date modified, and so on. This option uses part of the Sherlock search program. Notice that it also allows you to search the Web for information as well. See Figure 3-29.

FIGURE 3-29
Find File

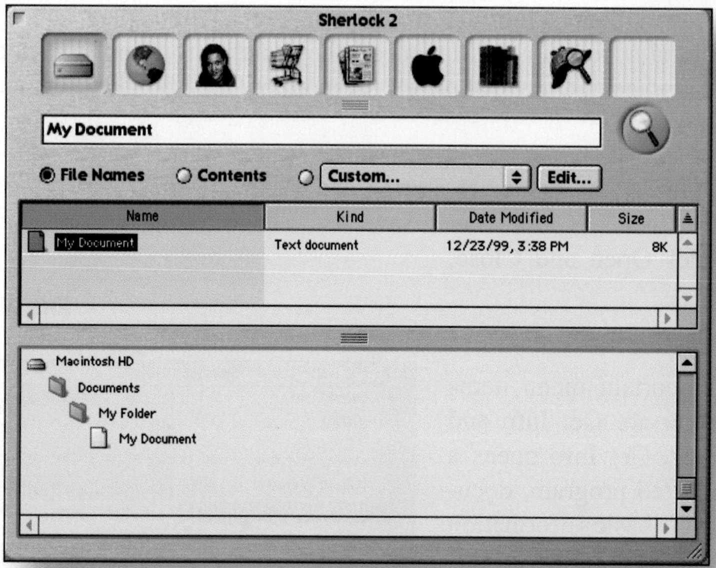

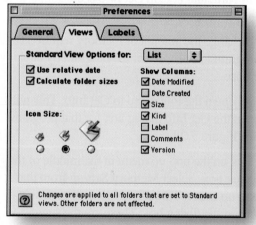

EDIT MENU

The Edit menu contains standard options such as Undo, Cut, Copy, and Paste. In a word processing program (such as Microsoft Word) these functions are pretty clear. In MacOS they are a little less so. Copy and Paste have to do with the filenames, not the files themselves. The Edit menu enables you to change other functions. For example, selecting Preferences from the Edit menu can change the Finder preferences. Among other things, the Finder preferences allow you to change the size of the icon representations and determine what other information (besides the name) is listed in list views. See Figure 3-30.

FIGURE 3-30
Changing the Finder preferences

VIEW MENU

In MacOS the View menu allows you to change what is displayed when you view the contents of a folder in a window. The contents may be viewed as a grid of icons, a semi-list of small icons, or a list. If viewed as a list, clicking on the column heading in the window can change the sort order. For example, to change to a chronological view of the files click on the heading Date Modified. The list will then change to chronological order, with the most recent files first. See Figure 3-31.

FIGURE 3-31

Windows can contain numbers of icons or lists of files

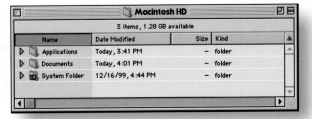

SPECIAL MENU

It is at this point, if not the View menu, where most programs cease to look like the Finder. Depending on the program, each will have its own unique menu from this point on (to the right). The MacOS has a Special menu for options not found under any of the other menus. Its functions are unique to MacOS, such as emptying the trash or shutting down the computer.

Shut Down and Restart can be implemented either from the Special menu or by pressing the On key on the keyboard. In fact, Shut Down and Restart both do the same thing—they bring up a dialog box asking if you're sure. See Figure 3-32. The only difference between the two is that the default in the dialog box is Shut Down for one and Restart for the other.

FIGURE 3-32

The Shut Down screen

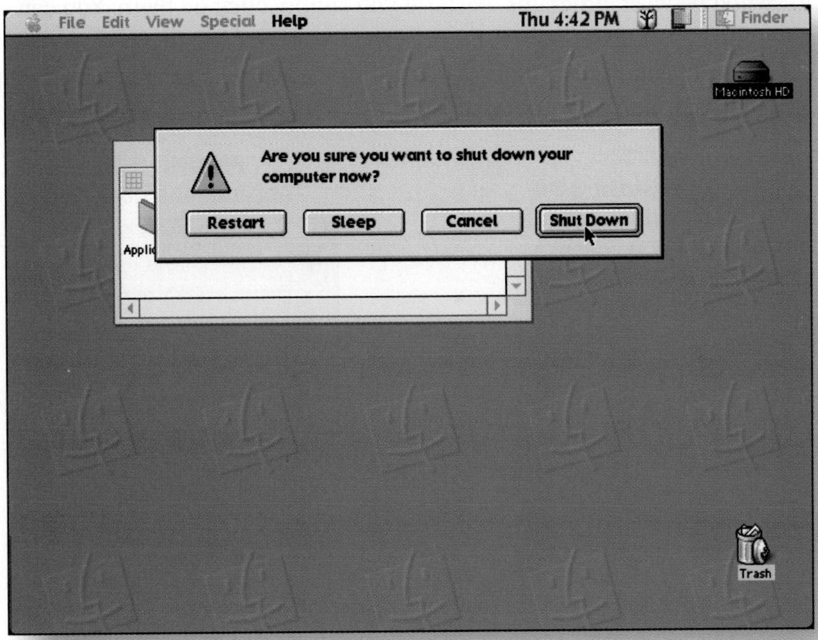

7 9

HELP MENU

Many programs (but not all) have a Help menu. The Help menu is usually the last menu of the group that starts at the left. Among other options it usually includes Show Balloons. Balloons are small bubbles (like the dialogue in a comic strip) that appear next to objects on the screen and explain their functions. See Figure 3-33. When you're first learning a program, balloons can give you a great head start; however, most users find them distracting. Once you understand what's going on with MacOS, you will want to turn balloons off by selecting Hide Balloons from the Help menu.

FIGURE 3-33
Balloon help

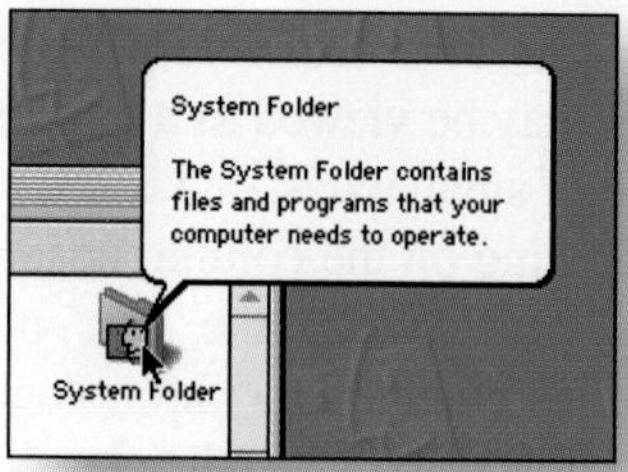

Programs may have their own help methods, such as indexes of help items, help menus based upon the context, and so forth.

THE APPLICATION MENU AND DOCK

As mentioned, on the far (right) side of the menu bar is the Application menu. See Figure 3-34. In addition to a list of all currently open programs, this menu offers other options. One is to Hide the current program. If you select this option, the current program, its windows, and other palettes become invisible, and its icon in the Applications menu becomes dimmed out. You can make the program visible again by selecting from the menu again. Another option is to make everything *but* the current program invisible. In this case, any windows or palettes from other programs disappear. Their invisibility is indicated in the Applications menu by their icons being dimmed out. As before, they can be made to reappear by selecting them in the menu.

Another interesting ability of the Applications menu is that it can be torn off the menu bar to become a standalone palette (or dock) of all the currently active applications (programs). See Figure 3-35. This makes it easier to switch between programs, because you simply click on them. You can also drag a file to an icon to open the file in that program.

One convention you will need to remember when using the Applications menu or Applications dock is that the Finder is another name for the MacOS.

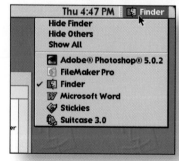

FIGURE 3-34
Applications menu

FIGURE 3-35
Applications dock

S TEP-BY-STEP ▷ 3.6

Matching the Menu Items to the Menu

1. Copy and cut out the following words (Note: Not every menu item under the menus is represented here—only the most common or important.): Chooser, Control Panels, Key Caps, Scrapbook, New Folder, Find, Print, Open, Close, Get Info, Cut, Copy, Paste, Clear, Select All, Undo, Empty Trash, Shut Down, Show Balloons, Help.

2. Across the top of a piece of paper, write the words Apple, File, Edit, View, Special, and Help. Be sure to set them far enough apart to allow you to place the cut out words beneath them.

3. Place cut out words beneath the appropriate menu without looking at the Macintosh menus. Explain in your own words to your partner why each belongs under the menu where it has been placed. After you're done, check the Macintosh menus to see if you were right. Change any that were wrong.

4. Extra credit: Place them in the correct order in the menus (without looking) and justify the reasons for placing them in this order).

Using Icons to Navigate

Icons—the little, named pictures that represent files on the MacOS—are the means by which you manipulate and navigate the filing system of MacOS. Typically, programs and documents are stored in folders. Of course, you can also store folders inside folders as well. In this way you can organize the material on your disks to make it easier to locate the information you're looking for. The only downside to this much flexibility is that it also makes it easy to lose things if you aren't organized.

The icons that represent the files on the disk can be clicked (to select them), double-clicked (to open them), or dragged (to move them). In addition, there are usually two or three other ways to do things: one with the mouse, another through a pull-down menu, and the third by means of shortcut keystrokes. These are detailed below.

Moving and Copying a File

Moving files is one of the easiest things to do on a Macintosh. To move a file you simply drag it to the new location. That's it. It makes little difference where you drag it to or from.

DRAGGING

If you move a file within a single window, it will simply move its position in that window (unless the window is set to display items in a particular order, such as alphabetical order).

If you move a file from one window to another on the same volume, the file will move to the new location and be removed from the previous location.

When you move a file to a folder icon on the same volume, the file will move to the folder and be removed from its previous location. When you open the folder to which the file has moved, the file will be located in a logical location in the folder's window. (For example, if the folder is not set to any particular order or arrangement, the new file will be put in the next available place in the window. If the window is set to arrange things alphabetically, the file will be placed in the correct alphabetical sequence.)

If the file is moved to a window or folder that is located on a different volume, the file will not move. Instead, it will be *copied* to the new window or folder. In other words, a copy of the file will be found in both the original location and in the location to which it was dragged.

You can force the Macintosh to copy a file when dragging from one location to another on the same volume (rather than a move) by holding down the Option key as you drag the icon. This will give the same result as when you move a file to a different volume: It will copy the file to the new location and also leave the original copy in place.

SPRING-LOADED CONTAINER ICONS

A feature added to MacOS as of version 8.0 is called *spring-loaded folders*. That means you can drag an icon to a closed folder or volume and pause for a second (while still holding down the mouse button); that folder or volume will open automatically and allow you to navigate down a number of nested folders without opening the folders beforehand. When you release the mouse button, the file is moved or copied to the folder or window. All other folders automatically close.

DELETING A FILE

There are three ways to delete a file. All have the same effect.

- *Mouse*: Move the file (by dragging it with the mouse) to the Trash icon on the desktop.

- *Menu*: Select the file with the mouse by clicking on it once; then select Move to Trash under the File menu.

- *Keyboard*: Use the mouse to select the file by clicking on it once; then press Command-Delete (press the Delete—or Backspace—key while holding down the Command key).

Once deleted, the file is moved to the Trash. It can still be retrieved from the Trash by double-clicking to open a window of the Trash contents and dragging the file out of the Trash window. Once the Trash is emptied, however, the file cannot be retrieved without special software.

OPENING A FOLDER, APPLICATION, OR DOCUMENT INTO A WINDOW

As with most things in MacOS, there are three ways to open a folder, program, or document. Obviously, each of these processes has a different effect. Opening a folder opens a window that displays the contents of that folder. Opening a program starts the program (this is the same as the Run command in other operating systems). Opening a document will open a window containing the document in the program that created it, if available. There are several ways to open a file:

- *Mouse*: Open a file by double-clicking it.

- *Menu*: Select a file by clicking it once with the mouse; then select Open from the File menu.

- *Keyboard*: Select a file by clicking it once with the mouse; then press Command-o (as you hold down the Command key, press the letter o).

Using Windows to View Contents

CLOSING A WINDOW

Closing a window is as easy as opening one. There are three ways to do it.

- *Mouse*: Click the close box of the window.

- *Menu*: Select the window by clicking anywhere in the window with the mouse, then select Close from the File menu.

■ *Keyboard*: Select the window by clicking anywhere in the window with the mouse, then press Command-w (as you hold down the Command key, press the letter w).

Not all programs support the Command-w key combination.

MOVING A WINDOW

As mentioned earlier, dragging windows by the title bar easily moves them. You can also drag by the outside border of the window, though earlier versions of MacOS did not support this.

RESIZING AND ZOOMING A WINDOW

Two window buttons mentioned earlier allow you to change the size and shape of the window. The first is the size box that is a set of diagonal lines in the lower-right corner of the window. Drag this button to change the location of the lower-left corner of the window. When you let go, the window will be resized accordingly. The zoom box will open the window to the optimum size when clicked. When clicked a second time it will return it to the size it was previously (with most programs and with MacOS).

Unique Features

Moving Information Between Applications

One of the powerful early advantages of Macintosh computers was a kind of compatibility between the data created by diverse programs. For example, from the earliest days of the Macintosh, you could create a drawing in a draw or paint program and place it into a word processing document. While this ability seems commonplace now, it was pioneered on early Macintosh computers.

With the ability to have several programs open at the same time, this is a particularly appealing feature of Macintosh. There are several ways to move data between documents and even between programs.

SAVING A FILE

The first and most basic way to transfer data between documents is to save the file to the disk and then open it from the new program. This method is the "least common denominator method"—when all else fails, this method will usually work.

CUT AND PASTE

A much more common way to move data is to copy (or cut) and paste the information from a document in one program to a document in another program.

To do this, first select the information in the first program. If the program is a word processor or text editor, you simply drag the mouse over the text you want to transfer. You will know it is selected because the type will be reversed (white on black instead of black on white or colored). In an object-oriented draw program, just click on the object you want to copy. The object indicates that it is selected by displaying *handles* (small black squares) at the corners of the object. If the data to be transferred is a bit-mapped graphic (such as that produced in a paint program), drag the mouse over the portion of the picture to be selected. You will be able to see that it is selected by the *marquee* that surrounds the selected material. A marquee is a box (or other shape) that has moving dotted lines around it.

■ Copy or cut the material to the clipboard. Do this by choosing Copy or Cut from the Edit menu, or press Command-c (for Copy) or Command-x (for Cut). See Figure 3-36. The *clipboard* is a file located in the System folder that temporarily holds the material you've moved. The clipboard can only hold one thing at a time, so if you copy or cut something else before pasting the current contents, the contents will be lost.

FIGURE 3-36
Cut, Copy and Paste in the Edit menu

- Move to the document where you wish to transfer the information. Select the position in which you want the new material to appear. In a word processor, for example, you would click in the text where you want the graphic to appear.

- Paste the material in the new location by selecting Paste from the Edit menu, or by pressing Command-v.

The advantage to this method is that it is quick (it's actually faster to do it than to explain it). It also allows you to place the material in the new document in the exact location where you want it to appear.

DRAGGING INFORMATION FROM ONE PROGRAM TO ANOTHER

A third method for moving information from one document to another is called **_drag and drop_**. Not all programs support this feature, but it works very much like moving files from one window to another.

- Select the material to be copied, as described above in Cut and Paste.

- Drag the selected material from the former window to its new location in the new document and release the mouse button (to drop the material).

- If drag and drop is supported, the material will automatically appear in the new position. Technically, this is identical to Copy and Paste.

PUBLISH AND SUBSCRIBE

A fascinating but rarely used feature of the MacOS is called _Publish and Subscribe._ (ActiveX on Windows is a distant relative of this method.) In Publish and Subscribe you are not moving actual content from one document from another: You are actually connecting the two documents so that when data in the copied document is changed, it is automatically updated in the pasted document. This method is particularly useful for reports in need of constant updates. Functionally it is very similar to Copy and Paste. Not all programs support Publish and Subscribe.

FIGURE 3-37
Publish and Subscribe

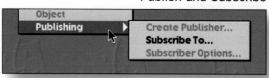

To do a Publish and Subscribe, select the material to be moved as described in Cut and Paste above. Select Publish under the Edit menu. (Sometimes it is found on the File menu.) Move to the new document and place the cursor in the location where you want the material to appear. Select Subscribe from the Edit menu. (This option is sometimes found under the File menu.)

A good example of Publish and Subscribe is using a spreadsheet like Microsoft Excel to create a budget, and a word processor like Microsoft Word to create a budget report in which some or all of the spreadsheet data will appear. When the spreadsheet is updated, the word processing document would automatically reflect the new figures in the spreadsheet.

Finder Preferences

The Macintosh can display information about the file structure in any one of several different ways, including icon and list views. The list view can be sorted by name, date, and several other criteria. To change the standard view, simply select a new view from the View Options menu option under the View menu.

Dragging Information to the Desktop

In addition to dragging files from one window to another, you can also place files on the desktop. These files are not really located on the desktop but in a special, invisible folder on the disk called *Desktop Folder*. The authors advise against putting too many things on the desktop as it soon becomes cluttered, which makes things hard to find.

Right-Clicking and Contextual Menus

Windows introduced a two-button mouse, with an alternate button that can pop up a context menu right under the mouse cursor. This menu will provide options about functions that can be performed at this point. A Macintosh computer that has a two-button mouse can do the same thing. But if your Macintosh only has a one-button mouse, do not despair. Simply hold down the Control key as you click. This technique is called *mouse keys* and can be used for many functions.

Aliases

An *alias* is a pointer to an actual file. The alias itself does not contain any information; it merely points to the real file, which does. Aliases can be safely deleted without affecting the original file.

Aliases are created by selecting the file (folder, program, or document), then pressing Command-m or selecting Make Alias from the File menu. An alternate will appear that has two differences in appearance from the original. The text of the alias will be in italic(s), and a small bent arrow will appear in the icon.

The alias can then be placed anywhere you like, and its name changed. Aliases are often used to make access simpler, such as placing them on the Apple menu or on the desktop. (Aliases are similar to Shortcuts in Windows.)

A Special Folder: The System Folder

One folder in MacOS is unique. Neither the name of the folder nor any of the folders or files inside it should be changed. This folder is the System folder. As you might guess, the System folder contains the files that make up the operating system. Five subfolders inside the System folder will be discussed here. They are the Apple Menu, Extensions, Control Panels, Preferences, and Fonts folders.

Most of these folders also have a counterpart disabled folder that has the same name but with (Disabled) added onto the name. Items in these folders are not active when the computer is started up.

THE APPLE MENU FOLDER

The items that appear in the Apple Menu come from this folder. To make an item appear in the Apple Menu, simply place it into this folder. A common trick is to make an alias of a program or document that is used often and place it in the Apple Menu folder so that it appears in the Apple Menu. Folders can also be placed here.

One important folder in the Apple Menu is Control Panels. Actually, it is an alias of the Control Panels folder, which is really in the System folder, but it gives you easy access to the Control Panels from the Apple Menu. The Control Panels are discussed in more detail on the following page.

EXTENSIONS AND CONTROL PANELS

The Extensions folder contains extensions to the operating system. Such things as add-on capabilities (for example, QuickTime for digital video) and printer drivers are found here. They are roughly analogous to .dll files in the Windows OS. Control panels are utility programs for changing the way things in the OS operate. On startup, both of these folders' contents are checked for important extensions to the operating system. For this reason, extensions are often targeted as causing problems when MacOS is having a hard time booting up. See the troubleshooting section further on in the chapter.

PREFERENCES

The Preferences folder contains the stored preference files for all programs on the Macintosh. These preference files are created when most programs are run. When you change your preferences for that program, the preferences file updates. (Some programs create their own folders of preferences and other program-specific information. These folders may appear as submenus in the Preferences folder, or they may appear in the System folder.) As mentioned for Extensions and Control Panels, corrupted preference files can occasionally cause problems. See the section on troubleshooting.

FONTS

Fonts available to all programs must be found in the Fonts folder. Some of the fonts in this folder are used for MacOS and cannot be removed or changed.

STEP-BY-STEP 3.7

Exploring the System Folder

1. Find and double-click on the folder called System folder on your boot volume to open it. (The boot volume is the icon located at the upper-right corner of the desktop.) The folders discussed below are located in the System folder.

2. Find the Apple Menu Items folder in the System folder and double-click on it to open it. Compare the contents of this folder with the Apple menu on the desktop. What do you notice about these two? Close the Apple Menu Items folder.

3. Find the Control Panels folder in the System folder and double-click on it to open it. Compare the contents of this folder with the Control Panels contents under the Apple menu. What do you notice about these two? Close the Control Panels folder.

4. Find the Extensions folder in the System folder and double-click on it to open it. Also, open the Extensions Manager control panel by selecting it from the Control Panels submenu under the Apple menu. Compare the contents of the Extensions folder with the list of extensions in the Extensions Manager. What do you notice about these two? Close the Extensions Manager control panel and the Extensions folder.

5. Find the Fonts folder in the System folder and double-click on it to open it. What fonts does your system have? What would you do to add a font to your Macintosh system? Close the Fonts folder.

6. Find the Preferences folder in the System folder and double-click on it to open it. If your Macintosh has an Applications folder, double-click on its icon and open it as well. Compare the contents of the two. What do you notice about these two folders? Which has more items: the Preferences folder, or the Applications folder? Why is that? Close the Preferences folder and the Applications folder if you have opened it.

7. Find the program called SimpleText on your Macintosh. Make an alias or shortcut of the SimpleText program icon. Find the Startup Items folder in the System folder and place the alias of SimpleText into that folder. Now reboot the computer. What happened? Why? Remove the SimpleText alias icon from the Startup Items folder and throw it into the Trash. Close all currently open windows. Now reboot the Macintosh again. What was different? Why?

Forked Files

A technical feature of early Macintosh computers that made them easier to deal with was known as the *forked file structure*. In this structure, every program and document was made up of two parts. The first was called the *data fork* and contained the basic information of the file. If it was a document, it was the document itself; if it was a program, it was the code for the program. The other portion was called the *resource fork*. It contained information about the file (such as who created it and what type of file it was), as well as resources used by the program (such as the contents of menus and dialog boxes). This arrangement made it very easy to attach certain documents to their programs. It also made it relatively easy to create different versions of programs for different languages, because most of the time all you needed to change were the menus and dialog boxes.

This structure has been carried on in MacOS X, although it is no longer part of the file itself because the operating system is based on Unix.

Macintosh File Structure Plus (MFS+)

The filing routines for MacOS use either *MFS+* (Macintosh Filing System Plus) or *UFS* (Universal-Unix Filing System). Both are true 32-bit filing systems that provide maximum flexibility in filing information.

General Troubleshooting

Despite the greatest precautions, computers sometimes fail. Macintosh seems more resistant than some computers to crashing because it is a single-vendor solution—that is, both the hardware and software come from the same company. Apple has the opportunity to work out the unique problems that may exist between a particular hardware configuration and the operating system.

That is not to say that MacOS does not have bugs. In addition, incompatibilities, corrupted files, and accidents can also cause problems. This section provides you with a basic set of procedures to try with simple operating system errors.

In earlier versions of MacOS when a program crashed, the entire computer would often also require rebooting. That is less likely with MacOS X because each program runs in a protected partition of the memory. If the program in the protected partition crashes, it will tend not to impact other programs or the operating system.

Crashing out of a Program

When a program *freezes* (refuses to respond to mouse or keyboard commands) the first thing to do is wait for 20 seconds. Occasionally, other programs take priority from the system that slows the entire system. When this happens, the computer can appear to freeze. Waiting for the computer to catch up will solve this problem (however, if it continues to happen, it may be a symptom of a more serious problem.

When waiting does not solve the problem, you may need to *crash out* of the program. In other words, you may need a way to quit the program when the Quit command does not work. Be forewarned that if you have to crash out of a program, data in any document that is open and has not been saved will be lost. To crash out of a program, press Option-Command-Escape (while holding down both the Option and Command keys, press Escape). A dialog box explaining that the program has unexpectedly quit will usually appear. (If it does not, or if this technique does not work, you must restart the computer.)

Ejecting a Disk

IBM PC-compatible programs have buttons to eject removable disks. The disadvantage to this is that disks can be removed before the computer is done using them, or without the computer's knowledge. On a Macintosh, only the operating system can eject a disk. This means that the computer knows what disk it has access to. Sometimes during a problem, you cannot eject a disk. When this happens you need a little tool which is easily made from a paper clip. Straighten one end of the paperclip and push it gently into the small hole you will find near the disk's opening. This will force the computer to eject the disk.

Restarting the Computer

The next technique to try when things go wrong is to simply restart the computer. This will often take care of the problem. Restarting the computer not only allows all programs to start again, it clears out memory and resets pointers.

To restart a Macintosh, hold down the On key for a second or two. If that does not work (if the computer has crashed), press the On key while holding down the Control and Option keys. This is known as a *warm boot*.

WITH EXTENSIONS OFF

Occasionally, you still have the same problem after you have restarted. This can sometimes be caused by a conflict among extensions. If problems persist after you have restarted—particularly soon after new software of any kind has been installed—you can test for an extensions conflict by restarting the computer again with extensions turned off. Do this by restarting the computer while holding down the Shift key. The welcome dialog box will let you know that it is starting without extensions. If the computer operates normally with the extensions off, that indicates that a conflict or other problem exists with the extensions or control panels.

RESTART TO EXTENSION MANAGER

Of course, with all extensions off, the computer may start just fine, but you can't test the problem because you need certain extensions on to test with. To work on the computer, you need to go directly to the extensions manager before continuing with the boot process; this will enable you to turn some extensions on and determine what the problem is. Hold down the Spacebar key as you reboot and you will immediately be taken to the Extensions Manager control panel. Make whatever changes you deem appropriate from there, and click the button that allows you to continue booting up. If your problem is an extension conflict, expect to reboot your computer several times while eliminating extensions one by one to determine the problem. (*Hint*: Have you installed anything recently that included extensions or control panels?)

RESTART FROM A CD-ROM

You may discover that the problem persists even with the extensions off, or you may decide that simply reinstalling the system would be more effective than trying to find the exact problem. Possibly the computer won't even boot up. If any of these are the case, you must tell the computer to reboot from something other than the hard disk. Insert your system CD-ROM into the CD-ROM or DVD-ROM drive and reboot your computer while holding down the C key. This will instruct the Macintosh to reboot from the CD-ROM. If there is no System folder on the CD, or if the System folder on the CD-ROM you inserted is not compatible with your Macintosh, you will see a blinking question mark on the screen when it looks for a disk from which to boot.

Rebuilding the Desktop

Rebuilding the desktop can solve many simple file problems. As the computer is used, icons and other materials are stored in special files so that operation is improved. These files can be come cluttered with redundant and unnecessary information. To clear them out, rebuild the desktop. This isn't as hard as it sounds. To rebuild the desktop, restart the computer and hold down the Option and Command keys while it boots. You will be asked in a dialog box if you're sure you want to rebuild the desktop. If you answer Yes, a process is started to clean up and rebuild it. This can take several minutes, so be patient. When it is complete, it is a good idea to restart the computer again.

Resetting the PRAM and Changing the Battery

Another problem that can cause your computer to seem erratic is related to Permanent Random Access Memory, or PRAM. The PRAM is used to remember important facts about your computer's configuration. To reset the PRAM, hold down the following keys while rebooting: Shift, Option, Command, P, and R. The computer will reboot itself while you do this. Allow it to reboot itself at least three times. Related to this is the system battery, usually located on the motherboard. On many Macintosh's there is a smal lithium battery that may need changing every 3 to 6 years. Contact your service representative to do this for you.

Deleting a Preferences File

When a single program that has been working suddenly has problems (particularly after a crash) you may need to delete its preferences. Remember that deleting a program's preferences means that they are forgotten—the program will return to its installed state. You find the preferences file for a particular program by looking in the Preference folder, which is inside the System folder. Look under the program's name or initials. Because you will be discarding potentially valuable preferences, it's a good idea to keep the old preference file just in case it is not the problem. Make sure the program in question is not running. Rename the existing preferences file, then restart the program. A new preferences file will be created. Test the program to see if that solved the problem. If it did, discard the old (renamed) preferences file—it is probably corrupt. If not, you can restore the old preferences file by discarding the new one and changing the name of the old one back to its former name.

Reinstalling Software

If throwing out the preferences file does not fix a problem with a program, try reinstalling the software from the original disks. (This is why it is so important to keep all those serial numbers, etc., when you are done setting up your computer.)

Reinstalling the System

If system-wide bugs continue to occur, your solution of last resort is to reinstall the operating system. If you are using an operating system that includes a minor update, you may need to install the operating system and the update separately.

An option when reinstalling a system is to do what is called a *clean install*. The difference between a typical install and a clean install is that MacOS courteously tries to remember all your settings and preferences when you install system software. Therefore, extensions that the install program does not recognize and preferences from all your programs that have ever been run on your system will be included in the new install. A clean install, on the other hand, puts the old operating system (with its extensions, control panels, preferences, and so forth) in a folder of its own, and installs a fresh, new system. The disadvantage to this is the loss of needed extensions and preferences. However, they are not really lost, just placed out of harm's way. You can restore them if you need to by moving them to the appropriate folder. We recommend caution in doing this, particularly if you have reinstalled your system because of a problem.

Special Tools

Sometimes a computer's problems are too sophisticated for the above techniques to be used. This is especially true when you do not want to lose important data. When this happens you will need to use some special tools, which may include Apple's Disk First Aid, Norton Utilities, TechTools, and others.

Some of the problems that these tools can fix include recovering data from damaged disks; recovering accidentally deleted files; defragmenting files (to speed disk access); and repairing directory errors.

Other specialty tools can help with other unique problems. Conflict Catcher can assist you in finding conflicts between extensions; it also identifies known conflicts. Others (Norton, Virex, and others) help identify and eliminate viruses.

We strongly encourage you to purchase one of the general-purpose tools before you need it. A regular backup is also an important safety measure for protecting your data.

Hardware Problems

Hardware problems that prevent you from booting up will give you what is known as a Sad Mac. A Sad Mac is a little frowny-faced Mac on startup (instead of the usual smiling one). A Sad Mac will often be accompanied by a number (just below the Sad Mac) and a tone. Note and report both of these to your repair vendor—they will help him or her identify the exact problem.

General Techniques for Optimizing

These are general techniques that will improve the performance of your Macintosh computer.

- Upgrade cautiously.

- Clean up the Apple Menu—Discard unnecessary items or disable them by placing them in another folder.

- Manage Control Panels—Discard unnecessary Control Panels or disable them by placing them in another folder. (The Extensions Manager can help you do this.)

- Manage Extensions—Disable unnecessary extensions by placing them in another folder. (The Extensions Manager can help you do this.)

- Delete unnecessary fonts.

- Clean up program folders—Get rid of programs you no longer use.

- Delete redundant SimpleText applications—Many installation programs install a version of SimpleText. Throw all of them away except the most current one.

- Delete unnecessary Read Me files.

- Discard unnecessary multimedia files (such as QuickTime movies, audio files, etc.) because they're large and waste disk space.

- Delete unnecessary color management files (unless you are doing high-end color).

Summary

In this chapter, you learned:

- Because the Macintosh is a complete system (hardware and software) from a single vendor, the available hardware configurations are more limited than those for other types of operating systems. The advantage to this approach is that the operating system and hardware are much better integrated. The major hardware devices with differences are the CPU, memory, and storage devices.

- Apple has worked very hard to make using the computer a pleasant experience. To accomplish this, they start with an easy-to-install operating system. In a newly purchased Macintosh, the system is already installed. The only times you will be required to install the operating system is if for some reason the system becomes corrupted (broken), or if you are upgrading the system to the next version. In either case, you insert a CD-ROM disc with the operating system on it, double-click the install icon, select Easy Install from the options, and answer the questions. Occasionally, an easy install is not enough. On rare occasions, you want to install some unique features, or avoid installing some features that you will never use. When this happens, your configuration has unique attributes that do not fit the easy install paradigm. Do a Custom Install to take more control of the installation.

- The most notable features of the desktop (when there are no windows open) are the menu bar across the top, the icons of disks or other volumes in the upper-right corner, and the trash can in the bottom right corner. The menu bar always appears at the top of the screen (not at the top of individual windows as in the Windows OS). The volumes (such as disks) always appear at the top right. They can be moved around the desktop, but when you reboot, they reappear at the top right. The Trash icon can be moved anywhere and will stay wherever you put it—even after rebooting.

- MacOS uses windows to show the contents of files and folders. When you double-click on a folder, a window opens to show you what's inside. When you double-click on a document, a window opens to display the document in the program in which it was composed.

- The ability to have several programs open at the same time is a particularly appealing feature of Macintosh. There are several ways to move data between documents, and even between programs. The four most common are by saving a file, cut and paste, dragging information from one program to another and Publish and Subscribe.

- Use the following special features in the Macintosh operating system: Finder preferences, dragging information to the desktop, right-clicking and context menus, aliases, the System folder, the Apple menu folder, extensions and control panels, preferences and fonts.

- Despite the greatest precautions, computers sometimes fail. Macintosh seems more resistant than some computers to crashing, because it is a single-vendor solution—that is, both the hardware and software come from the same company. Apple has the opportunity to work out the unique problems that may exist between a particular hardware configuration and the operating system.

VOCABULARY REVIEW

Define the following terms.

Apple menu	multitasking	windowshade
close box	resize button	zoom box
Finder	Trash	

CHAPTER 3 REVIEW QUESTIONS

MULTIPLE CHOICE

Circle the answer that best applies.

1. The user interface of the Macintosh operating system is called a:
   A. graphical user interface.
   B. command-line interface.
   C. menu-based user interface.
   D. mouse-driven user interface.
   E. keyboard-driven user interface.

2. Multitasking is the ability of:
   A. a user to use more than one computer at a time.
   B. a computer to have more than one user at a time.
   C. a computer to multiply columns of numbers quickly.
   D. a computer to run more than one program at a time.
   E. software to run on more than one brand of computer.

3. The installation of a new version of MacOS on a Macintosh would probably go in which order?
   A. Double-click on the Install icon, insert the CD-ROM, then reboot from the CD-ROM.
   B. Insert the CD-ROM, double-click on the Install icon, then reboot from the CD-ROM.
   C. Reboot from the CD-ROM, double-click on the Install icon, then insert the CD-ROM.
   D. Insert the CD-ROM, reboot from the CD-ROM (by holding the C key down), then double-click on the Install icon.
   E. Double-click on the Install icon, reboot from the CD-ROM, then insert the CD-ROM.

4. The Finder is Macintosh's name for what?
   A. The operating system user interface
   B. The Find function
   C. The Search and Find function
   D. A software robot that searches through your files
   E. An Internet search engine

5. When troubleshooting a problem on your Macintosh, what is the solution of last resort (before taking the machine to a repair shop)?
   A. Rebooting
   B. Resetting the PRAM
   C. Deleting a preference
   D. Crashing out of a program
   E. Reinstalling the system

TRUE/FALSE

Circle T if the statement is true or F if it is false.

T F   1. Apple Computer invented the graphical user interface.

T F   2. The mouse cursor on a Macintosh will change, depending on over what it is placed.

T F   3. To turn on a Macintosh, you flip the switch located on the back of the computer's CPU box.

T F   4. Restarting the computer is a universal troubleshooting technique.

T F   5. Almost all Macintosh programs have the same first three menus.

WRITTEN QUESTIONS

Write a brief answer to the following questions.

1. What are the three most common mouse actions?

2. What three keys on the keyboard of a Macintosh can change the output of other keys?

3. What is a main distinction between the Macintosh operating system and DOS?

4. What does it mean when you say the Macintosh is a complete system?

5. Give three of the general techniques to improve the performance of your Macintosh.

MATCHING

In the blank space match the following terms to the correct definition.

___ 1. multitasking

___ 2. alias

___ 3. windowshade

___ 4. kernel

___ 5. Finder

A. the central part of an OS

B. MacOS

C. more than one thing at once

D. in two places at the same time

E. roll up into the title bar

CHAPTER 3 PROJECTS

PROJECT 1

1. Open the folder **MacPractice 1** and create three new folders inside it. Name them **Folder A**, **Folder B**, and **Folder C**, or names of your choosing.

2. Position the window so it does not cover the icon for **MacPractice 2**.

3. Drag **Folder A** from the **MacPractice 1** window to the icon for **MacPractice 2**. Drop the icon for **Folder A** when the icon for **MacPractice 2** is highlighted and ready to receive the icon.

4. While holding down the **Option key**, drag **Folder B** from the **MacPractice 1** window to the icon for **MacPractice 2**. This will return the original of **Folder B** to **MacPractice 1**, while making a copy of it in **MacPractice 2**.

5. Hover over the icon for a second or two. If set up correctly, a window will automatically open under the icon, revealing the contents of **MacPractice 2**. Drop the **Folder C** icon in the open **MacPractice 2** window.

6. If it's not already open, open the window for **MacPractice 1** by double-clicking on the icon. Select **Folder B** by clicking on it once. It will change shading to indicate that it is selected. When it is selected, press **Command-d** (hold the Command key down while pressing the d key.) In this case, **Command-d** stands for duplicate. A folder called **Folder B Copy** will display in the window.

7. Place the cursor over the name of the icon **Folder B Copy** and click once. At first the icon will be selected, then (if you have left the cursor over the text name) the text will be highlighted. You can now change the name of that icon. Type in **Folder D**.

8. If you have followed these directions exactly, the contents of **MacPractice 1** should be **Folder B** and **Folder D**. The contents of **MacPractice 2** should be **Folder A** and **Folder C**.

9. Show your instructor the new folders for credit.

PROJECT 2

1. Restart your Macintosh.

2. Hold down the **Option** and **Command** keys simultaneously while the computer is booting up. You must hold them down until a dialog box pops up to ask you a question.

3. A dialog asks you whether you want to rebuild the desktop. Release the Option and Command keys and click or press **Return** to answer OK to the question. If you have more than one disk connected to your system, you may be asked the question for each disk.

4. If you've been having minor operating problems, this may have cleared them up. You may also notice some icons have changed, though their functions probably haven't.

5. Show your instructor the cleaned-up desktop for credit.

CRITICAL THINKING

1. Several kinds of career fields have adopted the Macintosh as their platform of choice. For example, Macintosh computers are more common in graphic design, animation, and even in Web development. Macs are also more prevalent in education, especially K-12. While this is becoming more and more an individual preference, why do you think this choice would be so field-specific? Write a short essay answering this question.

2. Select one of the fields that tends to prefer Macintosh computers and research it. Identify, if you can, the attributes of the career that would lead users to prefer Macintosh computers.

3. The Macintosh was the first computer to introduce cutting, copying and pasting at the operating system level. (That is, it was the first to allow users to cut, copy, and paste material from one program to another.) With CD-ROMs and the Internet making information so readily available, this creates some potential problems for the ethical use of information not originally created by the current user of the information (i.e. plagiarism). List some examples of ethical and unethical use of cutting and pasting and some ways that an unethical use can be made ethical.

4. While this brief introduction to MacOS could hardly make you an expert, friends with computer problems may call you for advice or help. Look at the following situations that describe problems on a Macintosh computer. What advice would you give to your friend to solve each of these problems?

Situation 1: Your friend calls and says that Corel WordPerfect no longer works on his computer. It just simply stopped working. You inquire whether he has upgraded the system or anything, and he has not. What would you recommend?

Situation 2: Several months later, the same friend calls and tells you his Macintosh seems to be getting slower and slower. What might you recommend for speeding it up if he does not have any high-level repair tools? What additional procedure might you recommend if he does have a high-level tool like Norton Utilities?

Situation 3: Another friend just installed a cool new shareware game, and now her computer will not even boot up. It acts like it is booting, then suddenly it stops and crashes, and she gets an error message. With this brief description, what would you guess the problem is? How might you go about fixing it?

Situation 4: Your first friend's little nephew accidentally spilled milk on his Macintosh. Now when he boots it up, he immediately gets a Sad Mac on the screen. The computer intones a funny sound, and a number appears below the Sad Mac icon. What should he do?

CHAPTER 4

MICROSOFT WINDOWS

Upon completion of this chapter, you should be able to:

- Describe the differences between the Windows 95 and Windows 98 operating systems.

- Install Windows 98 on your personal computer.

- Be able to use the basic fuctions of the operating system.

- Be able to use My Computer and Windows Explorer for file management.

- Use Windows 98's unique features to customize your use of the operating system.

⏱ **Estimated time: 10 hours**

folder

hard boot

icon

multitasking

shortcut

soft boot

taskbar

window

Introduction to Windows

Windows is a computer operating system designed to make using a computer easy and fun for anyone, regardless of his or her expertise. Unlike DOS or MS-DOS, which requires you to type in command lines to accomplish a task, Windows uses a *graphical user interface* or *GUI* (pronounced gooey), which allows you to easily customize your computer to match your personal computing needs. All you have to do is point and click with your mouse. Its improved features also help users to be more productive in the workplace.

The most common Windows operating systems today are Windows 95 and Windows 98. The Windows 95/98 operating system was designed by the Microsoft Corporation to replace Windows 3.1 and MS-DOS. It is more powerful and faster than Windows 3.1 and it allows you to do multitasking. *Multitasking* is the ability to run two or more programs at once, changing between windows with just a click of your mouse. It also was designed for *Plug and Play*, which means that when you install new hardware Windows will automatically detect and configure it for you. One of the other advantages to Windows 95/98 over its predecessors is that it allows you to use long filenames instead of the old 8.3 (8-character filename with 3-character extension) file-naming convention. This makes naming and finding your files much easier. The Windows 95/98 OS is compatible with MS-DOS based and older Windows-based programs. This means you can still run some of your older and MS-DOS-based software instead of having to go out and buy new programs to work with your operating system. All of this makes Windows 95/98 a powerful computing tool.

Differences between Windows 95 and Windows 98 Operating Systems

- The interfaces of Microsoft's Windows 95 and Windows 98 operating systems are almost identical, and unless you switch on the new features, most of them won't appear.

- With Windows 98 you can connect directly to the Web from anywhere on your computer. You can choose to view your desktop in Web style, which means it will look and act like the Web.

- The Windows 98 taskbar has a Quick Launch toolbar with icons for Internet-related features, as well as an icon that hides all windows and redisplays the desktop. The taskbar also has a pop-up menu available to add toolbars for typing a folder name or Web address, and for viewing all the icons on your desktop, or you can customize a toolbar with any icons you choose.

- The Start menu lets you access your Favorites folder, and the submenus stay visible longer than they did in the Windows 95 default settings, so it's easier to navigate them using the mouse.

- Windows 98 includes all of the drivers for newer devices, such as DVD drives, Universal Serial Bus (USB) scanners and keyboards, and FireWire digital cameras. You can also plug in devices while the system is running.

- Windows 98 improves on various system performance issues. Specifically, it has made program loading time, boot-up, and shutdown faster. It also initializes all device drivers more efficiently and supports systems with Fast Boot BIOS—initializing various devices only once instead of twice, which saves time.

- Windows 98 adds many Web-integration features, such as the Channel Bar, to your desktop. Most of them can be turned off so that your system looks just like Windows 95.

- As the PC and TV begin to converge, Windows 98 gives this development a push with its integrated Broadcast Architecture, which lets you watch TV on your PC and includes a number of other video enhancements.

Installation and Setup

Prior to Installation

PARTITIONING YOUR HARD DRIVE

Before you install your operating system you will need to partition your hard drive. You can make it all one large partition—drive C—or you can partition it into different sections—drives C and D, and so on. When you make multiple partitions, you allocate a certain amount of your hard drive space and assign it a drive letter. You also need to set up the partitions as one of the two types. The primary partition is the partition on which the bootable operating system will reside (the one your system boots to first). The other type of partition is the extended partition, which usually does not contain an operating system but instead is divided into logical drives to which you can assign a letter from D to Z. You can only have one primary partition, but you can have as many extended partitions as you want—up to 23. By partitioning your hard drive into different sections, you can install more than one operating system on extended partitions, so that you can do what is called *dual booting*—in which the computer gives you a choice of which operating system to load. For example, you can choose to load Windows 98 or Windows NT Workstation. To create multiple partitions, you need to use the DOS FDISK tool. For the details on using FDISK, refer to Chapter 2.

SYSTEM REQUIREMENTS

Before installing Windows 98 you need to make sure your computer meets the following system requirements:

- 486DX, 66 MHZ or higher processor

- 16 MB of RAM (but more memory will improve system performance)

- Adequate free space available on your systems hard disk. The amount of space needed will vary according to the type of installation you choose (whether it's the typical installation, the custom installation, or an upgrade from a previous operating system)

TABLE 4-1

Installation Method	Required Hard Disk Space
Upgrading from Windows 95 or Windows 3.1	120-295 MB
New Installation	140-355 MB

- VGA or higher-resolution monitor

- CD-ROM or DVD-ROM drive

- Microsoft Mouse or compatible pointing device

- A 3.5-inch high-density floppy disk to use for your startup disk during installation

Once you are sure you have at least the minimum system requirements, you are ready to do your installation. When you install Windows 98, it looks a lot like Windows 95 with a few minor changes.

Installation

The first screen you will see is the Installation Startup screen. See Figure 4-1. This screen gives you an overview of what steps will be taken to install Windows 98. The installation process is estimated to take 30-60 minutes.

FIGURE 4-1
Windows 98 installation

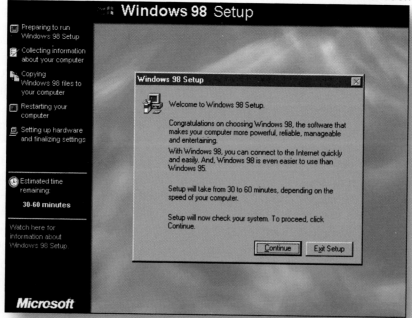

If you have the available hard disk space (approximately 50 MB), let the Setup wizard save your system files. By doing this you will be able to uninstall Windows 98 from the Add/Remove Programs applet in Control Panel, if for some reason you cannot get it working correctly.

At this point you may want to create a startup disk. The startup disk includes all the files necessary to boot your system, along with generic CD-ROM drivers that work with most CD-ROMs. You can use this disk to boot other machines as well as the system on which you created it. You can create this disk at another time if you choose. To create a startup disk, you will need to click Add/Remove Programs in the Control Panel, then click the Startup Disk tab.

Next the Setup wizard will begin copying the files from the installation CD. See Figure 4-2. Although the Setup wizard has already checked your hard drive for available space, the installation could still fail here. The Setup wizard tells you how much additional space you need to complete the install; if you do not have enough space, it lets you launch Explorer to delete files and make room without having to restart the installation.

FIGURE 4-2
Copying installation files

A series of screens are displayed while files are being copied. The screens being displayed will tell you about the enhancements that have been made to Windows 98 and go over a few of the new features. Once the files are copied, your system will reboot. See Figure 4-3.

This is the first of three reboots your system will make before installation is complete. If for some reason your system locks up, you can *soft boot* (press Ctrl+Alt+Del on the keyboard) and the installation will continue normally, or you can *hard boot* the system by actually powering it off.

Once your system has restarted, Windows 98 will attempt to locate and install all hardware on your system. Windows 98 examines the database of drivers available on the Windows 98 Installation CD and attempts to match the appropriate drivers to the hardware it finds. If it does not find the necessary driver it will use a driver already installed on your system.

FIGURE 4-3
Restart the computer

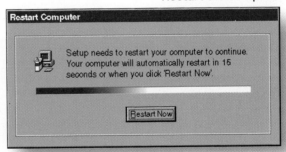

During the final stage of the installation, Windows 98 will walk you through the setup and configuration of various components such as your desktop, Control Panel, and help files. At this time the installer also begins the process of organizing your hard disk and tuning program performance. See Figure 4-4.

Microsoft has made it simple to install Windows 98 or Windows 95 by giving you step-by-step instructions to follow on your screen using the Installation wizard.

FIGURE 4-4
Windows 98 setup

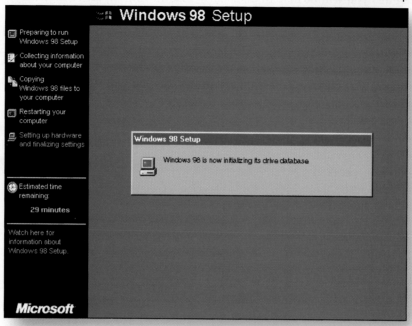

Basic Functions of Windows 98

Your Desktop

Your desktop is your main workspace. See Figure 4-5. Here you will find small pictures called *icons*. Icons are used as an easy way to open programs and documents. You will also find application

FIGURE 4-5
Your Windows desktop

windows, desktop components, and the taskbar. You can customize your desktop by changing the background colors, creating shortcuts to your favorite documents and programs, and adding toolbars.

Using Your Mouse

In Windows, you use your mouse to navigate your desktop. Your mouse is the tool you will use to open files, programs, and menus. You use your mouse by sliding it around on your mouse pad. As you move your mouse across your mouse pad you will see the arrow on your monitor move. Your mouse has two buttons on the top. The left mouse button is used to select or open a file, program, or icon. By single-clicking the left mouse button you will select the item. By holding down the left mouse button you can move items around your desktop or drop them into folders on your desktop. By double-clicking the left mouse button you can open a file, expand a folder to view its contents, or execute a program. The right mouse button is used to activate *context menus* (shortcut menus), which display several tasks that are commonly performed in that context.

Configuring Your Mouse

To configure your mouse to work best for you, click the Start button, click Settings, then click Control Panel. The Control Panel window will open on your desktop. Scroll down and double-click the Mouse icon. Click the Buttons tab. See Figure 4-6. From here you can check your double-click speed by double-clicking your mouse on the jack-in-the-box in the Test area. The jack-in-the-box will pop up when your double-click speed corresponds to the speed you have chosen. To adjust the double-click speed, move the slide arrow to the right or left depending on whether you want your double-click speed faster or slower.

You can adjust the speed at which your pointer moves across your desktop by clicking the Motion tab and choosing your most comfortable pointer speed from slow to fast. You can even have your mouse make mouse trails.

Click the Pointers tab. See Figure 4-7. From here you can change the size, color, and shape of different pointers to make them easier to see and use. You can use the Standard Windows scheme or choose another scheme from the drop-down list. To change your pointer, do the following:

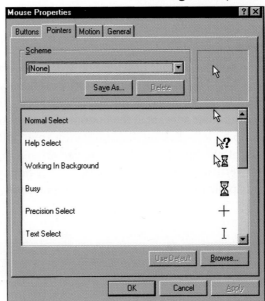

FIGURE 4-7
Selecting a new pointer

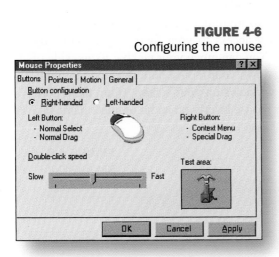

FIGURE 4-6
Configuring the mouse

- Select the pointer you want to change.

- Click the Browse button. A dialog box will appear with the available pointers. Choose one from the list.

- Click Open if this is the pointer you want, or click Cancel.

- If you change your pointer, choose Save As and name your scheme.

- Click the Apply button, then click OK. To return to your original pointers, click the Use Default button.

Note

When you click the Apply button, it causes your new settings to take effect. Clicking OK both applies your changes and closes the dialog box.

S TEP-BY-STEP ▷ 4.1

Using the Mouse

1. Point at any icon on your desktop and select it by clicking your left mouse button once. Notice how the icon highlights when it is selected.

2. Practice dragging your icons around your screen. To drag, point to the icon, click your left mouse button once and hold it down. Now slide your mouse across your mouse pad.

3. Right-click a blank space on your desktop. Point to **Line Up Icons** and left-click once. Windows arranges your icons for you.

4. Right-click the **My Computer** icon and view the shortcut menu. Click an empty area on your desktop to close the pop-up menu.

5. Double-click the **My Computer** icon to open its window. To close the window, click the X in the upper-right corner of the My Computer window.

Taskbar

At the bottom of your desktop you will see a gray rectangular bar. This is called your *taskbar*. See Figure 4-8. The taskbar displays any programs you have minimized for quick access between applications. It also can be customized with icons for easy access to your favorite programs. By default your taskbar appears at the bottom of your desktop. You can move your taskbar to any side of your desktop by left-clicking the empty grey area, holding down your mouse button, and dragging it.

By right-clicking the taskbar, you can arrange open windows on your screen, tiling them horizontally or vertically, or cascading them. (If you hold your mouse briefly on an incomplete name in a minimized application, the entire name will pop up.)

FIGURE 4-8
Your taskbar

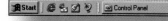

To access taskbar options, you can click the Start button, choose Settings, then choose Taskbar, or you can right-click the taskbar and click Properties. There are several options you can choose to customize your taskbar. Here is a brief description of the options you can choose.

■ *Always on Top*—When you check this box, your taskbar will be visible when any program is open. This gives you less screen space but makes switching between windows easier.

■ *Autohide*—When you check this box, the taskbar disappears when you click a window and activate it. This gives you more screen space. When you move your cursor to the very bottom of your screen the taskbar reappears.

■ *Show Small Icons in Start Menu*—When you check this box, it makes the icons on your Start menu smaller, leaving more room to add programs.

■ *Show Clock*—When you check this box, a small clock appears at the bottom right of your taskbar.

On the right side of your taskbar you will see the time and small icons to access programs that are automatically available when you turn on your computer. These icons give you easy access to programs that manage system resources and also let you access utilities that help to improve your computer's performance.

STEP-BY-STEP ▷ 4.2

Working with the Taskbar

1. Practice moving your taskbar around your screen.

2. Point your mouse at the small icons on the right side of your taskbar. Little pop-up boxes called ScreenTips display and tell you what each icon is.

3. Point your mouse at the time on the right side of your taskbar. Double-click with your left mouse button. A dialog box displays to allow you to change the time and date that appear on your taskbar. When changing the time on your taskbar, be sure to note whether you have selected A.M. or P.M. If you adjust the time and date, left-click Apply, then click OK. If you

haven't adjusted your time and date, just left-click the Cancel button.

4. Right-click the taskbar. Left-click Properties. Left-click the check box next to Show Small Icons in Start Menu to put a check in the box. Left-click Apply, and then click OK. Now click your Start button. Notice how the icons have changed.

5. Right-click the taskbar. Left-click Properties. Click the check boxes next to each of these options to turn them all on, then click OK. Notice the changes. Right-click the taskbar. Left-click Properties. Click again next to the options, turning them all off, and click OK.

Start Button

On your taskbar you will see a Start button. The Start button is one of the most useful items on your desktop. You can use the Start button to quickly find or open a document, start a program, access tools to help you customize and optimize your system, and shut down your computer.

FIGURE 4-9
The Start button

The Start Button

When you click the Start button you will see a menu. You can also open the Start menu by holding down the Ctrl key, then pressing Esc. You will also see a small black triangular shape next to some of the items on the Start menu. Point to one of these arrows with your mouse and a submenu will appear. If you are using Windows 95, you need to left-click once on the item you are pointing at for the submenu to appear. Click your mouse on an empty spot on your desktop to close the Start menu.

Below is a brief description of the options you have from the Start menu:

- *Programs*—This is where you will find all of the software programs installed on your computer.

- *Documents*—This is where Windows 95 stores shortcuts to the last ten documents you have opened. By clicking on the document name you can open it.

- *Settings*—This is where you can access the Control Panel. The Control Panel is where you can reconfigure your hardware and computer settings, as well as add and remove software. You also will find the Printers folder here. This is where you will add, configure, and remove your printers.

- *Find*—The Find option comes in handy when you know what you are looking for but don't remember where you put it. From the Find option you can search directories and drives for programs, files, and folders.

- *Help*—Here you will find a variety of help topics to choose from. You are given the option to choose from a specific topic, searching an index, or search with a keyword.

- *Run*—This command enables you to run a program from a floppy disk, your hard disk, or a network drive.

- *Shut Down*—This is where you will shut down, restart, or log off from your computer.

STEP-BY-STEP ▷ 4.3

Working with the Start Button

1. Click the **Start** button on your taskbar. Now, with your mouse, point to Programs. A submenu will appear. Point to **Accessories**, another submenu will appear. Point to **Calculator** and left-click it. You have now opened the Calculator program. To close the Calculator left-click the **X** in the upper-right corner of the window.

2. Click the **Start** button on your taskbar. With your mouse point to **Shut Down** and left-click. The Shut Down dialog box will appear, asking, "What do you want the Computer to do?" You are given the option to Shut Down or Restart your computer. You will also see three buttons across the bottom of the dialog box: Open, Cancel, and Help. Choose Cancel by pointing to the **Cancel** button with your mouse and left-clicking once.

FIGURE 4-10
Close Program dialog box

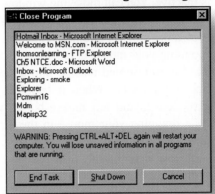

 Important

You should always use Shut Down when exiting Windows 95. Simply turning off your computer without shutting down properly can damage your programs. If your system has a frozen computer screen and mouse and will not let you access the Shut Down menu, try pressing and holding down the Ctrl, Alt, and Del keys at the same time. This will bring up your Close Program dialog box. See Figure 4-10. From here you can see what programs are not responding. Click that program and choose End Task. If this doesn't unfreeze your computer, try to choose Shut Down from the Task Manager. As a last resort, hit the Reset button on the front of your computer to reboot the system.

Windows

A *window* is the area or workspace you see when you open a program or application. This defined workspace is a movable and resizable area in which you will see information displayed that you can manipulate. At the top of each window you will see a title bar. This is the bar across the top of the window that displays the name of the program you are using. If you have two or more programs open on your desktop, you can make one active by left-clicking the title bar. You can tell which window is active by the color of the title bar. If it is dark it is active; if it is light it is inactive. You can move the window around the desktop by left-clicking the title bar, then dragging while holding down the mouse button. You can resize the window by pointing your mouse at the edge of the window. Your mouse cursor should change into a double-ended arrow. See Figure 4-12. When it becomes a double-ended arrow, click your left mouse button and hold it down while dragging your mouse in the direction you want to move the window edge.

FIGURE 4-11
Double-ended arrows

Vertical Resize	↕
Horizontal Resize	↔
Diagonal Resize 1	↘
Diagonal Resize 2	↙

In the top right of the title bar there are three control buttons. The left one is the *Minimize* button. Clicking this button keeps your window active, but reduces it to a rectangular icon on your taskbar. All programs that are running are displayed on the taskbar. If a program is active it will appear to be indented.

The middle button is the *Restore* button. It returns a full-screen window to window size, or returns a window back to full-screen size.

FIGURE 4-12
The window buttons

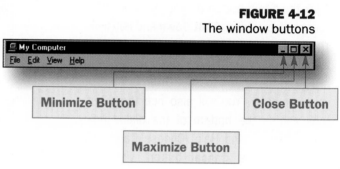

Minimize Button

Close Button

Maximize Button

The last button—the X button on the right—is the *Close* button. Clicking that button closes the active window or program.

SCROLL BARS

If you can't see all the information in a window, use the scroll bars at the right or bottom edge of the window to view more information. Click the up arrow to scroll up a page, or click the down arrow to move down the page. To scroll from side to side, use the right or left arrows on the scroll bar at the bottom of the window. Instead of using the arrows, you can also click the scroll box between the scroll bars and drag it left, right, up, or down.

STEP-BY-STEP ▷ 4.4

Working with Windows

1. To open a window, click the **Start** button on your taskbar. Move your mouse pointer up to **Programs** and left-click once to display the submenu. Point to **Accessories** and left-click once, revealing another submenu. Left-click **Notepad**. You will now see an application window on your desktop.

2. Practice moving the window around your desktop.

3. Practice resizing the window.

4. Practice minimizing and maximizing the window.

5. Now open a second application window. Click the **Start** button on your taskbar. Move your mouse pointer up to **Programs** and left-click once to display the submenu. Point to **Accessories** and left-click once, revealing another submenu. Left–click **Paint**. You should now have two application windows on your desktop.

6. Practice moving between the different windows by clicking their title bars. Minimize and maximize your windows. Notice how the applications appear on your taskbar when they are minimized.

7. Double-click the **My Computer** icon on your desktop. Practice resizing and moving the window.

8. Practice scrolling up and down your window and from side to side. Move the icons around in the window by left-clicking once on the icons and holding down the mouse button while dragging the icon around in the window.

9. Left-click **View** on the menu bar below the title bar. Change your icon view by left-clicking, in turn, the Large Icons, Small Icons, and List choices. As you click each view, notice the changes that occur in the window.

10. Close your windows by left-clicking the **X** button on the title bar of each window.

Changing the Name of an Icon

To change the name of an icon, left-click the icon you wish to change, right-click the same icon, and choose Rename from the submenu. See Figure 4-13. This will highlight the name of the icon so you can type a new name for it.

Using Help

To access Help, click the Start menu, then click Help. The Help Topics screen appears. This screen has three tabs to choose from: Contents, Index, and Search.

FIGURE 4-13
Changing an icon's name

HELP CONTENTS

Click the Contents tab. See Figure 4-14. From here you can click the topic you want to view. When you double-click a topic, subtopics appear. Double-clicking the subtopic displays the Help information in the right window pane. You can use the scroll bar to move up and down through the information.

To print a Help topic, click Options on the menu bar and click Print.

FIGURE 4-14
The Help screens

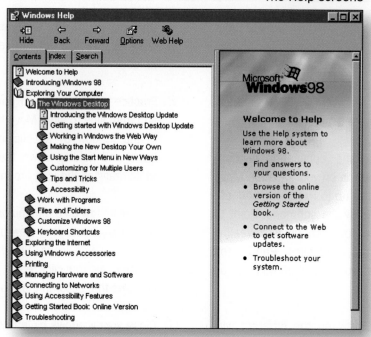

HELP SEARCH AND INDEX FEATURES IN WINDOWS 98

Click the Search tab. From here you can type a word related to the topic or information you are looking for, then click the List Topics button. The related Help topics appear in the Topic window. Click the topic you want to explore; Help displays the related text in the right window pane. Note that you might see subtopics displayed as blue hypertext. Single-clicking the hypertext displays additional information. You can use the scroll bar to move up and down through the topic's text.

To print the Help topic, click Options on the menu bar and click Print.

Click the Index tab. Type the first letter of a topic you are looking for. Help jumps to the section starting with this letter. You can then scroll down and find the section you need. Click the topic you want and then click the Display button. The topic appears in the right window pane.

File Management

In Windows 95 and Windows 98 you can manage your files and directories in both My Computer and Windows Explorer. It is easier to view or find a single file or directory using My Computer. When you want to move files or reorganize your directories, Explorer is your best choice.

When you view files and directories using My Computer, you choose a drive and view a list of folders and files in that drive. You view one window at a time. Each time you open a folder, another window opens. If you open several folders you will have several windows open on your desktop at the same time. See Figure 4-15. To avoid cluttering your desktop with windows, you can choose the Open each folder using the same window option, as described in the following section.

FIGURE 4-15
Desktop with several windows open

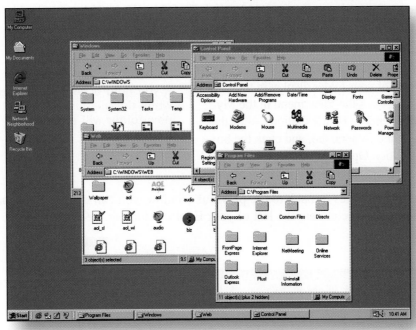

Windows Explorer provides a dual-pane view. See Figure 4-16. The left pane lists your drive and root folders. The right pane shows the contents of the selected folder. Explorer has tools available on its menu bar that My Computer does not. For example, you can use Find under the Tools menu to locate files.

FIGURE 4-16
Two panes in Windows Explorer

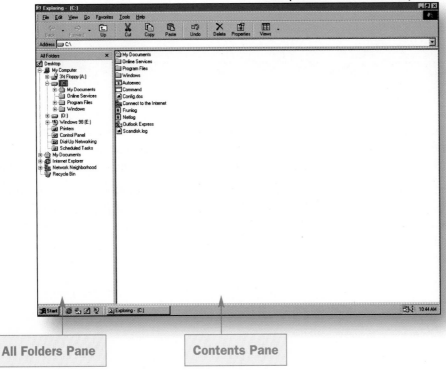

All Folders Pane

Contents Pane

My Computer: Navigating and Opening Files

■ To open a folder and view its contents, double-click the folder. Every time you double-click a folder, a new window opens to display the contents of the folder.

■ You can set your system so that when you open a new folder, the contents of your folder display in the same window. To do that, click the View menu in the My Computer window, choose Folder Options, click the Settings button on the General tab, and click the box to the left of the option Open each folder in the same window.

TIP

If you hold down the Ctrl key while double-clicking a folder, the new folder will open in the same window.

■ To move up your directories or back to the previous window, you can use the Backspace key or click the up-one-level icon near the left of your Explorer toolbar. See Figure 4-17.

FIGURE 4-17
Up-one-level icon

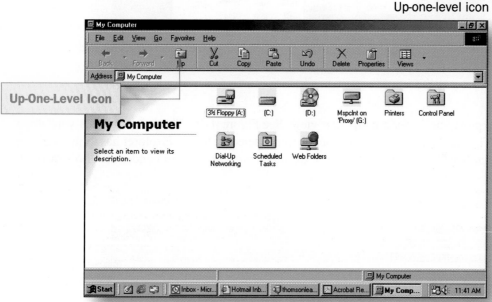

■ My computer has other icons on its toolbar you can use to make it easier to work in windows. There are icons for cut, copy, paste, undo, delete, to change views to large icons, small icons, list, and details. These same options are found on your menu bar under the File, Edit, and View menus.

■ You will also notice that you can view document files, program files, and other graphic and multimedia files when you open the folders. You can double-click any of these files and they will open in the program associated with them. When you double-click a program file, the program will start.

S TEP-BY-STEP ▷ 4.5

Using the My Computer Window

1. Double-click the **My Computer icon** on your desktop.

2. Practice navigating through different windows by clicking only folders, using the multiple window option.

3. Close all secondary windows and change your view options to a single window.

4. Left-click **View** on the menu bar of **My Computer**.

5. From the **View** drop-down menu, choose **Folder Options**.

6. A dialog box displays. On the General tab, click the Settings button, then click the box next to the option Browse using a single window.

7. Click **OK**.

8. Navigate through the Windows folder, first clicking a folder and then a subfolder. Navigate back up the Windows folder, using the various methods discussed above.

CREATING FILES AND FOLDERS

You can create files or folders in My Computer. A *folder* (also known as a *directory* in Windows terminology) is just a storage space for files, used for organizational purposes. Open the folder in which you want to create a document or folder, right-click an empty space in the window, and left-click New. Then, from the submenu, select the kind of document you want to create or select New Folder.

A new document or folder will appear with the name highlighted so you can rename it. Double-click the new file or folder to open it.

Note

Windows 98 filenames are not limited to eight letters or less, like Windows 3.1 or MS-DOS files. However, many punctuation marks are not allowed in filenames. To be safe, avoid using punctuation marks when naming your files.

S TEP-BY-STEP ▷ 4.6

Creating Files and Folders

1. Insert a floppy disk into your A drive. Open **My Computer** and double-click your **A:** drive icon, opening a window.

2. Right-click an empty space in the A drive window. From the shortcut menu, choose New, then choose Text Document.

3. Change the name of the file to **Test**.

4. Double-click your new file, **Test**. The file will open in Notepad. At the top of the file, type a couple of lines of text.

5. On the menu bar, click **File**, click **Save**, then close Notepad.

6. To close Notepad, click **File** on the menu bar and click **Exit**.

7. Right-click an empty space in your A drive window.

SELECTING FILES AND FOLDERS

Before you can rename, copy, or move a file or folder, you have to select the file or folder by left-clicking its icon. When a file or folder is selected it will highlight. See Figure 4-18. To deselect a file, click any empty space in the window.

To select multiple files

To select several files or folders at the same time, hold down the Ctrl key on your keyboard and click each file or folder icon you want to select. See Figure 4-19.

To select many files or folders that are in a row, click the first file; then, while holding down the Shift key, click the last file or folder you want to select. To select all files or folders in a window, click Edit on your menu bar and choose Select All; or you can press Ctrl and A on your keyboard.

8. Click **New**, then click **Folder** and rename the folder to **Student**. Repeat this step to create another folder. Name this folder **Your Last Name**.

9. Double-click the **Student** folder to open it. Inside the Student folder, create another new folder. Name the folder **Your First Name**.

TIP

To select most of the files in a window, select a few files that you do not want to select, click Edit on the menu bar, then choose Invert Selection. You can also choose Select All from the Edit menu, then hold down the Ctrl key while clicking a file to deselect it.

FIGURE 4-18
A selected object

FIGURE 4-19
Many files and folders selected

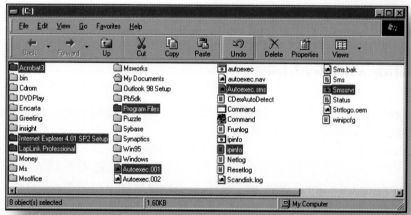

S TEP-BY-STEP ▷ 4.7

Selecting Files and Folders in My Computer

1. Click the **My Computer** icon on the desktop.

2. Click the **C:** drive and then double-click the **Windows** folder.

3. Click the **View** menu and set the view to **Details**.

4. Under the View menu, arrange all icons by type and then in your Windows directory, select all the **.txt** files.

5. Under the View menu, arrange all icons by name and then select all the files and folders beginning with the letter **D**.

6. Under the View menu, arrange all icons by date and then select all files created in **1997**.

7. Under the View menu, arrange all icons by size and then select all files smaller than **10 KB**.

8. Using two different methods, select all files, invert selection, and deselect all files.

Windows Explorer

Almost everything you can do in My Computer you can do in Windows Explorer. Windows Explorer has a dual-pane view, which you may prefer to use when copying or moving files. It also makes it easier to view the entire structure of your folders and files. To look at Windows Explorer, click the Start button on your taskbar, click Programs, and then click Windows Explorer.

 TIP

You may find it easier to right-click your Start button and choose Explore from the shortcut menu to start Windows Explorer.

In the title bar, Explorer displays the drive or directory that is open. It also displays it above the right pane, in an area known as the address bar. In Explorer's left window pane, you will see a list of the folders that are in the drive you have selected. A plus sign next to the folder means that the folder will expand and reveal more folders. A minus sign means that the folder is fully expanded. As you click folders in the left pane you will see their contents displayed in the right pane. You will see both files and folders displayed.

NAVIGATING IN EXPLORER

■ Using your mouse, you can drag the line between the two panes to make one pane smaller or larger. See Figure 4-20.

■ To expand or contract (open or close) a folder, double-click it.

■ To change the drive, use the drop-down arrow at the top of the right pane on the address bar. You can also use the Backspace key or the up arrow on the toolbar to change drives.

■ Notice there is a scroll bar in the middle that you can use to scroll through the root directory. On the right there is another scroll bar to scroll through folder contents.

■ You can press the Ctrl-Home key combination to go to the top of the page, or Ctrl-End to go to the bottom. You can also use the PgUp and PgDn keys on your keyboard to move page by page through either the right or left pane—depending on which one is active.

FIGURE 4-20
Explorer window

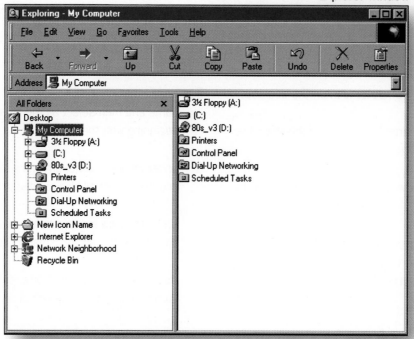

COPYING FILES IN EXPLORER

You can use either Explorer or My Computer to copy files. There are many methods you can use for copying files: right-click and choose Copy, click an icon on a toolbar, or click Edit on the menu bar and choose Copy. You can also press Ctrl-C on your keyboard or drag your files from one folder to another. As you gain more experience, you will become more comfortable using the drag-and-drop method. Initially, you may prefer the other options.

Whatever method you use, you must first select the file or files you want to copy. It will be easier to copy the file or files if you make the target directory visible in your left pane before you select the file or files you want to copy. Click with your mouse in the right pane to select the file. Use one of the following methods to copy your file.

Menu Bar

■ Select the file you want to copy. Click Edit on the menu bar, and then choose Copy. See Figure 4-21.

■ Navigate to the directory folder where you want to place your copied file or files. Select the file you want to copy.

■ Choose Edit again on the menu bar, then choose Paste.

116

FIGURE 4-21

Copying files using the Edit menu

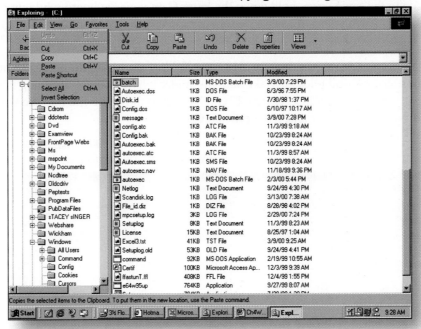

Right-click

■ Right-click the file you want to copy. Choose Copy from the shortcut menu.

■ Find the directory where you want to move your file or files; choose Select or Open to open the directory.

■ Right-click the destination directory, and choose Paste from the shortcut menu.

Keyboard

■ Select the file you want to copy. Hold down the Ctrl key while you press the letter C. This copies the file.

■ Find the directory where you want to move your file or files, then Select or Open it.

■ Hold down the Ctrl key as you press the letter V. This pastes the selected file to the new location.

Toolbar

■ Make sure your toolbar is visible. Click View on your menu bar and choose Toolbar if it is not already chosen.

■ To select the file you want to copy, click the Copy icon on the toolbar.

■ Find the directory where you want to move your file or files, then select or open it.

■ Click the Paste icon on your toolbar.

Drag and Drop

■ Make sure both directories are visible when using this option.

■ First left-click the file you want to copy.

■ To Copy a file to the same drive, hold down the letter C on your keyboard while dragging the file; then, holding down your left mouse button, release it in an empty place in the same folder. See Figure 4-22.

■ To Copy to a different drive, just drag the file to the folder you want it in while holding down your left mouse button, and release. Make sure the folder where you are dropping the file is highlighted (i.e., shows that it is selected). If you happen to move the file into the wrong folder, just click Edit on the menu bar and choose Undo Copy.

FIGURE 4-22
Copying files using drag and drop

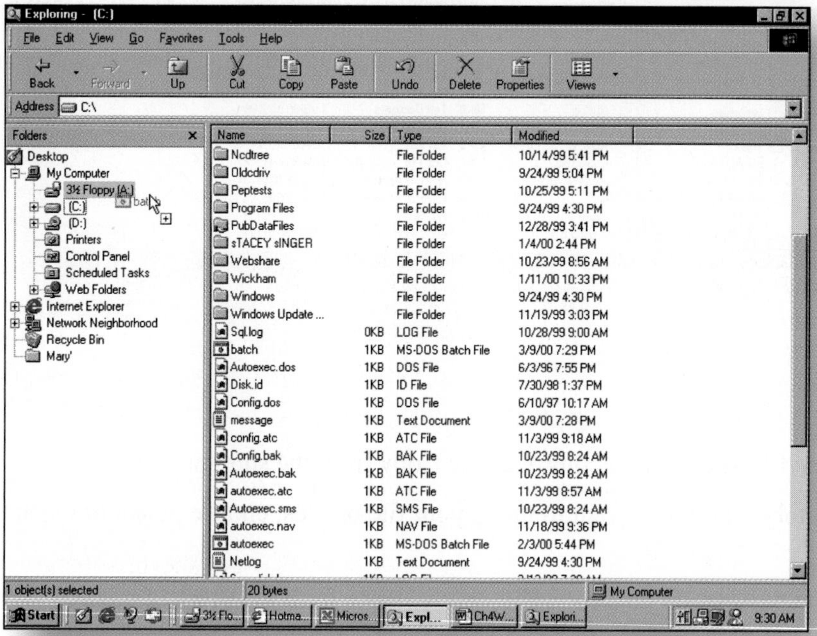

STEP-BY-STEP 4.8

Practice Copying Files in Windows Explorer

1. Using the menu bar in Explorer, copy your **Test** file to the A drive and paste it into your **Student** folder on drive A.

2. Using the toolbar, copy the **Student** folder into the personal folder labeled with your **Last Name**.

3. Create a new text document in your **Last Name** folder. Rename it **Practice**.

4. Use Ctrl-C to copy and Ctrl-V to paste your **Practice** file into your **Student** folder.

5. Practice dragging and dropping your **Practice** file and your **First Name** file into different folders.

MOVING FILES IN EXPLORER

You can move files in either Explorer or My Computer, using methods that are similar to copying. For example, let's look at the Test and Practice files being created in this chapter. To move these files, either right-click and choose Move; click an icon on a toolbar; click Edit on the menu bar and then choose Move; or press Ctrl-X on your keyboard to cut the file or folder and then press Ctrl-V to paste it. You can also drag your files from one folder to another by holding down the right mouse button as you drag. When you release the file into the destination folder, you will see a shortcut menu asking you if you want to Copy Here or Move Here. As you gain more experience, you will become more comfortable using the drag-and-drop method. Initially, you may prefer the other options.

Again, whatever method you use, you must first select the files you wish to move. It will be easier to move files if you make the target directory visible in your left pane before you select the file or files you want to move. To do this, click with your mouse in the right pane to select the files. Use one of the following methods to move your files.

Menu Bar

■ Select the file you want to move. Click Edit on the menu bar, then choose Cut.

■ Navigate to the folder where you want to place your file. Select the folder.

■ Again click Edit on the menu bar, then choose Paste.

Right-click

■ Right-click the file you want to move. Choose Cut from the shortcut menu. See Figure 4-23.

■ Find the folder where you want to move your file and select or open it.

■ Right-click the destination folder, and choose Paste from the shortcut menu. See Figure 4-24.

FIGURE 4-23
Cut in the shortcut menu

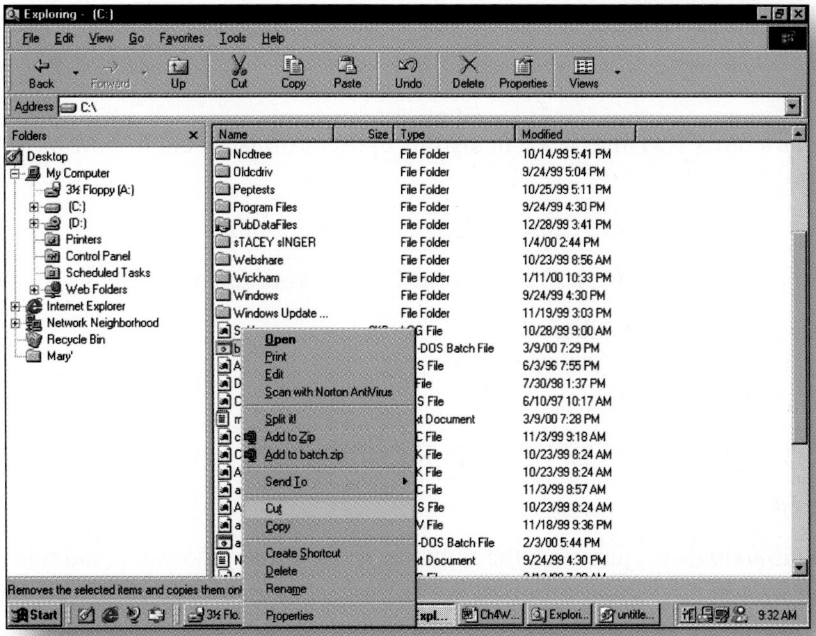

FIGURE 4-24
Paste in the shortcut menu

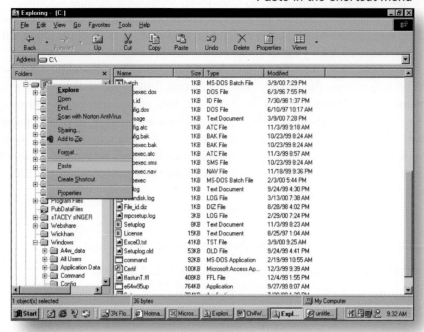

Keyboard

■ Select the file you want to copy. Hold down the Ctrl key while you press the letter X. This will cut the file.

■ Find the folder where you want to move your file, and either select or open it.

■ Hold down the Ctrl key while you press the letter V. This will paste the file to the new location.

Toolbar

■ Make sure your toolbar is visible when using this option. If it isn't, click View on your menu bar and choose Toolbar.

■ Select the file you want to move. Click the Cut icon on the toolbar.

■ Find the directory where you want to move your file; select or open the file.

■ Click the Paste icon on your toolbar

Drag and Drop

■ Make sure both directories are visible when using this option.

■ Left-click the file you want to move.

■ To move to a different drive, just click the right key in the folder you want, and release. A shortcut menu appears, giving you the option to Move Here; click it. Make sure the folder in which you are dropping the file is highlighted, showing that it is selected. If you happen to move the file to the folder, click Edit on the menu bar and choose Undo Move.

Deleting Files

You have several options for deleting files and folders.

■ Select the file or folder and press the Delete key on your keyboard.

■ Right-click the file or folder and choose Delete from the shortcut menu. See Figure 4-25.

■ Select the file or folder and click the Delete icon on your toolbar.

■ Drag and drop the file into the Recycle Bin on your desktop (or the Recycle Bin in the left pane of Windows Explorer).

When you delete a file it goes to the Recycle Bin. You can later permanently delete the item from the Recycle Bin.

Note

If you delete an item on a floppy disk it is NOT sent to the Recycle Bin. The file is removed from the disk and cannot be recovered. When you delete a folder, you are deleting all of the files in that folder.

FIGURE 4-25
Deleting files using the shortcut menu

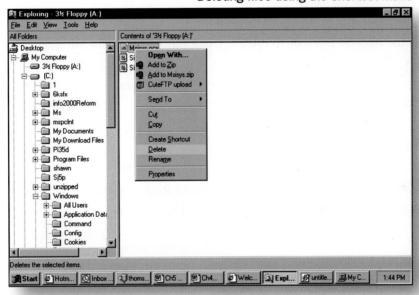

STEP-BY-STEP ▷ 4.9

Practice Moving and Deleting Files

1. Move the **Test** file to your desktop using the drag-and-drop method. Now delete the Test file from your desktop.

2. Double-click your **Recycle Bin** to view the deleted file.

The Recycle Bin

Windows 95 and Windows 98 recycle files rather than permanently deleting them. Each time you delete a file you are sending it to the Recycle Bin. This gives you the option to later restore the file to its original location or to permanently delete it by emptying the Recycle Bin. When the Recycle Bin is empty, its icon on your desktop appears empty. When there are items in your Recycle Bin, its icon appears full.

When you are sure you want to permanently delete a file you can easily empty the Recycle Bin by right-clicking it and choosing Empty Recycle Bin. See Figure 4-26.

You can also disable the Recycle Bin by right-clicking it, choosing Properties from the shortcut menu, and checking the box next to Do not move files to Recycle Bin. Remove files immediately when deleted.

FIGURE 4-26
Emptying the Recycle Bin

USING THE RECYCLE BIN

To empty the Recycle Bin

■ Right-click the Recycle Bin icon, and choose Empty Recycle Bin from the shortcut menu.

■ Double-click the Recycle Bin icon to open it. Click File on the menu bar and choose Empty Recycle Bin.

■ Double-click the Recycle Bin icon to open it, select the files you want to delete, then press the Delete key on your keyboard.

To restore files

■ Double-click the Recycle Bin icon to open it, select the file you want to restore.

■ Select the file you want to restore. Right-click, choose Restore from the shortcut menu. Your file will now be restored to its original location. See Figure 4-27.

FIGURE 4-27
Restoring files from the Recycle Bin

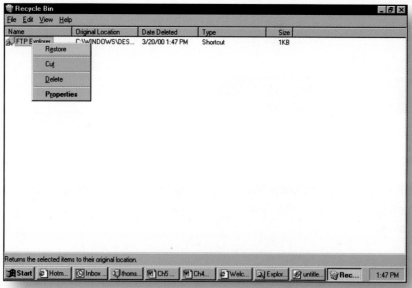

MICROSOFT WINDOWS

To change Recycle Bin properties

- By default the Recycle Bin uses 5% of your hard drive. If you need to save hard drive storage space you can change this default setting in the Recycle Bin properties.

- Right-click the Recycle Bin icon and choose Properties from the shortcut menu.

- To be asked every time if you are sure you want to delete an item, go to the Recycle Bin Properties and check the Display delete confirmation box.

Use the Global tab to change properties for all drives, or use each drive tab to change properties for individual drives. (This means reserving a different percentage of space for each drive). See Figure 4-28.

You can adjust the amount of hard drive space reserved for your Recycle Bin by going to Properties and moving the size indicator to the percentage you want to use. Click Apply to accept the change, and then click OK.

FIGURE 4-28
Changing the Recycle Bin properties

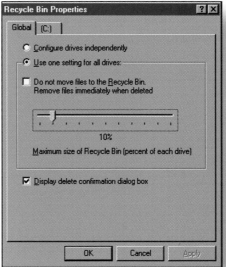

S TEP-BY-STEP ▷ 4.10

Practice Working with the Recycle Bin

1. Create a new text document on your desktop. Right-click your desktop, choose **New**, choose **Text Document**, and name the file whatever you want. Drag and drop it into the Recycle Bin.

2. Double-click the **Recycle Bin** to open it.

3. Select the text document, click File on the menu bar, and choose **Restore**. The document returns to your desktop.

4. Delete your file from the desktop again. Open up the Recycle Bin, click **File** from the menu bar, choose **Empty Recycle Bin**. When the window is empty, close the Recycle Bin.

5. Create a new text document on your desktop. Drag and drop it into the Recycle Bin. Right-click the **Recycle Bin** and choose **Empty Recycle Bin**.

Finding Files or Searching

In Windows you can search for files based on the filename, date, or a portion of the filename. See Figure 4-29. To start a search, click the Start button on your taskbar, choose Find, and click Files or Folders. The Find: All Files dialog box opens on your desktop. You can also access Find from Windows Explorer under the Tools menu. Another way is to right-click the My Computer icon and choose Find from the shortcut menu.

When you do a basic search you enter the filename or a portion of the filename using a wildcard. See Figure 4-30. You also are given the option to choose which directories you want to search, or you can search your entire computer. The search results will be listed in a window at the bottom of the Find dialog box. This window functions like a screen in Windows Explorer or My Computer, allowing you to open, move, copy, and delete files.

FIGURE 4-29
Find on the Start menu

FIGURE 4-30
The Find dialog box

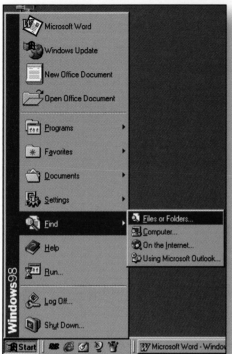

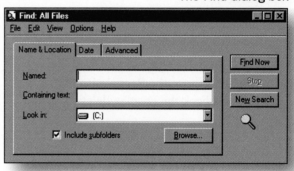

If you don't know the exact name of the file or folder you are looking for, you can use what is called a *wildcard*. Wildcards are question marks or asterisks that stand for the characters you are missing. Examples of wild ards are given in the following table.

TABLE 4-2

Example	Explanation	Sample Files Found
abcd???.doc	This would find all files that begin with the letters abcd, have three unknown characters after that, and end with the extension .doc.	abcdefg.doc abcdhhh.doc abcduip.doc
*.txt	This would find all files that end with the extension .txt.	letter.txt fax.txt memo.txt

You can also save your search criteria by clicking File on the menu bar and clicking Save Search, or clicking Options on the menu bar and choosing Save Results.

Did You Know?

In MS-DOS you had to place the wildcard at the end of a filename. In Windows 95 you can put the wildcard at the beginning, middle, or end of a filename.

STEP-BY-STEP ▷ 4.11

Finding Files

1. Open Windows Explorer.

2. Make sure that you are exploring the contents of drive C.

3. Right-click on the **Contents** pane in an empty area.

4. Choose **New** from the shortcut menu and then choose Create a New Text Document

5. Name the new text document **myfile.txt**.

6. Open the Start menu and click **Find**, then click **Files or Folders**. In the Named box, type the name of the file you are searching for: **myfile.txt**.

7. Check Include Subfolders to search all subfolders on your hard drive. By default, the Look in box will list drive (C). If you wanted to search another drive or folder, you could set the new drive/folder name here. For this exercise, just leave it on drive (C).

8. To begin your search, click the **Find Now** button.

9. When the filename appears in the bottom window, click the **Stop** button to stop the search.

10. You can treat this file as you would any file in a window: open, move, rename, copy, or delete it.

ADVANCED SEARCHING

You can also locate files by size, date, or type.

To search for files by date, open Find, click the Date tab, and enter the criteria you want to search for. See Figure 4-31. You can choose to search for all files or all files modified, created, or accessed between specific dates, or in the last number of months or days.

To search for files by type, click the Advanced tab. From the Of type drop-down box, choose the type of file you are searching for and click Find Now. To seach for files by size, indicate the size of the file you are looking for in the Size is boxes and click the Find Now button. See Figure 4-32.

FIGURE 4-31
Searching for files by date

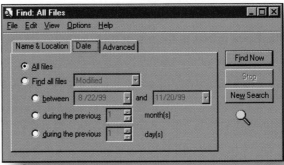

Using the Advanced Search Options

1. Search for all files created after yesterday's date and before tomorrow's date.

2. Search for all icon files on your computer. Click the **Advanced** tab and then, in the Of Type drop-down box, choose **Icons**.

3. Search for all .tmp files in your programs directory that were created or modified in the last five months.

4. Search for all files on drive C that are at least 500 KB in size.

FIGURE 4-32
Searching for files by size

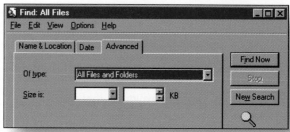

Unique Features of Windows

Creating Shortcuts on your Desktop

Creating *shortcuts* is a very useful function in Windows 95 and Windows 98. Shortcuts help to save time and increase productivity by making your most commonly used programs and documents easily accessible from your desktop. A shortcut is simply a quick way to open a file or folder or start a program without having to go to its permanent location. Shortcuts also take up very little file space because they are only pointers to the original icons. Shortcuts look identical to the original icons they represent except they have a small arrow at the bottom.

To create a shortcut for a program, file, or folder that is not on your desktop:

■ Right-click your desktop, choose New, and then click Shortcut.

■ Click on the Browse button.

■ Make sure the Files of type field indicates All Files. This will allow you to view all files.

■ In the Look in box at the top of the dialog box, click the drop-down arrow and choose the drive or folder where the program or file is located.

■ Once you have found the program or file for which you are making a shortcut, double-click it or click Open, then click Next.

■ At the next screen, type in the name for the shortcut. Click the Finish button.

■ The shortcut icon will be created on your desktop.

■ You can also change the appearance of your shortcut icons by right-clicking them and choosing Properties. Click the Shortcut tab, click the Change Icon button, choose the icon you want and click apply, then click OK. See Figure 4-33.

You can also create a shortcut for a program, folder, or file by opening My Computer. Navigate through the windows until you find the item you want to create a shortcut for, right-click the icon and choose Create Shortcut. You can also right-click the icon; while holding down the mouse button, drag the icon to your desktop and release, then choose Create Shortcut from the shortcut menu.

FIGURE 4-33
Creating shortcuts

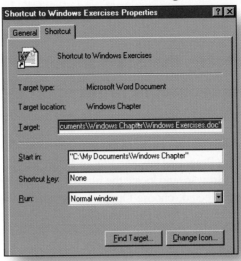

STEP-BY-STEP ▷ 4.13

Creating Shortcuts

1. Double click **My Computer**, create shortcuts on your desktop to Control Panel, drive C and drive A.

2. Create shortcuts on your desktop to the files and folders you created on your floppy disk.

3. Create a new folder on your desktop. Drag and drop all of your shortcuts into this folder.

RENAMING A SHORTCUT

When you create a shortcut it is automatically named "Shortcut to..." (followed by the name of its related file, program, or folder). You can right-click the icon and choose Rename from the shortcut menu to change this, or remove the "Shortcut to" portion of the name. See Figure 4-34.

REPAIRING A BROKEN SHORTCUT LINK

If you move the original file, folder, or program that a shortcut is pointing to, you will be prompted to click the Browse button and show Windows the new location of the file. Once you do this, Windows will modify the shortcut icon to point to the new location.

To Change A Shortcut Icon

■ Right-click the icon, choose Properties, then click the Shortcut tab. Click Change Icon.

FIGURE 4-34
Changing the name of
an icon

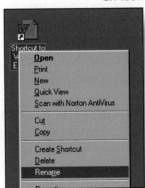

- In the dialog box, use the scroll arrows to view the icons you can choose from.

- Choose the icon you want, and click OK. In the original dialog box, click OK. Click your desktop and the new icon will appear.

Modifying the Start Menu

ADDING SHORTCUTS TO THE START MENU AND TASKBAR

You can also place shortcuts at the top of your Start menu, above Programs. To add a shortcut to the top of your Start menu, drag an original icon or a shortcut and drop it on the Start button on your taskbar. You can also add shortcuts to the Start menu by right-clicking the taskbar, then clicking Properties and the Start Menu Programs tab. See Figure 4-35. Next click the Add button, click Browse, and locate the file you want to add. When the file has been selected, choose Open, then click the Next button. You will be asked where to place the icon. Click the Start folder above Programs, click the Next button, name the program, click the Finish button, and then click OK.

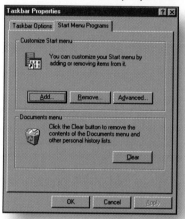

FIGURE 4-35
Start menu properties

REMOVING SHORTCUTS FROM THE START MENU

To remove a program from the Start menu, right-click the taskbar and again choose Properties and the Start Menu Programs tab. Next click the Remove button, click Browse, and locate the file group or file shortcut you want to remove. When the group or file has been selected, choose Remove; you will be asked to confirm whether or not you want to delete the shortcuts. If you are sure you want them removed, click yes and the shortcuts will be placed in the Recycle Bin. Click Close when finished removing shortcuts from the Start menu.

STEP-BY-STEP ▷ 4.14

Adding Shortcuts to the Start Menu

1. Add **WordPad** to the top of your Start menu.

2. Add **Control Panel** to the top of your Start Menu. Drag it from **My Computer**.

3. Open **WordPad** by using your Start Menu, then close WordPad.

4. Remove **WordPad** and **Control Panel** from the top of the Start menu.

CUSTOMIZING THE PROGRAMS MENU

You can customize the Programs menu just as you can the Start menu. Right-click the taskbar, click Properties, click the Start Menu Programs tab, and click the Advanced button. The Explorer window will appear. Double-click the Programs folder in the right pane of Explorer. You can now view the contents of your Programs menu. From here you can create new folders or shortcuts, or rename existing folders and programs. You can also drag icons or files from Explorer, My Computer, or your desktop and drop them into directories. When you have made the changes you want, close Explorer's Start menu, click the Apply button, then click OK.

CUSTOMIZING YOUR STARTUP FOLDER

In the Programs folder there is a special folder called StartUp. See Figure 4-36. In this folder you can put programs and documents that you want to open whenever you start your computer. Some people like to put their email program or word processor in this folder. Many programs that you install will automatically place themselves in your StartUp folder, and you may want to remove them. To remove programs from the StartUp folder, use Windows Explorer and locate the StartUp folder. The path to the StartUp folder is C:\Windows\Start Menu\Programs\StartUp. View the contents of the StartUp folder and delete whatever program shortcuts you do not want opened when Windows starts.

FIGURE 4-36
The StartUp folder

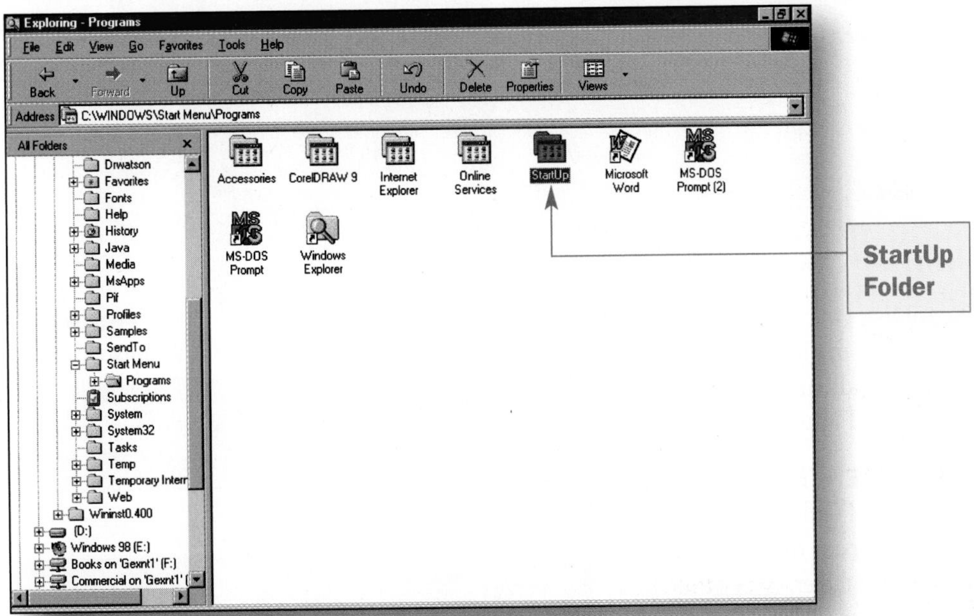

System Maintenance

Windows has built-in tools to help you maintain and improve your system's performance. Your computer, just like everything else, needs to be tuned up every once in a while to keep it running smoothly.

The two most commonly used tools to improve your systems performance are ScanDisk and Disk Defragmenter.

SCANDISK

You use ScanDisk to check your hard drive for physical and logical errors. ScanDisk will search your hard drive, find the errors, and then fix the errors. ScanDisk gives you the option to do a complete scan or just a partial scan. It also gives the option to choose which drive you want to scan.

To start ScanDisk click the Start button; then click Programs, Accessories, System Tools, and ScanDisk. See Figure 4-37.

The ScanDisk dialog box will display on your desktop. From this box you have the option to choose which drive you want to scan, the type of scan test you want to perform, and if you want ScanDisk to automatically fix errors as it finds them (or have the program prompt you for the appropriate action to take).

129

FIGURE 4-37
Starting ScanDisk

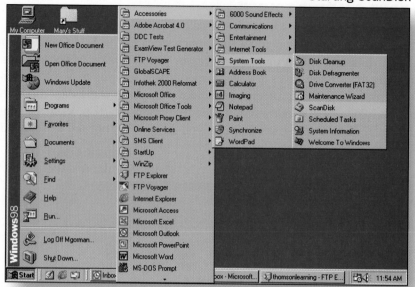

As ScanDisk is running, it will indicate the files it is checking with the Checking folders indicator at the bottom of the window. See Figure 4-38.

DISK DEFRAGMENTER

You use Disk Defragmenter to consolidate the unused space on your hard disk so that programs run faster. Every time you delete a file it makes a small section of unused space on your hard drive. When you run Disk Defragmenter, the program finds all the used space and pushes it together, leaving all of the unused space at the bottom of your hard drive. By doing this, it allows programs to access data on your hard drive faster because it doesn't have to search as much of your hard drive to find unused space.

To start the Disk Defragmenter program, click the Start button, then click Programs, Accessories, System Tools, and Disk Defragmenter. See Figure 4-39.

The Select Drive dialog box will appear on your desktop. From this dialog box, choose the drive you want to defragment and click OK.

The defrag process usually takes 20 to 45 minutes to complete.

FIGURE 4-38
ScanDisk working

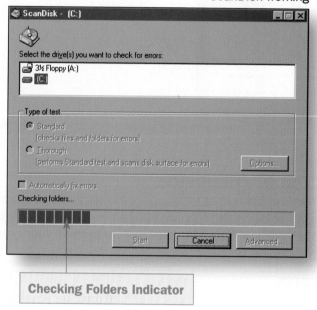

Checking Folders Indicator

FIGURE 4-39
Starting Disk Defragmenter

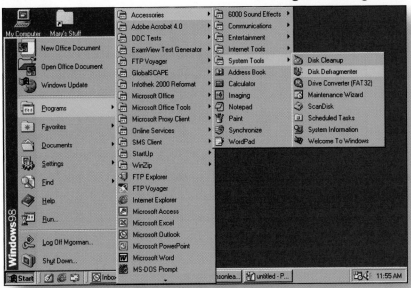

DELETING .TMP FILES

Deleting your temporary (.tmp) files is another way to improve system performance. To start the process, click the Start button and choose Find. In the Named field type *.tmp and click the Find Now button. All of your TEMP (.tmp) files will appear in a window on the bottom of the Find dialog box. On the menu bar, click Edit and choose Select All, then press the Del key on your keyboard. This process removes all the TEMP files from your system. Once you do this, make sure to empty your Recycle Bin so the files are permanently removed from your computer.

Display—Customizing your Desktop

Windows 98 gives you a variety of options for customizing your desktop. You can change the appearance of fonts, background and wallpaper properties, the color of toolbars and menus, and choose from a variety of screen savers.

DISPLAY PROPERTIES

You can access your display properties in two different ways: You can right-click your desktop and choose Properties from the drop-down menu, or you can click the Start button on the taskbar, choose Settings, then choose Control Panel, and double-click the display icon. See Figure 4-40.

After you have done this, the Display Properties dialog box will appear on your desktop.

The first tab you will see is the Background tab. From here you can choose a variety of patterns from the Patterns list and also different wallpaper from the Wallpaper list.

The second tab is the Screen Saver tab. From here you can pick from a list of screen savers that are preloaded when you install Windows. You can also determine the number of minutes you want your system to wait before the screen saver starts. If you click the Settings button next to the Preview button, a Properties dialog box for the screen saver will appear and you can customize it even further. If you click the Preview button, Windows will give you a quick preview that shows the chosen screen saver.

The third tab is Appearance. From here you can choose from a long list of color schemes for your desktop. You can also customize the fonts, font size, icon size, icon spacing, and colors of your

FIGURE 4-40
Open the display properties

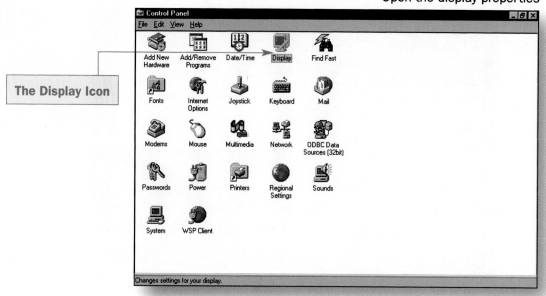

The Display Icon

active and inactive title bars, menus, message boxes, scrollbars, and windows. Once you have made the changes you want, you can save your customized windows scheme by clicking the Save As button. When the Save Scheme box displays, enter a name for your scheme and click OK. Later, if you want to delete a scheme, all you have to do is highlight the scheme and click the Delete button.

The fourth tab is the Effects tab. From here you can change your icons; choose to hide icons when you are viewing your desktop as a Web page; view large icons on your desktop; show icons using all possible colors; animate windows, menus, or lists; smooth the edges of screen fonts; and show window contents while dragging.

The final tab is Settings. See Figure 4-41. From here you can adjust the type of colors you view, whether it is in 256 colors, or 16-bit, 24-bit, or 32-bit color. The color choices you see in the drop-down box will depend on the type of display drivers on your system. You can also adjust the screen area size—which also depends on your display drivers. The screen area can vary from 640×480 pixels to 1024×768 pixels. If you click the Advanced button a dialog box displays, showing you what type of video drivers you are using and giving you the option to change them.

FIGURE 4-41
Changing the settings

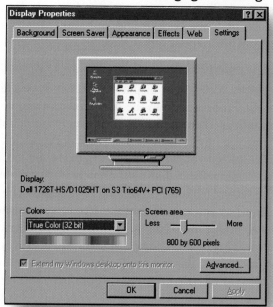

S TEP-BY-STEP ▷ 4.15

Changing the Display Properties

1. Click the **Appearance** tab to change the background color of your desktop.

2. Click the **Background** tab and change the wallpaper on your desktop. Use both the tile and center display options.

3. Click the **Screen Saver** tab to change your screensaver.

4. Click the **Appearance** tab to change your appearance color scheme.

5. Practice making your own color scheme for Windows and then delete it.

6. Click the **Effects** tab, then change your desktop appearance to show large icons.

7. Click the **Settings** tab, then change the screen area to view at 640 × 480 pixels. Now change it back to its original setting.

The Control Panel

The Control Panel is where you will find everything you need to customize your computer, from changing the date and time to setting up your own network. You can add and remove programs; install hardware; add new fonts; customize your display, keyboard, and mouse; add printers; and much more. To access the Control Panel, click the Start button on your taskbar, click Settings, and choose Control Panel. See Figure 4-42.

FIGURE 4-42
The Control Panel

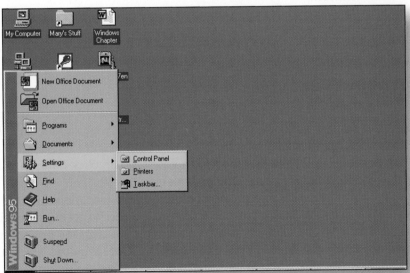

ADDING NEW HARDWARE

The first thing you need to do when adding new hardware is to read the manufacturer's instructions and physically install the hardware. Make sure that you read the documentation that comes with your new device and that you know how to change the interrupt request (or IRQ) and any input/output (I/O) settings that might need configuring. Usually Windows 98 will automatically reset the hardware's IRQ and I/O settings for you; in case it doesn't, you will want to know how to do it yourself. Once this is done you are ready to start your computer. Often upon installing new hardware, your computer automatically launches the Add New Hardware wizard when it is restarted. It will ask you questions about your new hardware to assist Windows with the installation. If it does not, you will need to initialize the Add New Hardware wizard yourself using the Control Panel. Follow these steps to start the Add New Hardware wizard: To access the Control Panel, click the Start button on your taskbar, click Settings, and choose Control Panel. Next find the Add New Hardware icon and double-click it.

This will start the Add New Hardware wizard. See Figure 4-43. Click the Next button and the Add New Hardware wizard will give you the option to select your new hardware from a list or it will search out new hardware for you. It is recommended that you let Windows try to find the new hardware for you. If it does not find it, you will be prompted to choose the hardware from a list. Once it has found the new hardware, Windows will see if it has the appropriate drivers for your new device. If it does not have the driver available in its driver database, you will be prompted to tell Windows where to find the driver. This is when you will use the driver disk that came with your new hardware. Under normal circumstances you would just insert the driver disk into your floppy drive and change the

FIGURE 4-43
The Add New Hardware wizard

location box to search the A drive. Windows will install the new drivers and tell you that your hardware has been successfully installed, prompting you to restart your system.

ADDING AND REMOVING PROGRAMS

You can do several things from Add/Remove Programs in the Control Panel. You can add and remove programs, add and remove Windows components, and create your startup disk. To add or remove programs, use the first tab—Install/Uninstall.

To access the Control Panel, click the Start button on your taskbar, click Settings, and choose Control Panel. Find the Add/Remove Programs icon and double-click it.

The Add/Remove Programs Properties screen will appear on your desktop, displaying the programs you have installed on your computer. To install a program from here you need to put the installation floppy disk or CD in the appropriate drive and click the Install button. This will start the Installation wizard. Windows will search the installation disk and locate the Setup program. Once Windows has done this, you will click the Finish button and Windows will start the install process. You will be prompted by on screen instructions and wizards to complete the installation.

To uninstall a program, click the Start button on your taskbar, click Settings, and choose Control Panel. Next find the Add/Remove Programs icon and double-click it. In the window at the bottom of the Install/Uninstall window, find and select the program you want to uninstall. Only the applications that have uninstall programs will be displayed in this list. Click the Add/Remove button. This will start the InstallShield wizard, which will walk you through the uninstall process. You can also use the Add/Remove button to reinstall programs or to add various components to an application using the same steps.

Windows Setup

The next tab is Windows Setup. From this tab you can add and remove a variety of components that come with Windows. You can add additional screen savers, wallpaper, networking tools, accessibility features to assist the disabled, and several other components.

To find out if a component is installed all you have to do is look at the check box next to the component. If there is a check in the box it is installed; if there is a check in the box but it is shaded, then only some of the components are installed. You can view the components that are installed and those that are not by highlighting the shaded component and clicking the Details button in the bottom of your window. You can then check which components you want from the details list. If a component does not have a check next to it, it is not installed.

Startup Disk

The final tab in the Add/Remove Programs Properties box is the Startup Disk tab. From here you can create a startup disk for your computer. You will need a 3.5-inch, formatted floppy disk. Just insert the disk into your floppy drive and click the Create Disk button. Windows will then format the disk and copy the needed system files to the disk. It is highly recommended that you always have a startup disk for your computer. If you experience problems with Windows 98 after it has been installed you can use your startup disk to help recover your installation. The startup disk is a bootable floppy disk that has several system files copied to it. You use it by placing it in your floppy drive and booting your computer. Your computer will boot to an MS-DOS prompt and from here you can access utilities and maintenance instructions. This is also a good reason to know at least your basic MS-DOS commands from the earlier chapter. If you do not know any MS-DOS, you will not be able to use the startup disk to recover your system.

ADJUSTING THE DATE/TIME

To access the Date/Time, click the Start button on your taskbar, click Settings, and choose Control Panel. Next find the Date/Time icon and double-click it. See Figure 4-44.

From here you can change the date and time displayed on the taskbar. You can also adjust your time for the appropriate time zone you live in and set it to automatically change for daylight savings time.

FIGURE 4-44
Adjusting the date and time

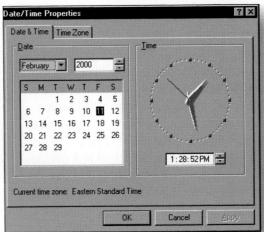

ADDING FONTS

To add custom fonts, click the Start button on your taskbar, click Settings, and choose Control Panel. Next find the Fonts icon and double-click it.

The Fonts dialog box will appear on your desktop. See Figure 4-45. From here you can add or delete fonts. To add a new font, click File on the menu bar and choose Install New Font from the drop-down menu. The Add Fonts dialog box pops up. Now you tell Windows where to find the new fonts you want to add—whether they are on a floppy disk or in a directory on your hard drive.

FIGURE 4-45
The Fonts dialog box

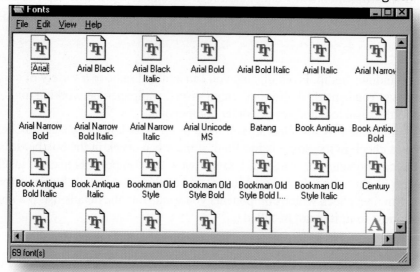

Select the fonts you want to add from the List Fonts window and click OK. The new fonts are now added to your main fonts folder.

CUSTOMIZING YOUR KEYBOARD

To customize your keyboard, click the Start button on your taskbar, click Settings, and choose Control Panel. Then find the Keyboard icon and double-click it.

In the Keyboard Properties dialog box, click the Language tab. From this tab, you can change the language your keyboard supports, or you can click the Speed tab to adjust the speed at which a character on the keyboard repeats itself. You can also adjust how fast your cursor blinks. See Figure 4-46.

FIGURE 4-46
Customizing the keyboard

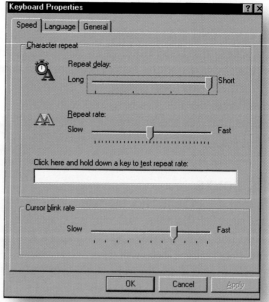

SETTING UP PRINTERS

Setting up and installing new printers is a simple process in Windows. As with adding new hardware and software, Windows has a Print wizard to walk you through the steps of installing a new printer. First, click the Start button on your taskbar, click Settings, and choose Printers; if you wish, you can choose Control Panel and double-click the Printer icon. The Printers dialog box displays. Now click the Add Printer icon. The Add Printer wizard appears on your desktop and walks you through setting up your new printer. See Figure 4-47.

- The next box asks if it is a local printer or a network printer. See Figure 4-48. In this case, choose Local Printer.

- Then the wizard will want you to specify the manufacturer and model of the printer you are installing. Click the Next button.

- The next dialog box asks you which port you want to use for the printer. If you do not have any other print devices attached to your computer, Windows defaults to LPT1. Click Next.

- The Print wizard now asks you to name the printer. Give it whatever name you want—just try to use something that will make it easy to identify if you decide later to install additional print devices.

FIGURE 4-47
Add New Printer wizard

- The final dialog box will ask you if you want to print a test page. When you are actually installing a new printer, you will want to say yes so you can verify that the printer is working correctly. If you are doing this for practice, choose No and just click the Finish button. Windows will install your new printer and tell you the installation was completed successfully.

FIGURE 4-48
Local or network printer

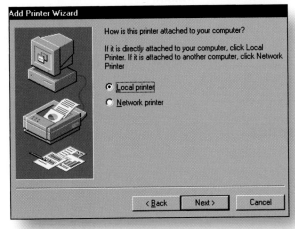

 **Note**

If the printer you are installing is not listed, you can click the Have Disk button and insert the driver disk that came with the printer into your floppy drive. Next tell Windows to look in your floppy drive for the print drivers by selecting A: from the Copy Manufacturers files drop-down box.

Summary

In this lesson, you learned:

- The differences between the Windows 95 and Windows 98 operating system. The interfaces of Microsoft's Windows 95 and Windows 98 operating systems are almost identical; unless you switch on the new features, most of them won't appear.

- How to use the basic functions of the operating system, including the desktop, the Start menu, and the mouse; navigating in Windows, and utilizing the Help feature.

- How to manage files in the operating system using My Computer and Windows Explorer. You can create files and folders directly in these windows by right-clicking. You can then copy, move, rename and delete these files in a variety of ways, some of which are mouse actions and keyboard combinations.

- When compared to other operating systems, Windows has many unique features. Among them are the ways you can customize the operating system to suit your own personal preferences.

VOCABULARY REVIEW

Define the following terms.

folder	multitasking	taskbar
hard boot	shortcut	window
icon	soft boot	

CHAPTER 4 REVIEW QUESTIONS

MULTIPLE CHOICE

Circle the answer that best applies.

1. You can resize a window by:
   A. clicking File on the menu bar and choosing Resize window.
   B. double-clicking the box in the upper-right corner of the window.
   C. putting your mouse on the edge of a window; when it turns into an arrow, drag your mouse while holding down the left button to change the size.
   D. putting your mouse on the edge of a window; when it turns into an arrow, double-click your left mouse button to resize the window.

2. How can you customize your desktop appearance? Choose all that apply.
   A. Right-click your desktop and choose Properties. The Display Properties dialog box will appear.
   B. Click the Start button on the taskbar, click Settings, then click Display properties.

    C. Double-click the My Computer icon, double-click Control Panels, and then double-click the Display icon.

    D. Drag a picture file from Explorer and drop the picture onto your desktop.

3. To create new folders you:
   A. open My Computer, choose the storage device you want the folder on, click File on the menu bar, and choose New Folder.
   B. right-click your desktop, click New, then in the drop-down menu choose New Folder.
   C. open Windows Explorer, choose the storage device you want the folder on, right-click in the right pane, and choose New and then Folder.
   D. All of the above.

4. To open a file you:
   A. click File on the menu bar and choose Open.
   B. open My Computer, double-click drive C, find the file you want to open and double-click it.
   C. open Windows Explorer, navigate to the file you want to open, select the file, and choose Open from the File menu.
   D. All of the above.

5. Windows has a number of tools you can use to improve the performance of your computer. Which of the following are Windows tools?
   A. Hard Drive Optimizer
   B. Performance Manager
   C. ScanDisk
   D. Disk Defragmenter

TRUE/FALSE

Circle T if the statement is true or F if it is false.

T   F   1. Windows 98 is a 16-bit operating system.

T   F   2. By single-clicking the left mouse button you can select an item.

T   F   3. Desktop icons are displayed on the taskbar.

T   F   4. You can set the clock by double-clicking the clock on the taskbar.

T   F   5. You should shut down your computer by pushing the power button.

WRITTEN QUESTIONS

Write a brief answer to the following questions.

1. How can you manage files and folders in Windows?

2. What are some of the differences between Windows 95 and Windows 98?

3. What are some of the different ways you can customize your desktop?

4. What are the minimum system requirements you must meet in order to install Windows 98?

5. How do you create a startup disk?

MATCHING

Match the following terms to the correct definition.

___ soft boot
        Restarting your computer by turning the power off and then back on, using the power button.

___ hard boot
        The main workspace on your computer.

___ hard drive
        Restarting your computer using Ctrl+Alt+Del.

___ mouse
        Small picture that represents a file, disk, menu, option, or program.

___ multitasking
        A mode of operation that allows you to perform two or more tasks at the same time.

___ desktop

___ icon
        Device used to navigate your desktop and windows.

        Physical device that stores all data on your computer.

CHAPTER 4 PROJECTS

PROJECT 1

1. Put your floppy disk into the floppy drive.

2. Open Windows Explorer.

3. Create a new text file on your floppy disk called **Mine**.

4. Create another new text file on your floppy disk called **Yours**.

5. Create a new folder on your floppy disk called **Windows**.

6. Create another new folder on your floppy disk called **98**.

7. Copy the **Mine** file into the **Windows** folder.

8. Move the **Yours** file into the **Windows** folder.

9. Copy the **Yours** file from Windows to the **98** folder.

10. Rename the **Yours** file in the 98 folder to **New yours** file.

11. Delete the **Yours** file from the Windows folder.

12. Delete the **Mine** file from your floppy disk.

13. Turn in your floppy disk to your instructor for credit.

PROJECT 2

1. Start Windows 98 Help.

2. Find information about the Paint Accessory Program in Windows 98.

3. What is the Paint program used for?

4. Through Help, launch the Paint Accessory Program.

5. Close Paint.

6. Return to Windows 98 Help.

7. Find information about the Disk Cleanup utility.

8. What is this program used for?

9. Through Help, launch the Disk Cleanup utility.

10. Use Disk Cleanup on the C drive to delete all files in the Recycle Bin and all temporary internet files.

11. Close Help.

CRITICAL THINKING

1. Anyone reading the newspaper or watching the news on television knows that the United States government is currently engaged in an antitrust suit against Microsoft. First of all, what is a trust? What is the major issue surrounding this suit and do you think that the government has a valid suit against Microsoft?

2. When searching the want ads, why do you think a knowledge of Windows is listed as a basic job skill? Why did Windows become so popular as a standard operating system?

WINDOWS NT WORKSTATION

OBJECTIVES

Upon completion of this lesson you should be able to:

■ Walk through a basic installation of Windows NT Workstation from the CD-ROM.

■ Understand the basic functionalities of NT, including maneuvering in the operating system, resource management, and file management.

■ Use the unique control panel icons of Windows NT.

■ Apply the User Manager to create and manage users.

■ Set file and folder permissions.

■ Use Network Neighborhood to share a network device.

⏱ **Estimated Time: 10+ hours**

VOCABULARY

compression

FAT

hardware compatibility list

NTFS

partition

permissions

registry

User Manager

What Is Windows NT Workstation?

Windows NT (now called Windows 2000) is Microsoft's version of Windows for the multiuser server platform. In 1993 when Windows 3.x was the version used on stand-alone PCs, Microsoft created a networked version called Windows NT 3.1 (which stands for New Technology). A *network* is a system of computers that are interconnected by telephone wires or other means in order to share information.

Windows NT is not designed for use by individual users. Rather, it was aimed at corporate users working on networked computers. Unfortunately, the market did not readily accept Windows NT 3.1. The second version of NT, 3.5—even though it still had the look and feel of Windows 3.x—began to challenge Novell NetWare in terms of networking market share. NT Version 3.5 was the first to offer two separate versions: Workstation and Server. Advances in Windows 95/98, with its overhaul of the graphical user interface, were incorporated into the next version of Windows NT, 4.0, which became a big hit. Because many users were already familiar with the Windows 95/98 interface, no retraining was needed to learn the NT interface. Now NT posed a real threat to Novell's networking market share.

As mentioned earlier, there are two different classifications of Windows NT: Workstation and Server. This chapter will concentrate on the Workstation implementation of NT, but it is important that you understand the difference between the two. By offering a combination of Workstation and Server software, Microsoft's goal is to provide a total client/server solution for businesses. Workstation is designed for use on every desktop PC in the network, with Server as the back-end product used for sharing resources and security. Workstation generally serves as a desktop operating system, whereas Server is mainly used if your machine is a source for files, applications, or print services. Workstation can also handle this function, but only at the most basic level: It can only handle ten inbound client sessions at a time. This means that only ten computers (called workstations) can simultaneously access shared resources (such as a printer or files) from a machine that has NT Workstation on it, whereas Server can handle unlimited inbound client sessions. If you constantly reach the limit of ten inbound client sessions, then the purpose of sharing resources is defeated. In this case, Server is the better option. Also, if a business solution includes remote access (where users will be accessing shared resources through a modem), Workstation is limited to one remote access session at a time, whereas Server can sustain 256 remote access sessions at a time.

Installing Windows NT

Before you Begin

Before installing Windows NT Workstation, you need to address several issues to ensure that your installation process is as smooth as possible. Specifically, you must make sure that you meet the minimum recommended hardware requirements, that your hardware is on Microsoft's hardware compatibility list, and that your partition scheme is compatible with Windows NT.

MINIMUM RECOMMENDED HARDWARE REQUIREMENT

The advance of technology means that there are minimum hardware requirements for today's networking software, and NT Workstation is no exception to this rule. The minimum requirements for NT Workstation are as follows:

- Intel processor 486/333 or higher

- 12 MB of RAM (although 16 to 32 MB is preferable)

- 120 MB of free hard drive space

- CD-ROM drive or access to a network CD-ROM or share

- VGA or higher resolution graphics card

- Microsoft mouse or compatible device

TIP

Remember that these are the minimum requirements for Windows NT. If you are running many applications, it is recommended that you exceed the minimum requirements in order to obtain the most productivity from Windows NT Workstation.

In addition, the following hardware is recommended in order to get the most out of Windows NT Workstation:

- Intel Pentium, Pentium Pro, Pentium II, Pentium III Processor

- 32 to 48 MB of RAM

- 2 GB of free hard drive space

- CD-ROM drive

- SVGA or higher resolution and a 3-D graphics card

- Microsoft mouse

- Internet connectivity

HARDWARE COMPATIBILITY LIST

Before selecting Windows NT Workstation, you want to make sure that your hardware is listed on the *hardware compatibity list* (HCL) provided by Microsoft. In order for a manufacturer's hardware device to appear on the HCL, it must pass tests given by Microsoft that ensure no conflicts will occur when Windows NT Workstation is installed. To find the most current HCL, check out Microsoft's website (*www.microsoft.com*). This information is updated periodically by Microsoft to ensure that your installation of NT is as smooth as possible.

Once you have found out that your hardware is on the HCL and compatible with NT Workstation, you should make sure that you have the required device driver handy. Earlier, you learned that a device driver is a small program used to enable communication between the operating system and the device itself. Unlike Windows 98, Windows NT is not Plug-and-Play enabled, which means that you cannot just plug a new hardware device into a PC running Windows NT Workstation and expect the device to work. During installation, Windows NT Workstation will try to recognize all of your hardware devices, but if it does make a mistake, you will be required to install the correct driver for the device.

Partitioning the Hard Drive

A *partition* is a logical division of a disk drive. It is common to partition a drive before installing Windows NT Workstation. Once you partition the drive, you will need to decide which partition will be the active one (the partition from which the operating system will boot) and which will be the system partition. Once you finish partitioning the drive, it is ready for formatting.

There are two major types of file systems: *file allocation table* (FAT) and *new technology file system* (NTFS). The newest version of FAT, called FAT32, is used primarily for MS-DOS as well as Windows 3.x and 95. The FAT file system is good for smaller hard disks (2 GB or less), but does not provide any file or directory security. The FAT file system also requires that your filenames follow the original DOS 8-character limit, followed by a three-letter extension (commonly termed the 8.3 filename convention). It also does not provide for the security features in Windows NT Workstation. A disk formatted with the FAT32 file system cannot have Windows NT Workstation installed on it (Windows 2000 does support the FAT32 file system with some limitations).

The NTFS file system is the best choice for Windows NT Workstation. It allows the user to take advantage of the features that make NT so popular, such as Windows NT security, when using the NTFS file system. NTFS allows the user to specify access levels to files and directories on the network and on one PC. Also, NTFS will not allow a user running a different operating system to access files on the NTFS partition. NTFS also supports filenames of up to 255 characters.

TIP

To see whether your disk is FAT or NTFS, right-click the disk icon in My Computer and check its properties. The name of the file system is listed on the General tab under File system.

Installation

Now that you have prepared to install the Windows NT Workstation operating system, there are many installation options from which to choose. You can install from the hard drive of the local computer, from a CD-ROM drive, or from the network. In this discussion, we cover only one of the installation options: installing from a CD-ROM.

STEP-BY-STEP ▷ 5.1

Beginning the Installation from the CD-ROM

1. Place the CD-ROM into the drive.

2. At the command prompt, change to your CD-ROM drive by keying **D:** (If this does not work, try keying **E:** at the command prompt).

3. Key the command **cd I386** and then press **Enter** to change to the I386 directory.

4. Key the command **WINNT32.EXE /B** to begin the setup utility.

The setup program copies the actual files to your local hard drive. (Installation is quicker if the files are accessed from the hard drive rather than the CD-ROM.) When the files are copied, the text portion of setup begins to ask you questions about setting up Windows NT Workstation and tries to identify all of your hardware. The installation program tries to locate your processor type, motherboard type, file system, hard disk, the amount of free space on your hard disk, and the amount of memory for your system. If NT Workstation does not recognize all your hardware and you do not install the correct drivers when asked to do so, this almost guarantees that your installation of NT will fail.

The next stage of the installation is the partition selection. Here you select on which partition you want to install Windows NT Workstation. It is wise to install on an NTFS partition to take full advantage of NT's security features. You should partition the disk before beginning installation; otherwise it is a tedious and difficult process.

In the next stage, the installation program examines the hard disk to make sure that it has no physical problems. Finally, the graphical portion of the setup begins. A wizard walks you through this stage of the setup process.

STEP-BY-STEP ▷ 5.2

The Graphical Portion of Setup

1. Select **Typical** as your configuration option and then click **Next**.

2. Enter your name and your organization name and click **Next**.

3. Enter the default administrator password and confirm it when prompted. DO NOT FORGET THIS.

4. Select **Yes** to create an Emergency Repair Disk.

5. Select **Install the Most Common Components** and click **Next**.

6. Select **Wired to Network** and click **Next** to continue. Windows NT should find your network adapter card if your card is on the hardware compatibility list.

7. Select **TCP/IP and DHCP** and click **Next**.

8. Select **Workgroup** and click **Next**.

9. Click **Finish**.

10. Enter the correct time zone and date/time properties and then click **OK**.

11. Insert a blank disk to create the Emergency Repair Disk. When the disk is complete, remove it from the drive.

12. The sytem should reboot and then log in to Windows NT using the administrator setting you created in step 3.

Basic Functionality

The Basic Boot Process

Windows NT Workstation has a number of tasks to perform before it is ready to process information. When power is applied, the computer looks at a special chip on the motherboard called the *BIOS*, where it finds all the instructions it needs to start. Then the computer makes sure all the hardware required to boot is actually attached to the computer.

The next step is to start loading the operating system (OS) from the hard drive. If everything works correctly, your PC begins loading the rest of NT at this point. Before you can open a file or run a program, though, you'll have to log in.

Logging In

Logging in is the process of identifying yourself to the computer. You do this by entering a unique user name and password combination. To do this, press the Ctrl, Alt, and Del keys simultaneously. This brings up the login screen, and opens a dialog box where you type your user name and password. If you don't have a user name, you will need to obtain one from your network administrator. Your administrator can also explain how to set your password.

At this point NT performs *user verification*. It attempts to match your login name and password with a known list of users. If it makes a match, your personalized startup files load now. Windows keeps track of everything you've asked it to do, including what color you want the background to be and where you want all your icons to sit.

Once the computer has verified that you are allowed to use the machine, it also sets some rights. Rights are merely rules, such as what file access you have, what network access you have, and to which printers you can print. NT administrators specify just what the user can and cannot access. These are not the only rights you can have; you can be assigned additional rights at any time.

The reason for logging in is simple: NT acts like a security guard. You have to show your identification, and then NT has to check the list of names to make sure it's OK for you to come in. The password, which only you should know, is as good as a photo ID. When the system administrator first created an account for you, he or she added your name to the list of authorized users and gave you a password. Once you log in, NT will run for a minute and then drop you onto the desktop where all the work actually takes place.

If you have forgotten your password, just ask your administrator to help you set a new one. This will allow you to regain access to your account.

 Did You Know?

With most other PC operating systems, the Ctrl+Alt+Del key combination restarts the computer. If the Windows NT login dialog box appears when you press these keys, you can be certain that Windows NT is running.

CHANGING YOUR PASSWORD

For security's sake it is best if you change your password every two or three months. This decreases the likelihood that someone will be able to access your system. It also makes you more aware of what is going on in your system. To change your password, press Ctrl+Alt+Del to display the login dialog box. Then click the change password option (remember, unless you are told otherwise, you always click with the left mouse button). You will be asked to enter your old password for verification and then you must type the new password twice. Make sure to write it down.

Here are some rules for protecting your password.

- Make the password long enough (at least 8 letters) to prevent random guessing by a stranger.

- Avoid the obvious: Don't use your birthday or your Social Security number or the names of your kids as a password.

- Mix numbers, letters, and symbols; nonsensical combinations are much harder to guess.

- If you must use a real word, use something that you won't forget and no one else could possibly guess, like the name of the sled you had when you were a child. You might try putting the capital letter somewhere other than the first letter—i.e., RosebUD.

- Change your password regularly, at least as often as you change the oil in your car. Your system administrator may require that you change passwords every six weeks or so.

- Don't forget: A good lock is sometimes more effective than a password. Use the keyboard lockout on the front of many machines. Someone can hack into your system if he or she can use the keyboard.

- To change your password, you first have to enter your old one. Then type the new one, and type it again to make sure you didn't make a mistake the first time.

What do you do if you can't change your password? Your system administrator may have placed additional restrictions on your account. For example, the administrator may have told NT that your password has to be at least 10 characters, or that you can't reuse any of the last four passwords you've used. If you have trouble, ask your system administrator whether any of these restrictions apply to you.

The Graphical User Interface

When you first log in to Windows NT Workstation, you will feel like you are using Windows 95. The desktop contains the familiar icons, My Computer, and the Recycle Bin. The taskbar is at the bottom of the desktop with the Windows Start button at the left end and the system tray icons at the right end. When you open a window, you'll see the close, minimize, and maximize buttons at the right end of the title bar. See Figure 5-1.

This is done on purpose to make new users familiar with the interface. If you are comfortable using Windows 95/98, you will be comfortable using Windows NT Workstation. All of the objectives discussed in Chapter 4 about maneuvering in the Windows 98 operating system hold true. However, there are some major changes under the hood, which will be discussed later in this chapter.

THE START BUTTON

By default NT places a horizontal bar, called the taskbar, across the bottom of your screen. This bar displays the icons for the applications that are running. It enables you to quickly switch to a new application by clicking its icons instead of minimizing windows. On the right end of the taskbar you will see a clock and possibly a few other small icons; this area is called the system tray. On the left end of the taskbar you will see the Start button. See Figure 5-2.

FIGURE 5-1
The Windows NT desktop

FIGURE 5-2
The Start button

Start
Button

Place your mouse pointer (the on-screen arrow) over the Start button and click. This opens a menu that contains several options. To open the Programs submenu, hold your mouse pointer over Programs until the submenu opens. Or you can click the Programs option to open the Programs submenu immediately. Try it both ways. Until you learn some shortcuts, this is where you will select all your programs. Try opening a few. As you install new programs, the list will become longer. Don't be afraid to play around; there isn't anything you can break. If you find yourself in unfamiliar territory, just close the window and start again.

STEP-BY-STEP ▷ 5.3

Using the Start Button

1. Click the **Start** button in your taskbar.

2. Click **Programs** from the Start menu.

3. Click **Accessories** from the submenu.

4. Open the **Paint** accessory program, then close it.

5. Repeat steps 2 through 4, except this time open and close the **Notepad** accessory program.

THE MY COMPUTER ICON

When you open the My Computer window, you see icons for each of the disks in your system, as well as a number of folders. See Figure 5-3.

Hold your mouse pointer over one of the folders and notice that a message box, called a ScreenTip, pops up to show how you can use the folder.

Folders and files are stored on disks, which act just like file cabinets (and seem to fill up just as quickly). How much free space is left on your hard disk? To find out, open the My Computer window, click the Control Panel icon, click the System icon, then click the Performance tab. You'll see a listing of your system specs, including its free resources.

You can also use My Computer to ask Windows to attach an electronic label to your disks. To name a floppy disk, you would insert a disk into drive A, click the A: drive icon, choose Properties from the File menu, and type the name for the disk into the Label: field. Now the next time you insert the floppy disk you'll know it contains budget data before you even open it.

Finally, My Computer is one of many places in Windows where you can find, copy, or delete a file. In fact, many of the functions of My Computer are the same as those available in Windows Explorer.

Your office equipment claims a few icons here as well. For example, printers and modems get special icons that let you adjust their settings. Imagine how awkward life would be if you had to lug your monitor down the hall every time you wanted to show someone this quarter's budget spreadsheet. That's why printers are the most important pieces of computer hardware, next to your PC, and that's why they get their own folder in the My Computer window.

FIGURE 5-3
The My Computer window

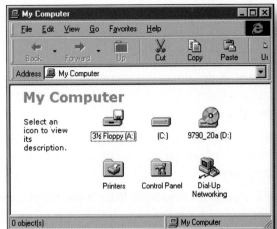

STEP-BY-STEP ▷ 5.4

Using the My Computer Icon

1. Insert a floppy disk into drive A.

2. Double-click the **My Computer** icon to open it.

3. Double-click the **A:** drive icon to view the contents of your floppy disk. How many folders are on your disk? How many files on your disk?

4. Click the A: drive icon to highlight it.

5. Click the **File** menu in the menu bar, then click **Properties**.

6. In the label area of the dialog box, add a label to your floppy disk that describes its contents.

THE FIVE BASIC ICON TYPES

NT uses five types of icons to represent everything in your computer. The icons give you important clues about the type of object with which you are working.

- *Folder*: Folders represent special files that are capable of holding documents and programs. Use them the same way you would with real file folders. You can even "nest" folders inside other folders in an unlimited series.

- *Document*: A document might consist of a simple note, or it might be a complex combination of graphics, links, and text. Electronic documents are similar in many ways to documents in the real world.

- *Program*: Programs (also called applications) are the parts of NT that actually do the work. They can be spreadsheets, word processors, games, and so on. Programs usually have custom-designed icons.

- *Device*: Device icons provide links to the hardware of your computer—the mouse, keyboard, monitor, and so forth. The icons link to special utilities that allow you to configure the hardware.

- *Shortcut*: Shortcuts are special links. They are really just a set of instructions telling the computer where the program actually exists. Every time you click a shortcut, the icon redirects the computer to the program. The purpose of shortcuts is to provide convenient access routes to a program from various places on your computer (from your desktop, for instance). You can identify shortcut icons by the little arrow in the lower-left corner of the icon. Shortcuts are available in Windows 95 and up. Once you learn how convenient they are, you'll find yourself using them everywhere.

 Did You Know?

To quickly change an icon's label, select the icon, press the F2 key, and then start typing the new name.

USING SHORTCUTS

Consider this scenario: You, Mr./Ms. Sales Manager, have three customers who place large orders frequently. You keep each customer's sales records in a separate manila folder. You also have a product catalog the size of a phone book that you use, no matter which customer you're working with. If you make three copies of that catalog and put one in each client folder, you've created a big problem the next time you revise your catalog. You have to remember to put the latest copy in all three client folders, or you might wind up sending the wrong merchandise or charging the wrong price.

The solution is to store the catalog in its own folder, then store a note in each client folder that tells you where to find the catalog. That's how shortcuts work. They act like little notes that tell NT to find something stored elsewhere on the disk (or even on another computer) and open it up. Shortcuts use only a small amount of disk space, and they can point to just about anything: programs, documents, printers, and drives—even a location on the Microsoft Network.

CREATING SHORTCUTS

One of the most useful places to create a shortcut is right on the Windows NT desktop. For a program you use every day, like the Windows Calculator, why should you have to rummage through the Start menu? You don't want to move the program out of its home in the Windows

 Note

When you drag and drop a program to create a shortcut, NT calls the new icon Shortcut to .. [the program's original name]. You can delete the two extra words if you like, or even completely rename the shortcut. Calling it Word, for example, uses less screen space than calling it Shortcut to Microsoft Word for Windows.

folder, but you would like to be able to start it up by just double-clicking an icon. Here's how: If you already know where the program is stored, just open its folder or highlight it in Windows Explorer. Drag the icon using the right mouse button, and then drop it onto the desktop, choosing Create Shortcut(s) from the menu that pops up.

Another way to create a shortcut to an item is to use the Create Shortcut dialog box. See Figure 5-4. Right-click your desktop and from the menu choose New and then Shortcut. In the dialog box, click the browse button to locate the program you want to create a shortcut to. In the final step, type the name you want to give the shortcut.

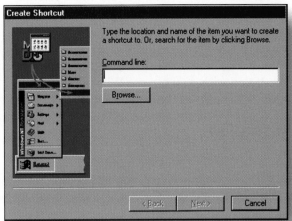

FIGURE 5-4
The Create Shortcut dialog box

STEP-BY-STEP ▷ 5.5

Creating Shortcuts

1. Right-click the desktop.

2. Click **Browse** in the dialog box.

3. Double-click the **Windows** folder in the Browse dialog box.

4. Double-click the file **Calc.exe**.

5. Click **Next**.

6. Rename the shortcut **Calculator**.

7. Click **Finish**.

File Management

Windows NT has an update to the file system. You no longer need to have all those cryptic filenames. You can now have names up to 255 characters long. This means you can have filenames like "thank you letter to Bob 06201999.doc". This name has more meaning. But don't use the longer filenames as an excuse to get sloppy. You still need to develop a filing system to keep things orderly and easy to find.

You should be aware of one thing when dealing with longer filenames. If the file is copied to an older machine that doesn't support long names, the older machine will truncate the filename. (Don't worry; if the file is copied back to a newer machine that supports long filenames it will have the longer name again.) Truncating follows a rule. The machine preserves the first six characters, then adds a tilde ("~") the number 1, and then the extension. For example, our thank you letter to Bob would truncate to "thank y~1.doc". If you need to type in the filename on a machine that does not support long filenames, just type it in the way you see it, not the long version. It will work fine.

Windows NT still uses the file extensions you used to see in DOS and Windows 3.x. For the most part the usage is the same. However, NT does not normally display the extensions. People used to check the extension to know what type of file it was. Now different file types have different icons, so an extension would be duplicate information. If you wish, you can use Windows Explorer options to ask NT to display the extensions.

STORAGE DEVICES

Files go in folders, and folders go on drives. As the number of files on your computer builds up, you'll be glad to have a logical filing system that lets you find documents when you need them. If you expect Windows NT to help you organize your work, you need to understand two of its most important building blocks: drives and folders.

WORKING WITH HARD DISKS

Your disk drives work just like filing cabinets. To keep your files organized you use the computer equivalent of manila folders. But just like the filing cabinets in your office, you have to do a little prep work before you place your data into folders. The challenge is to make sure there's enough free space on the disk and that the files are organized properly.

CHECKING FREE SPACE ON A STORAGE DEVICE

Every time you save a file to a hard disk, it gobbles some of the empty space on that disk (which is measured in megabytes, or millions of bytes); sooner or later you'll fill up most of that space. As the disk reaches its capacity you will notice your computer starts running slowly, and eventually you won't be able to open or save new documents. That's why you should keep an eye on free disk space. It's especially important to check how much space is left on a disk when you're planning to install a new program.

> **TIP**
>
> You can make an icon's name up to 255 characters long, and you can even use some punctuation marks: periods, commas, semi-colons, ampersands, parentheses, and dollar signs. However, there are a handful of characters you can't use in an icon's name: `" \ / * ? | < >`

> **TIP**
>
> You can choose from four different ways to arrange the drives in the My Computer window. Pull down the View menu and choose Arrange Icons. Now you can sort the entries in the window by drive letter, type, size, or amount of available free space.

S TEP-BY-STEP 5.6

Determining Free Space on a Storage Device

1. Double-click the **My Computer** icon on your desktop to open My Computer.

2. Click the **C:** drive icon. The total disk capacity and free space appear in the status bar at the bottom of the My Computer window. (If the status bar isn't visible, pull down the **View** menu and click **Status Bar**.)

3. Close the window.

4. To see a graphical display of free disk space, right-click the hard drive icon, then choose **Properties** from the pop-up menu. Above the pie chart, you can see exactly how many free megabytes are left, as well as the total megabytes on your hard disk. See Figure 5-5.

OUT OF ROOM

One of the realities of owning a computer is that sooner or later, you'll have more files than your hard disk can hold. If you've been checking your free disk space regularly, you'll get some advance warning. Otherwise, you'll just get an error message when you try to save a file. At that point you have three choices:

■ *Clean some files off your hard disk.* The cheapest solution to an overstuffed hard disk is to delete the files you don't need. Try emptying your Recycle Bin first. There are disk utility programs you can purchase that will also clean up some of the other files that cause your hard drive to be cluttered.

■ *Get a new hard disk.* You'll need a few hundred dollars to purchase this and you'll also need to find someone who'll install it for you. If you replace your hard disk, you will have to reinstall all your software, including NT.

■ *Software compression of your files.* You can tell NT to pack one or more files, a folder, or even an entire drive so that they take up less space. This option is to be used at your own risk. Compression is such a risky affair, it is not recommended at all. Use it only under dire emergencies. There are two reasons. First, if you do this and something goes wrong, none of the data will be retrievable. The "key" used to compress/uncompress the files is stored on the hard drive along with the rest of your data; if something happens to your data, chances are it will damage the "key" as well. Second, if you are running out of space, you should solve the problem correctly, by adding a second hard drive or upgrading to a bigger hard drive. Compression is only a temporary bandage that buys you a little time. Even with compression you will soon run out of space.

HOW COMPRESSION WORKS

Compression replaces small file containers with one big container that holds all your files. It separates each file from the one before it and after it with a special character. The result is that there is almost no wasted space. The tradeoff is that in order to find anything NT needs to start at the beginning of the file container and read through each file until it reaches the one it wants. This results in a huge slowdown. It can be as much as

FIGURE 5-5
Graphical display of free disk space

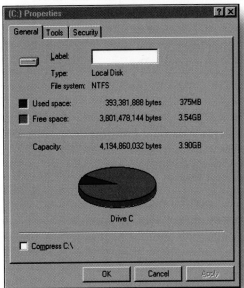

 Did You Know?

A byte is one character, and mega means million. So a megabyte is a million characters, right? Not exactly. Your PC can only count by powers of 2, so a megabyte is actually 2 to the 20th power, or 1,048,576 bytes. Of course, not all the storage space is used for data. Some of it is used by your system to keep track of the files and some special attributes. So it's practical to "round off" a megabyte of storage at an even million.

TIP

You might have more free disk space than you think. Check the Recycle Bin first. If it's filled with files, simply emptying it might clear enough room to let you finish whatever you're doing. (To empty it, just right-click the Recycle Bin icon and select Empty Recycle Bin from the shortcut menu.)

100:1 when compared to the noncompressed method. So you are trading off speed and a little bit of wasted space for no wasted space and slower performance.

DOS in Windows NT

If you learned to use a PC running MS-DOS, you might not initially know your way around a Windows environment. But once you learn a few landmarks, you will be off and running. Later, if something should go wrong with NT, you will be able to use DOS to fix it. For this reason, it's always handy to know a little DOS in order to use NT effectively.

Whenever you want to use DOS in a Windows environment, you have a choice of two command lines. Both are accessible from the NT Start menu. The first looks like the familiar DOS prompt. To reach it, click the Start button, then click Programs and choose MS-DOS Prompt from the menu. The C:\ prompt in this window does everything a DOS user would expect, and then some. See Figure 5-6. Unlike old-fashioned DOS, which fills your entire screen, the Windows NT Command Prompt displays in a window that you can resize and move around your screen. You can type the name of any program at the command prompt, and the program will start right up. You can even run some of your older DOS programs, although some of them won't work properly with Windows NT.

FIGURE 5-6
MS-DOS screen in Windows NT

Command Prompt
Microsoft(R) Windows NT(TM)
(C) Copyright 1985-1996 Microsoft Corp.

C:\>

STEP-BY-STEP ⟹ 5.7

Using MS-DOS in NT

1. Click the **Start** button.

2. Click **Programs** and then **MS-DOS Prompt**.

3. At the command prompt, key **NOTEPAD**. The program should start just as if you selected it using the Windows Start button.

4. Close Notepad and return to MS-DOS.

5. At the command prompt, key **DEFRAG**. Again the Disk Defragmenting program should start, just as if you selected it using the NT Start button.

6. Exit Defrag.

7. At the command prompt, key **EXIT** to return to NT.

Shutting Down Your Computer in NT

To turn off your computer, first click the Start button, then choose Shut Down from the menu. NT will start to terminate all applications that are still running. If you have any data that hasn't been saved, you will be asked to save it. Once all processes have stopped, NT will display a message that it is OK to turn off your computer. If you turn off the power without doing a shutdown, you may lose vital data or damage the system. If you aren't sure whether the computer can be turned off, ask someone.

Unique Features of Windows NT

The Control Panel

The Windows NT Workstation Control Panel is where most of the configuration of your operating system takes place. Configuration is the process of adjusting the settings to make the operating system perform as you want it to. If you have used Windows 95 or 98, you will find that many of the icons in the Control Panel are unchanged. See Figure 5-7. However, NT offers a few new ones, including Tape Devices and Servers. This discussion will describe the icons.

FIGURE 5-7
The Control Panel window

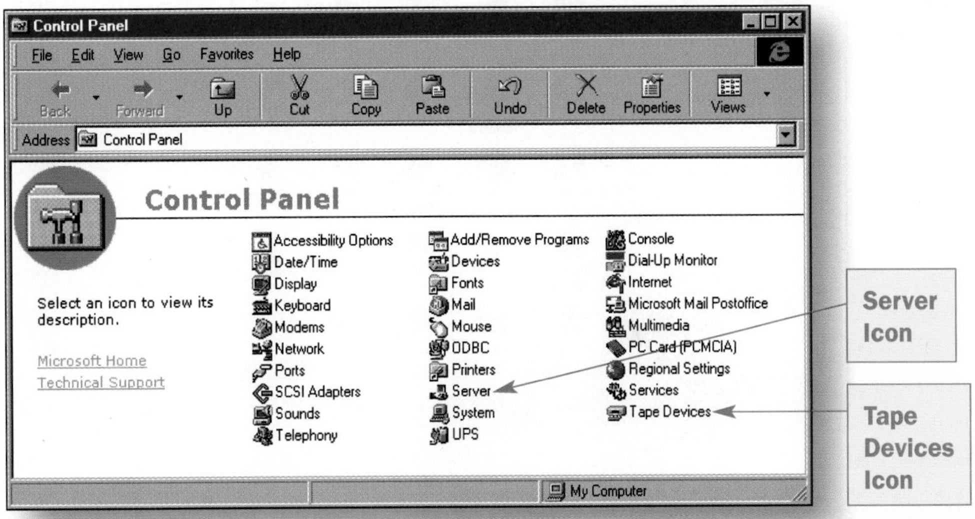

STEP-BY-STEP ▷ 5.8

Accessing the Control Panel

1. Click the **Start** menu, click the **Settings** option, and then click **Control Panel**.

2. Or click the **My Computer** icon on the desktop, then click the **Control Panel** icon.

TAPE DEVICES ICON

In order to use the built-in backup capabilities of Windows NT Workstation, you need to have a tape device installed on the sytem. When you click the Tape Devices icon, you will be ready to install and configure your device to back up information. See Figure 5-8.

TIP

It is common to find other icons in the Control Panel besides the ones with which you are familiar. Sometimes when you install new hardware or software, it will create an icon in the Control Panel for you. The idea is to centralize all of your configuration options into one location.

FIGURE 5-8
The Tape Devices icon

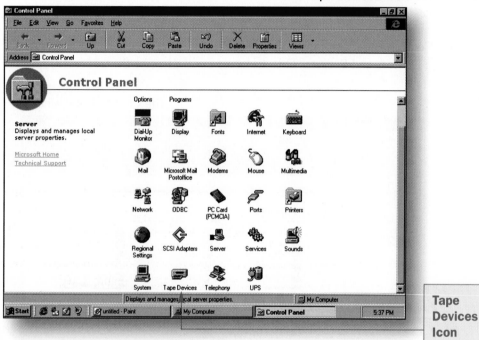

Tape Devices Icon

STEP-BY-STEP 5.9

Installing a Tape Device

1. Open the **Control Panel**.

2. Double-click the **Tape Devices** icon in the Control Panel to open it.

3. Click the **Drivers Tab** and then click **Add**.

4. Select your tape device from the list of manufacturers and models available.

5. If your device is not listed, make sure you have the driver disk that came with the device and click **Have disk to install the appropriate drivers**.

6. Click **OK**.

7. Restart the machine so the new changes will take effect.

THE SERVER ICON

The Server icon in the Control Panel is needed if you are making shared resources (also called *shares*), such as a printer, accessible to users at other machines. This gives you an idea of what shares are available to users and who is currently accessing the shares. Because you have resources that others are using, it is completely legitimate for you to know who is accessing them and how many times they have accessed them. The Usage Summary dialog box gives you the following information (see Figure 5-9):

FIGURE 5-9
The Usage Summary dialog box

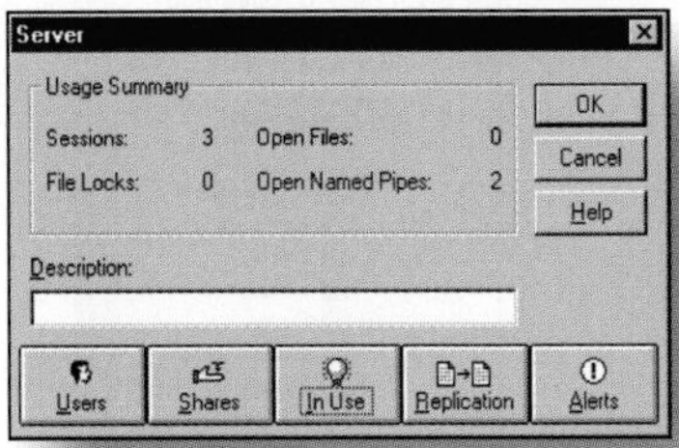

- *Sessions* are the number of users currently connected to your machine.

- *File Locks* are the number of files locked in use by users.

- *Open Files* are the number of open files and their users.

- *Named Pipes* allow one process to communicate with another.

The Shares button displays all of the shares that are currently available and the number of users connected to each share. You can also see how long a user has been using a shared resource. If there are users connected that you no longer want connected, you can highlight the user name and click the Disconnect button.

THE WINDOWS REGISTRY

While you are configuring your operating system using the Control Panel, a system file called the Windows *registry* is keeping track of these changes. The registry stores your software and hardware configuration settings. However, a new user can be overwhelmed by the registry and it is extremely easy to corrupt your system if you change things you do not understand. For the work in this chapter, use the Control Panel to make any system changes, but understand that all changes you make via the Control Panel are stored as command lines in the registry file. See Figure 5-10.

Managing Users

A Windows NT computer requires that all users have an account. Each user account is created with a unique user name and password.

DIFFERENT TYPES OF USERS

Windows NT includes the following predefined groups (chances are, you already belong to one of them).

- *Administrators* includes everyone who has the right to log on and act as an administrator. Some administrators keep two accounts—one in this group, which they can use when they need to do system maintenance, and another account, for everyday use, that has more restricted user rights.

TIP

Don't be surprised if your system has more than one administrator. In most companies, several people have the right to act as administrator on a given PC; that way, someone's always available to help with a problem, even if the regular system administrator is out sick or on vacation.

FIGURE 5-10
The registry

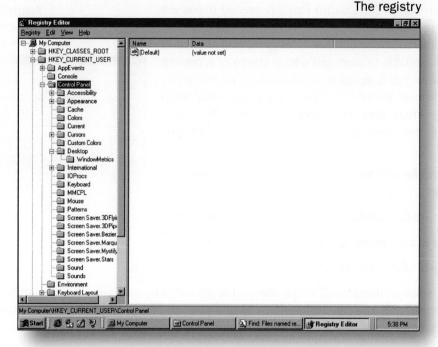

- *Everyone* has the fewest amount of rights of any group. Typically, users in this group get the right to log in at a specific machine and shut it down, and that's all.

- *Users* have restricted rights, not because they're not trusted, but because administrators want to keep them from accidentally deleting important files or stumbling into areas where they don't belong.

- *Power users* are assumed to be more experienced and are allowed to share files and folders with other users, and to create new user accounts on their own computers.

- *Guests*, as the name implies, are allowed to log in at a machine and use it temporarily. A guest account might be created to allow visitors to log in and use a few programs and a shared printer, storing their files in a special folder not shared by anyone else.

- *Backup operators* are allowed to get around file and folder security, but only for the purpose of making backup copies of important data files.

CREATING USERS

One of the responsibilities of the administrator is to decide upon a unique naming scheme for the user names he or she creates. One common scheme is to use someone's first initial of the first name, followed by their full first name. For example the user name for Joe Smith would be JSmith. Whatever the administrator decides to do, it should be simple and consistent.

User Manager is the tool employed to create new users. See Figure 5-11.

FIGURE 5-11
User Manager dialog box

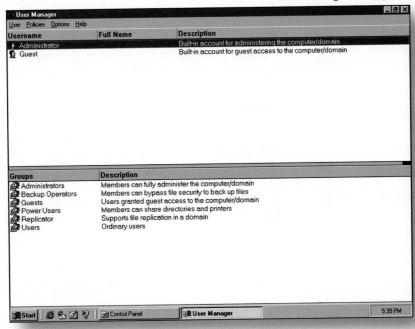

When creating a new account the administrator must enter information specific to that account. See Figure 5-12. Each account is assigned an ID by Windows NT. This security ID is unique to every account and this is part of the access token when the user logs in. To start User Manager, click the Start button, click Programs, and then click Administrative Tools and User Manager. Table 5-1 describes what you see in the User Manager dialog box.

FIGURE 5-12
Adding a new user

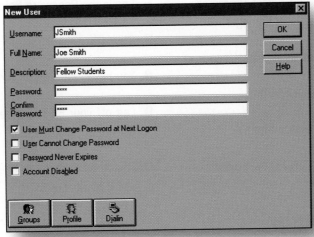

TABLE 5-1

BOX	DESCRIPTION
Username	A unique name up to 20 characters in length
Full Name	The name of the user
Description	A brief description of the user's account
Password	Passwords are case-sensitive and cannot be more than 14 characters in length
Confirm Password	Re-enter the password to make sure it is correct
User Must Change Password at Next Logon	Forces the user to change the password the next time they log in. This option is turned off once the user changes their password
User Cannot Change Password	Keeps the user from changing the password
Password Never Expires	Keeps the password from ever needing to be changed
Account Disabled	Prevents anyone from using the account

STEP-BY-STEP 5.10

Creating a New User

1. Click the Start button and select Programs, Administrative Tools and User Manager.

2. Click the User menu and select New User.

3. In the Username field key JSMITH.

4. In the Full Name field key Joe Smith.

5. In the Description field, key Fellow Student.

6. Leave the Password field blank.

7. Click OK.

8. You have just created a new user.

9. Log off your NT machine and log back in as user name JSMITH and no password.

10. NT will prompt you to change JSMITH's password. Make it JOE.

Windows NT Security

Security is a main element of a network. One advantage of using Windows NT Workstation over Windows 95/98 in a networked environment is NT's security capabilities.

Windows NT security has four main parts:

■ **Logon process** is the way in which the user gets initial access to the system.

■ **Local Security Authority** creates security access tokens, authenticates users, and manages the security policy.

- **SAM database** manages all users accounts. When a user logs in, the information is validated by comparing it to the SAM database.

- **Security Reference Monitor** verifies that a user has access to a requested object, such as a folder or file.

When a user presses Ctrl+Alt+Del to log in, the security process begins. The user is prompted for a user name and password. This information is passed to the Local Security Authority, which verifies this information against the SAM database. If the user is verified, the Local Security Authority creates an access token which acts as the user's ID badge. Once the user presents an ID, it is no longer needed to gain access to the system.

ACCESSING OBJECTS

Now that you are logged in to the system, how does NT know what you can and cannot access? If you choose to use the NTFS file system then the administrator can grant file and folder **permissions**. With NTFS the following permissions can be set to folders:

- **No Access** does not allow users any access to this file.

- **List** allows users to view the files and subfolders in the folder, but they cannot use anything within.

- **Read** allows users to read files in the folder, but they cannot save any changes to the file.

- **Add** allows users to add new files to the folder, but they cannot view any existing files or folder.

- **Add & Read** allows users to list, read, and write new files to the folder. However, they cannot save changes to any existing files.

- **Change** allows users to read, change, modify, and delete the existing files in the folder.

- **Full Control** allows users all of the rights allowed with Change, as well as the ability to change permissions and take ownership of the files and folders.

To set permissions on a file or folder, you can use Windows Explorer. See Figure 5-13.

FIGURE 5-13
Setting permissions in Windows Explorer

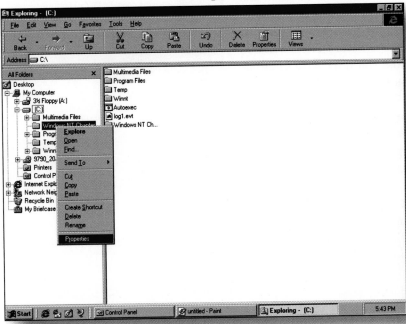

Setting Permissions

1. Open **Windows Explorer**.

2. Double-click **C:** in the **All Folders** pane of Windows Explorer to view the contents of your hard drive.

3. Right-click the **Contents** pane and choose **New, Folder** from the menu.

4. Name the new folder **Windows NT Class**.

5. Right-click the **Windows NT Class** folder and choose **Properties**.

6. Select the **Security** tab and then click the **Permissions** button. See Figure 5-14.

7. Now click the **Remove** button to remove the group Everyone from having access to this directory.

8. Click the **Show Users** button; select your user name from the list and click the **Add** button.

9. On the **Type of Access** drop-down menu, select **No Access**.

10. Return to Windows Explorer and try to access the folder. What happens?

11. Return to **Properties** and explore what happens when you choose the other types of access to the Windows NT Class folder. Do you notice the differences between the types of access?

Network Neighborhood

Most NT computers are connected to a *network*. In an office environment this allows fellow employees to share information and resources. You can even share with people in different offices in other parts of the world. If you double-click the Network Neighborhood icon on your desktop, you'll see a list of all the computers that you are allowed to access. See Figure 5-15.

Computers may be arranged in groups of "like" departments. For instance, the engineering and finance departments may have separate groups. This helps filter out information you really don't need. It also helps with security. You may not want anyone outside of the engineering department to view a new product design until you release it. At the same time, a departmental listing makes it easier to locate a particular machine, because you'll have a shorter list to look through.

FIGURE 5-14
Setting permissions

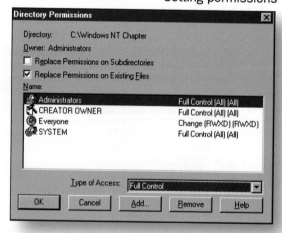

STEP-BY-STEP ▷ 5.12

Viewing the Network

1. Double-click the **Network Neighborhood** icon.

2. You should see a listing of all the machines on the network.

Network sharing is a multifaceted process. You can work with others' files, and share your own files, hard drive, and printer with others as well. You can tell if your printer or hard drive has sharing enabled. If it is shared, you'll see a hand beneath the printer or hard drive icon instead of the normal printer and hard drive icons. It should look as though the hand is holding the device. See Figure 5-16. If it isn't shared, you can quickly share it by right-clicking the device and selecting Properties from the menu. Select the Sharing tab at the top of the pop-up window. You can enable sharing and even password protection for the information, so only certain people can access it. You may also want to specify a name to use for the shared device. For instance, you can call one computer on your network "Walrus", another "Thing2", and a printer "Big Al". Some people have commented that network administrators name their machines as though they were pets. There is a very good reason for this: It's much easier to remember a name like "Walrus" than "ad1256f".

3. Ask your instructor which machine is yours.

4. Double-click the icon for your machine. Is there anything inside it?

FIGURE 5-15
Example of Network Neighborhood icon

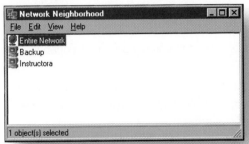

FIGURE 5-16
Icon of a
shared printer

MAPPING A SHARED NETWORK DRIVE

To *map* a shared network drive to a drive letter, just look in the Network Neighborhood. Double-click a computer icon and, when the list appears, select the name of the share you want to connect to. Then choose Map Network Drive from the shortcut menu. See Figure 5-17. When the dialog box appears, just pick any free drive letter from the list and click OK.

Let's say you want to map a drive to drive D on your boss's computer, Excalibur. You would look in Network Neighborhood for Excalibur, and browse to its drive D. Then pick any free drive name (say, J:) and map that drive name to D: on Excalibur. From now

FIGURE 5-17
Mapping a network drive

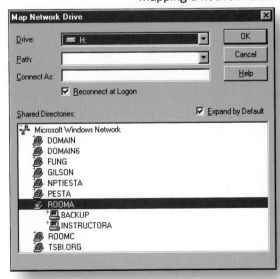

on, you can click drive J to get to D: on Excalibur. To tell NT that you want to continue to use this mapped drive letter every time you log in to your computer, check the Reconnect at Logon box.

STEP-BY-STEP 5.13

Mapping a Network Drive

1. Open the **Network Neighborhood** icon.

2. Find the name for your neighbor's computer.

3. Double-click the computer name to open it.

4. Right-click the icon for the CD-ROM drive (most likely D:) and click **Map Network Drive**.

5. On your computer, click the drive letter that you would like to use to represent your neighbor's CD-ROM drive.

6. Check the **Reconnect at Logon** option and then click **OK**.

7. Open Windows Explorer.

8. In the All Folders pane, you should see the mapped drive that you just created.

To disconnect a drive mapping, right-click My Computer, select the mapped drive and right-click it, then choose Disconnect from the shortcut menu.

ON YOUR OWN

As you work with NT, ask yourself what you need to accomplish, then look for ways NT can help you do it. You might also ask others what they have done to solve a particular problem.

Some of the obvious things NT can help you with are the routine tasks of the everyday office. Word processing, email, faxing, music, spreadsheets, contact lists, and even games are made easier. There's almost no end to what you can do. Jump in and explore a bit.

Summary

In this chapter, you learned:

- To install Windows NT: First you need to make sure you have a working hard drive and CD-ROM. Remember that you should know all the system resources beforehand, if possible. Make a list to keep track. Check the hardware compatibility list to ensure your hardware is compatible with NT. Partition your hard disk to the NTFS file system, so you can fully utilize the power of NT security. With the CD-ROM in, key WINNT32.EXE /B to begin the setup utility. Answer the questions to complete the setup of your particular machine. When the system reboots, you can now log in for the first time as the Administrator.

- NT uses many of the same functions you learned in Windows 98. You move around the operating system using your mouse and your keyboard. The main workspace is the desktop, where you work with windows and dialog boxes to perform tasks. As in Windows 98, you use My Computer and Windows Explorer to manage your files by cutting, copying, pasting, and deleting them.

- The Control Panel contains most of the icons you learned in the Windows 98 chapter as well as a couple of new ones, including the Tape Devices and Server icons. The Tape Devices icon allows you to install a tape device on your system, in order to back up your information on the PC. The Server icon tells you what shared resources are available to other users and who is accessing the shares.

- There are six different types of NT users: Administrators, Everyone, Users, Power Users, Guests, and Backup Operators. The User Manager utility allows the administrator to create new users for the system.

- Security is a key element of Windows NT Workstation. The four main processes associated with NT security are the logon process, the Local Security Authority, the SAM database, and the Security Reference Monitor. When a disk is formatted with the NTFS file system you can set folder and file permissions. The permissions available for folders are: No Access, List, Read, Add, Add and Read, Change, and Full Control. User access to a folder depends upon the permission assigned to the folder.

- The Network Neighborhood icon shows the computers you have access to. Here you can create maps to drives on other computers you would like access to. Right-click on a share in Network Neighborhood and choose Map Network Drive from the menu to access the resources on that drive.

VOCABULARY REVIEW

Define the following terms.

compression	NTFS	registry
FAT	partition	User Manager
hardware compatibility list	permissions	

MULTIPLE CHOICE

Circle the answer that best applies.

1. The two different classifications of Windows NT are:
   A. User and Administrator.
   B. Server and Workstation.
   C. MS-DOS and PC.
   D. Workstation and Playstation.

2. One of the recommended hardware requirements is:
   A. a 486 processor.
   B. 12 MB of RAM.
   C. 120 MB of free hard disk space.
   D. 32–48 MB of RAM.

3. The NTFS file system is the best choice for Windows NT because:
   A. It follows the limitations of the 8.3 file naming convention.
   B. It takes advantage of NT's security features.
   C. It is good for smaller hard disks.
   D. You can have Windows 95/98 loaded on the machine.

4. Which one of the following is a good reason not to compress your hard drive?
   A. It will make the computer run faster.
   B. It will free up some space on the hard disk.
   C. It will make the computer run slower.
   D. You can back up files that are compressed.

5. When assigning the permission list to a folder, the user has what permissions?
   A. The user can view the files and folders within the folder, but cannot access any of them.
   B. The user has no access to the folder.
   C. The user can list, read, and write new files to the folder.
   D. The user can add new files to the folder, but cannot access any existing files.

TRUE/FALSE

Circle T if the statement is true or F if it is false.

T F 1. Windows NT requires the use of the mouse.

T F 2. The Server icon in the Control Panel displays shared resources and who is accessing them.

T F 3. A user with the designation of Everyone has full rights to make changes to the machine.

T F   4. The SAM database manages all user accounts.

T F   5. To map a network drive, you can use Network Neighborhood.

WRITTEN QUESTIONS

Write a brief answer to the following questions.

1. Name the five types of icons.

2. What does NT stand for?

3. Name the different type of users and explain what rights each type has.

4. What is the desktop?

5. Discuss the four processes in NT security.

MATCHING

Match the following terms to the correct definition.

___ 1. compression

___ 2. hardware compatibility list (HCL)

___ 3. NTFS

___ 4. partition

___ 5. registry

A. A system file where all configuration changes to Windows NT are recorded.

B. The coding of data to save storage space.

C. A logical division of a disk drive.

D. A list available from Microsoft that shows what hardware devices are acceptable for use with Windows NT Workstation.

E. New Technology File System

PROJECT 1

1. Create a folder on your floppy disk named **Windows NT Section**.

2. Open the **Notepad** accessory program.

3. Write a short memo to your instructor describing what you have learned in the past few weeks about operating systems.

4. Save the file as **Operating System** in your Windows NT folder on drive A.

5. Close Notepad.

6. Open **My Computer** and view the contents of A:.

7. Create a shortcut on the desktop to your **Windows NT Section** folder.

8. Open Windows Explorer.

9. Create a Read permission to the **Windows NT Section** folder.

10. Can you access the **Operating System** file? Can you save any changes to the **Operating System** file?

11. Change the permission on the **Windows NT Section** folder to List.

12. Can you access the **Operating System** file now?

PROJECT 2

1. Open the **My Computer** window. Under the Help menu, choose **About Windows NT**.

   - To whom is NT licensed?

   - How much physical memory is available?

   - What percentage of system resources is free?

2. What does that tell you about the operating system?

3. Work with a partner (who is on a separate computer); both of you create a folder on drive C called **I Love Windows NT**.

4. Using **Network Neighborhood**, map a drive to that folder on your partner's computer. Label the drive with whatever letter you wish. Make sure you can locate the folder at login.

CRITICAL THINKING

1. As always in the information world, software companies are improving their technology and introducing better operating systems. Windows 2000 was recently released to the public. Research the improvements of Windows 2000 over Windows NT and Windows 98. What are the different advantages of the operating system?

2. There are many types of certification available from Microsoft for Windows NT. Research Microsoft's website at *www.microsoft.com* to find information about these. What is the major track of certification for Windows NT? How will certification benefit you if you plan to follow a career in networking?

NOVELL NETWARE

Introduction

Over time, desktop computers became popular because they were easier to use than mainframes. Their cost savings and productivity increases could not be ignored. However, even though they provided a cheaper solution than mainframes, they had comparatively limited computing power. In 1983, a new player named Novell entered the market and realized the potential of connecting all those computing resources and sharing them. This was the beginning of the *local area network* (*LAN*). A LAN is a network of interconnected workstations sharing the resources of a single processor or server within a relatively small geographic area.

In the beginning only large computer mainframes had been networked. A network was very expensive to purchase and maintain. The technology was complicated, and training was difficult and limited. This helped fuel a standoff between users and administrators. Users felt that the system was too cumbersome to use and had too many restrictions. Administrators countered that the users abused and destroyed parts of the system. This "us" versus "them" mentality wasted time and resources.

Novell's idea was to connect all those cheaper PCs to the mainframe. The users would get to use the simpler interface and all the data could be passed back to the mainframe for processing. The user was relieved of the usage issues and the administrators could tell the work was getting done. The idea appealed to both camps, so they looked for a way to make it happen.

In the early days, the fact that the DOS operating system had no native network capabilities was a big obstacle. How would you enable it to print to a remote printer, access/save remote files, and communicate among the various hosts on the network? To solve this problem, engineers decided not to re-invent the wheel: They turned back to the mainframes and looked at how they did it. In fact, since the system had to be compatible with the mainframes, why not use the same system?

Mainframe communications had two components: software and hardware. The software took the form of *drivers*—programs that told the computer how to access the network. A driver is configured for use between the host computer and network card. At the other end, a sort of universal connector is created between the network card and the network. This is an optimum solution. Programs could be designed to use this universal connector. This kept the hardware design as simple as possible, which improved its reliability and ease of installation.

To enable DOS to use the communications hardware of a mainframe was fairly easy. In its initial conception, the PC had been loosely based on the mainframe. The peripherals just had to use a different physical connector to plug into the computer. Making the software work was more difficult. This is where Novell got clever. They figured out a way to install certain programs into DOS and make up for its deficiencies. These programs are referred to as *extensions* to the OS. The first couple of versions weren't very friendly by today's standards, but they worked well enough. The programs allowed smaller companies to implement low-cost networks and enhance their productivity. This in turn enabled them to spend more money on networking devices—which allowed them to save money and increase productivity. The self-sustaining cycle is responsible for much of the networking world as we know it. It also changed the way networks are defined. As networking became more prevalent, it went from one local area network (LAN) to groups of networks, and then to networks of networks (called wide area networks, or WANs). Throughout this evolution, software has gone through many revisions, while the hardware has stayed relatively the same.

Customers

The following list of some Novell customers shows how popular the idea of networking is with large corporations.

- *Automotive*: Allied Signal, Daimler Chrysler, Ford, General Motors, Michelin, Nissan, TRW Automotive, Volvo

- *Banking and Finance*: ABN Amro Bank, American Express, Banc One Corp., Bankers Trust, California Federal Bank, Chase Manhattan, Citicorp, Deutsche Financial Services, First Union, J.P. Morgan, NationsBanc, PostBank, ReliaStar Financial Services, State Street, UBS Switzerland

- *Consumer Products and Retail*: American Home Products, Blockbuster-Australia, Colgate-Palmolive, Domino's Pizza, Eddie Bauer, Hallmark Cards, Jenny Craig International, LensCrafters, Nintendo, Pepsico, Safeway Stores, Wal-Mart

- *Education*: Duke University, Loyola University, Minnesota Department of State Colleges and Universities, Purdue University, New York University, University of California at San Francisco, University of Southern California

- *Electronic Systems and Engineering*: Andover Controls, Fluor Daniel, Raytheon

- *Energy*: Aramco, Mobil Oil, Occidental Petroleum, Pemmex Oil

- *Government*: California Department of Transportation, Environmental Protection Agency, German Ministry of Education, States of Arizona, California, Michigan, North Carolina, Ohio and Texas, U.S. Census Bureau, U.S. Postal Service, U.S. Department of Defense, U.S. Department of Justice

- *Healthcare and Pharmaceuticals*: Bristol-Myers Squibb, Foundation Health, Helix Health, Kaiser Permanente, Pfizer, United Healthcare

- *Industrial*: BASF Corporation, Hoechst Celanese, Litton/Solar Turbines, Whirlpool Corporation

- *Semiconductors*: National Semiconductor Corporation, SGS Thomson Microelectronics

- *Services*: EDS, KPMG Peat Marwick, Saatchi & Saatchi, Young and Rubicam

- *Telecommunications*: 3Com, Air Touch Cellular, ALLTEL, AT&T, British Telecommunications PLC, Nortel, Telecom Italia, WorldCom

- *Transportation and Shipping*: American Airlines, FedEx, Lufthansa SA, Southwest Airlines, United Airlines, United Parcel Service, and Virgin Atlantic

What Is a Network?

Simply stated, a *network* is a group of computers (or *workstations*—sometimes called *hosts*) that can communicate with each other, share hardware resources (such as hard disks or printers), and access remote computers or other networks. With Novell software there is also a server involved. (Some types of networks do not require a server. In peer-to-peer networking, all workstations act as the client and server at the same time.)

A basic Novell NetWare network consists of a server, client workstations, and printer(s). Each is connected to the network with cabling and a network board. More complex networks might include routers, hubs, switches, and gateways. See Figure 6-1.

FIGURE 6-1
A typical network

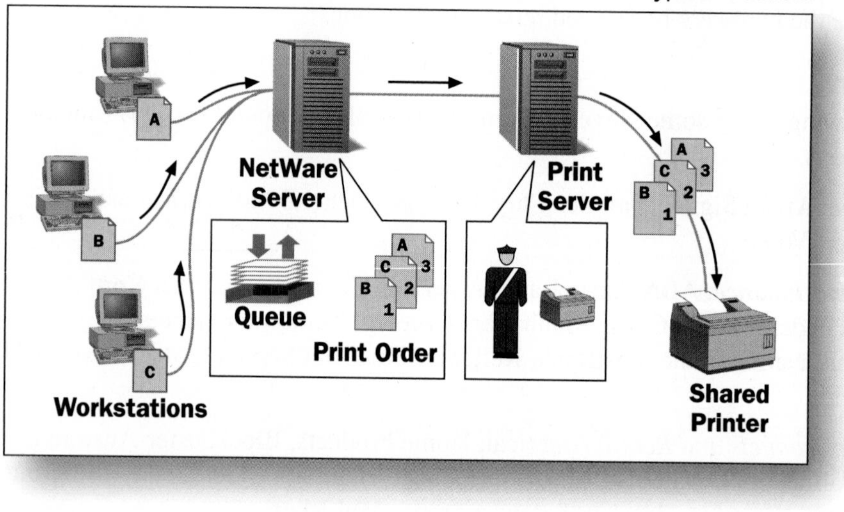

The actual communication between the different devices is done by first translating the data into a common protocol and then sending it across the network card into the network for use. A *protocol* is the set of rules that govern transmission between two machines or pieces of software, which lets them coordinate without ambiguity. Every device on the network does not natively speak the common protocol. This is because the protocols can be changed by the network engineers to fit their purposes or improve security. (For instance, if hackers can't talk to the network, they can't hack it.) The drivers that are loaded into each machine have instructions on how to encode the information into the protocols and then translate back again.

As stated earlier, today's PC networks are based on the networks developed for mainframes. Their protocol, called IP for Internet protocol, is the same protocol used by the Internet. NetWare's transport protocol is IPX—an extension of the IP protocol (IPX stands for Internet protocol extension). This means that it has certain extensions that allow the IPX protocol to do things not planned for in the IP protocol. The IP and IPX protocols are not compatible, but they can be run at the same time on a network without interfering with each other.

Each time a machine needs to send/request information, the data is translated into the protocol and sent across the network in small chunks called *packets*. This is very similar to sending a multipage letter one page at a time. The network doesn't send larger chunks because the machine with the largest chunk would tie up the network. Sending the data in uniform packets gives other machines a chance to send their data. This means the network resources are shared more equally.

- *Server.* The server manages the communication on the network. Because many users will access and use the server, a NetWare server should contain a fast processor and large amounts of disk space (usually over 20 GB) and memory.

- *Client Workstations.* Client workstations are computers running operating systems such as DOS, Windows, or Mac. To connect to the network, each client workstation requires Novell Client software and a network board, as described below.

- *Printers.* Because many users need access to printers, placing printers on the network is cost-effective. Printers connect to the network with a network board or through a dedicated print server.

Network boards (also called LAN cards, network adapters, and network interface cards or NICs) provide the connection between the computing device and the network. Each device on the network must have a network board. Network boards are designed for specific network architectures such as FDDI, token ring, or Ethernet. The following paragraphs describe each of these architectures.

FDDI, or fiber distributed data interface, uses fiber-optic cable in two concentric rings. See Figure 6-2. If one ring is broken, all communications fall back on the unbroken ring. Data flows clockwise in one ring and counter-clockwise in the other ring. This means that data has a maximum distance of only half the ring to travel. This high-speed (128 MB/sec) network is used almost exclusively as a backbone to connect separate networks into a wide area network (WAN). FDDI allows data to be transmitted a much greater distance than other technologies allow. Distance is measured in kilometers, versus 300 meters for Ethernet. FDDI is based on earlier token ring networks and uses a token to pass information.

FIGURE 6-2
Fiber distributed data interface, or FDDI

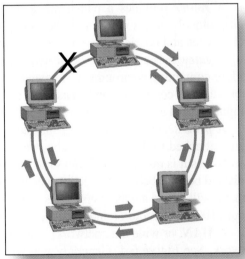

A *token ring* is a type of network that connects all machines on the network. See Figure 6-3. They are connected in a ring, similar to holding hands in a circle. It comes in two speeds, 4- and 16-megabit. In both cases, traffic is controlled by means of a *token*. The token is not a physical object, but a special bit configuration. When the network starts, the server has the token. No other machine is allowed to do anything until it receives the token. First the server looks at the token for any information addressed to it. If there isn't any, the server attaches any messages it may want to send and passes the token to the first workstation. The first workstation repeats the process. It looks at the token for any messages addressed to the first workstation. It removes these from the token and attaches any messages it wants to send. It then passes the token to the next machine.

The process repeats until the server gets the token back. This technology has an extreme amount of overhead to manage. But information can flow very rapidly—almost as fast as newer technologies—because the traffic is controlled better. Usually speeds are approximately 86% of the maximum possible speed, even on large networks. The downside to this technology is that the whole network stops working if one machine fails.

FIGURE 6-3
Token ring

Ethernet technology comes in different types: 10Base2, 10Base-T, 100Base-T, and 5base-T (ThickNet). The parts of the name refer to the speed at which data is transmitted across the media and the types of media used. The number at the beginning of the name indicates the data speed: For instance, 10 means ten megabits/sec, and 5 means five megabits/sec. The number at the end of the name refers to the type of connection. For example, 2 refers to a coaxial cable (similar to cable TV) used to connect the hosts; T refers to connection made to a backbone, through an 8-conductor cable that looks physically like the letter "T". Ethernet technology is extremely fault-tolerant. If one machine stops working, the rest of the network continues to work without problems. The downside is that it has almost no traffic management. As a result, the network usually only performs at 20% of maximum possible speed. However, because it is cheap and easy to implement and maintain, it is still the dominant network technology today.

Cabling connects each device on the network. The cable can be coaxial, twisted-pair, or fiber-optic, depending on the network architecture (physical layout and technology used). For certain network types, you need cable both for the main network trunk and also for attaching individual computing devices to that trunk. The attachment cable is often called a drop, patch, adapter, or transceiver cable. Generically, the cabling is referred to as the transmission media.

A *router* provides a path from a device on one network to a device on another network. Multiprotocol routers can handle several protocols at the same time. Routers can filter different packet types and restrict certain network addresses from reaching other networks.

A *gateway* is a computer dedicated to providing a network with access to a different type of network or computing environment. A gateway computer needs at least one network board, plus software to provide the conversion and translation services to communicate with the other network. Gateway computers need a considerable amount of disk storage and memory.

A *print server* is a computer that does nothing but pass print requests from the network to a printer attached to the computer. The computer is capable of handling multiple printers at one time. Many times it is not financially feasible for the company to dedicate a computer to this task. A small, dedicated box has been developed that accomplishes the same task at a much lower cost. The downside is that it will not do anything else. This is considered acceptable because even a cheap new computer is about $1000 with monitor and software, but a print server device starts at about $100 complete.

A **WAN**, or wide area network, is where two or more networks are connected to create a larger network. See Figure 6-4. Generally you will see this in large companies that want to connect their regional offices to the corporate office.

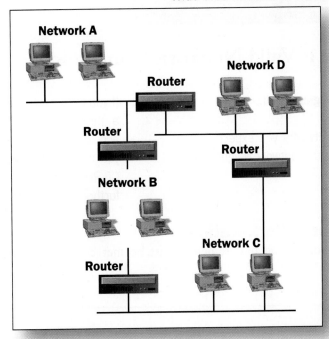

FIGURE 6-4
Wide area network or WAN

Installing NetWare

Understanding What a User Might See

If this is a new client software installation or an upgrade from older client software, the software is installed or upgraded when a user logs in. The new software is copied to the client machines. The workstation must be restarted to make the changes active. Users might see system messages set up by the administrator as their workstations are upgraded, depending on how you set up the installation.

If workstations already have current client software, the client login runs as usual. For the most part the client software is invisible to the user. The difference between a client machine and a non-client machine is that the file menus of a client machine may have extra options. The client machine may also show hard drives and printers that are not physically attached to the computer.

Before installing the client software, make sure the client workstation has sufficient resources and the required software. If not, the installation won't finish. The complete hardware and software setup for client workstations might require you to complete one or more of the following tasks:

- Check for a valid network connection.

- Check client workstation requirements.

Checking for a Valid Network Connection

1. Open **Network Neighborhood**.

2. Check that the networks you expect to see actually appear in the Network Neighborhood window.

3. If you have never installed a client or created a network connection, you may not have access to Network Neighborhood. Therefore, you must install the client software from a CD-ROM. See Installing Clients from CD-ROM further on in this chapter.

Preparing Client Workstations

Certain client workstation requirements must be met before installing or upgrading Novell client software. See Table 6-1 for these requirements.

TABLE 6-1

OPERATING SYSTEM	HARDWARE REQUIREMENTS
Windows 95/98	486 processor or better
	Minimum 28 MB free disk space
Windows NT	Must meet the minimum requirements for Windows NT
Windows 3.1x and DOS	386 processor or better
	A memory manager
	Minimum 15 MB free disk space
	Minimum 8 MB RAM

The Network Board

Novell Client for Windows NT and Novell Client for Windows 95/98 support Network Driver Interface Specification (NDIS) drivers. This is a set of standards set forth by Novell to ensure that all products capable of running Novell software are compatible. For specific information about installing the network board, refer to the board manufacturer's instructions.

IMPORTANT: Open Data-Link Interface (ODI) drivers are not installed on Windows 95/98 or Windows NT. ODI drivers are an early/primitive form of network driver. They have been upgraded to the newer and more powerful NDIS drivers. If you are upgrading an older version of the client and you have ODI drivers currently installed, these drivers are still supported. If you are installing for the first time, NDIS drivers will not be installed. If you do not already have the necessary NDIS driver, you might need to obtain it from the Windows 95/98 CD-ROM or from the network board manufacturer.

Novell Client for DOS and Windows 3.1x supports ODI drivers. For information about installing the network board, refer to the board manufacturer's instructions.

Checking for Incompatibilities

WINDOWS 95/98

The following network components are not compatible with Novell Client for Windows 95/98:

- Microsoft Client for NetWare networks

- Microsoft file and printer sharing for NetWare networks

- Microsoft Service for Novell Directory Services (NDS) software

- Novell NetWare workstation shell 3.x (NETX)

- Novell NetWare workstation shell 4.0 and later (VLM) clients

- Novell Internetwork Packet Exchange (IPX) ODI protocol (the 16-bit module for the NETX and VLM clients)

These network components conflict with Novell Client for Windows 95/98. If any of these network components are installed, the client installation program detects the conflict and removes the conflicting network components.

WINDOWS NT

For up-to-date information about software incompatibilities, read the Novell Client for Windows NT readme file, WINNT.TXT, or contact Novell directly.

DOS AND WINDOWS 3.1X

There are no known incompatibilities.

Installing Clients from CD-ROM

If you plan to install the Novell Client software on a small number of workstations, or if the workstations are not yet connected to a network, installing from the Novell Client CD-ROM works best.

If you plan to install the Novell Client on several workstations on the network, consider using one of several network installation options. A network installation can upgrade existing client software or install new client software. The Novell Client Setup utility helps you install Novell Client software on Windows-based workstations. When you use this utility, you can select the client you want to install from a list of available clients. Administrative options are also available.

S TEP-BY-STEP ▷ 6.2

Installing Clients from Windows

1. Insert the Novell Client CD-ROM. If the Novell Client Setup utility does not automatically launch, run **WINSETUP.EXE** from the root of the CD-ROM.

2. Select a language for the installation.

3. Select a platform for the installation.

4. Select the software to install. This starts the installation utility for that software.

5. Follow the on-screen instructions.

6. For help during the installation, refer to the online help that accompanies the software or contact your network administrator.

INSTALLING CLIENTS FROM DOS

The DOS-based installation installs the necessary files for Novell Client for DOS and Windows 3.1x files and allows you to select from several optional utilities.

If you previously installed the client software in Windows and you are using multiple location profiles, you should update using the Windows installation. Location profiles maintain information about your working environment for each workstation you work in, or for each networking environment in a location.

The DOS installation does not support Novell dial-up services or locations and it disables previously installed versions of the Locations Manager.

Note

During the installation of NetWare, if you are not sure of your particular network settings, see your instructor or network administrator for the necessary information.

STEP-BY-STEP 6.3

Installing from DOS

1. Insert the Novell Client CD-ROM.

2. From a DOS prompt, switch to the drive where the Novell Client CD-ROM is located.

3. Change to the **PRODUCTS\DOSWIN32** directory, and then key **INSTALL**.

4. Press **Enter** to accept the license agreement.

5. Select the options you want to install on the workstation.

6. Press **F10** to continue.

7. If you want to return to the previous screen or cancel the installation, press Esc at any time before the program begins copying files.

8. Configure the options you are installing.

   a. Depending on the options you have chosen, various configuration screens appear. Use the arrow keys to move to a new field and press **Enter** to edit the field.

   b. Press **F10** to save your changes and continue.

   c. Depending on the type of network board you have installed in the workstation, select the 16-bit or 32-bit LAN driver type. DOS and Windows 3.1 will use the 16-bit drivers. Windows 95/98 can use either, but better performance and reliability are obtained with 32-bit drivers. Windows NT, Linux, and Macintosh must use the 32-bit drivers.

   d. Review the Installation Configuration Summary. To make necessary changes, use the arrow keys to move to a new field and press **Enter** to edit the field.

9. Press **F10** to continue. The program copies the appropriate files to your workstation and sets up the workstation to run the Novell Client software.

10. To exit Install, press **Enter** to return to DOS or press **Ctrl+Alt+Del** to reboot the workstation.

The Novell Client for DOS and Windows 3.1x software does not load until the workstation restarts.

INSTALLING CLIENTS FROM THE NETWORK

If you plan to install the Novell Client software on multiple workstations, you can install from the network by copying files to the server and modifying the login script. The login script is a predefined set of instructions the network uses to connect to the various printers and hard drives. It also sets user access, based on rights set by the administrator. One network installation method is explained here. There are additional network installation options that might better suit your networking environment. You should evaluate these methods before deciding which is best for you.

Even if your network has workstations on multiple platforms (this generally refers to the OS being used; i.e., a machine running Windows is referred to as a Windows platform), you can install and upgrade the client software on all platforms when users log in. The process requires five tasks:

- Create a folder on the NetWare server.

- Copy Novell Client files and other required files to this folder (workstations can then read the files during login).

- Grant rights to the new folder.

- Create or update the appropriate configuration file (INSTALL.CFG, SETUP.INI, NWSETUP.INI, or UNTENDED.TXT) for each platform-specific client. These files are on the installation CD-ROM.

- Create or modify the appropriate login script.

Let users know in advance about the upgrade so they understand what is happening and why their work environment is changing.

Creating a Folder

Log in to a server as Admin or log in as a user with Admin equivalence. You need rights to copy files to a network folder that all users can access. You also need rights to modify login scripts. Create a folder that will hold the client files; for example, create a client folder in the SYS:\PUBLIC network folder, which has the name SYS:\PUBLIC\CLIENT.

Copying Files

There are several subdirectories that need to be copied from the PRODUCTS directory on the Novell Client CD-ROM to the client system. Copy the WINNT, WIN95, DOSWIN32, and ADM32 directories to a new folder on your hard drive. The files in these directories will be used by the setup program to install the client and various services.

If you are installing the client in only one language or if your network does not have enough space to accommodate multiple language directories, you can delete the language directories you do not need from the NLS directory under each client directory. To ensure that you have all necessary files, copy the entire client directory and then delete only the extra language directories. Some steps in the installation process are conditional, meaning they only occur in certain circumstances. Any time a step in the process is labeled conditional, you only have to do it if you meet that condition.

- (Conditional) If you are installing Novell Client for Windows 95/98, copy Windows 95 .CAB files to the Win95 directory. The files are on the Microsoft Windows 95/98 CD (and Upgrade CD) in the Win95 folder.

- (Conditional) If you are installing Novell Client for DOS and Windows 3.1x and you will be using the DOS installation utility (INSTALL.EXE), create a LOG directory in the new folder.

The login script executes commands that create a LOG file in the LOG directory. The LOG file indicates whether the client update was successful. It is also useful in tracking down problems because it is a record of what happened and when.

Assigning Rights

Rights are the network's way of controlling who has access to what. For instance, you would never give anyone outside of the payroll department rights to view salary information. Rights also guarantee that new users automatically get the basic utilities they need to do their job. Rights are an impartial system of controlling access, which are assigned by the system administrator, then managed by the network.

Notice that only the administrator or someone with equal status can assign rights. As a general user you will not be able to do this. The exception is in your own private directory. Here is an example of the process an administrator might follow.

- Create a Group object called Client in the NDS tree.

- Place into that group users whose workstations need to be installed or upgraded.

- Make sure that the group has Read and File Scan rights to the new folder you created.

- If you created the new folder in SYS:\PUBLIC, the new folder should have Read and File Scan rights already associated with it, but you should make sure that these rights have not been changed.

Administrators assign rights by using NetWare Administrator—a utility to which only they have access. It allows the administrator to define and shape the network as needed. For an in-depth discussion on the topic, you can read the user manuals on the Novell Client installation CD-ROM.

Updating Configuration Files

If you are using the default settings to install the clients, you do not have to create or modify the configuration files. You can bypass this process and proceed to Creating or Modifying the Login Script.

Each platform-specific installation utility reads a configuration file in order to get information such as where to copy drivers during installation and what is the most recent version number. This file must be placed in the same directory as the installation utility. See Table 6-2 to determine what configuration file to use with your system.

TABLE 6-2

PLATFORM	CONFIGURATION FILE
Windows 95/98	NWSETUP.INI and a Novell Install Manager-generated text file
Windows NT	Novell Install Manager-generated text file
Windows 3.1x	SETUP.INI
DOS	INSTALL.CFG

UPDATING WINDOWS 95/98 AND WINDOWS NT CONFIGURATION FILES

You can use Novell Client Install Manager, a GUI-based utility, to configure the client properties. This method eliminates the need to configure each workstation manually. After you have created the configuration file with Install Manager, use the /U command-line parameter in the login script to call the configuration file and set the properties.

S TEP-BY-STEP ▷ 6.4

Configuration File

1. Start the Novell Client Install Manager (NCIMAN.EXE).
   a. For Windows 95/98, the Install Manager is located in the SYS:\PUBLIC\CLIENT\WIN95\IBM_LANGUAGE \ADMIN directory you copied to the server.
   b. For Windows NT, the Install Manager is located in the SYS:\PUBLIC\CLIENT\WIN95\IS386\ADMIN directory you copied to the server.

2. Do one of the following:
   a. For Windows 95/98, click **File > New File > Windows 95** to create a new file.
   b. For Windows NT, click **File > New File > Windows NT** to create a new file.

3. Modify the installation options as needed.
   a. In the Installation options list box, double-click the configuration option you want to modify.
   b. In the Property pages, set the parameters and then click **OK**. The values you set appear in the right list box.
   c. (Conditional) If you change properties for Novell Client for Windows NT or Windows 95/98 and intend to use the configuration file created with Novell Client Install Manager to upgrade existing client software, you must change the major or minor version parameter. If you are installing for the first time, proceed to Step 4.

   d. The client is updated only if the version numbers have changed. If the version numbers have not changed, even if parameters in the configuration file have been changed, the client and the new properties will not change.
      i. For Novell Client for Windows 95/98, you must change the version number in the NWSETUP.INI file. Open NWSETUP.INI and search for the Client Version section. The version number consists of four numbers, each separated by a decimal point (for example, 2.5.0.0). The third number is the major version number; the fourth number is the minor version number. Increase either number by one to install a new version.
      ii. For Novell Client for Windows NT, change the version number with Novell Client Install Manager by clicking **Installation > Client** and increasing the major or minor parameter by one or more.

4. Click **File > Save**. You can save the file with any filename you want to use. For example, you could rename the file **UNATT_95.TXT**.

5. Copy this file to one of the following directories:
   a. SYS:PUBLIC\CLIENT\WIN95\IBM_LANGUAGE directory (for Windows 95/98)
   b. SYS:PUBLIC\CLIENT\WINNT\I386 directory (for Windows NT)

This file is then used with the /U command-line parameter in the login script to call the configuration file and set the properties during installation.

UPDATING DOS AND WINDOWS 3.1X CONFIGURATION FILES

You can control the Windows-based install program (SETUP.EXE) by modifying the SETUP.INI FILE, and you can control the DOS-based install program (INSTALL.EXE) by modifying the INSTALL.CFG file. However, the defaults work fine for most installations.

Evaluating Other Network Installation Options

There are additional network installation options that might better suit your networking environment. You should evaluate these methods before deciding which is best for you. The following section gives a brief overview of the other network installation methods and information on where to find complete documentation about them.

USING OTHER WINDOWS 95/98 INSTALLATION OPTIONS

You can use the following methods to install Novell Client for Windows 95/98 software:

- *MSBATCH*: Use this option to install and configure Novell Client for Windows 95/98 without your having to be present. This is called an *unattended installation*. The administrator has created a file with a listing of all options to install on the system. The installation program uses this file to know how to install the client. This process saves a great deal of time, especially if you need to install the software on multiple workstations. This is usually how it is done in the real world. An administrator will create one disk that works the way he wants and then make many copies (for example, let's say 20 copies.). He will then take a row of 21 machines and start at one end. He will stick a disk in the first machine. While the first machine is booting he will move onto the next machine, repeating his actions. He continues down the row until all 21 machines have been booted. Hopefully, by the time he reaches the last machine the first one is complete and ready for use. He then collects the disks and repeats the process on another row. Think of it as a sort of assembly line.

- *Automatic Client Upgrade (ACU)*: Use this option to automatically upgrade multiple workstations from the Microsoft Client for NetWare Networks to Novell Client for Windows 95/98.

USING OTHER WINDOWS NT INSTALLATION OPTIONS

You can use any of the following methods to install Novell Client for Windows NT software:

- *Unattended install*: Use this option to install and configure Novell Client for Windows NT without having to be present. This feature saves a great deal of time, especially if you need to install the software on multiple workstations. By preconfiguring installation options with Novell Client Install Manager, you can install both Windows NT and Novell Client for Windows NT, or Novell Client for Windows NT by itself, on one or more workstations over the network.

- *Automatic Client Upgrade*: Use this option to automatically upgrade multiple workstations from the Microsoft Client for NetWare Networks to Novell Client for Windows NT.

- *Windows NT Network control panel*: Use this option if you want to use the Network control panel to install Novell Client for Windows NT as you would other services.

USING OTHER DOS AND WINDOWS 3.1X INSTALLATION OPTIONS

There are two additional network installation methods for installing the Novell Client for DOS and Windows 3.1x:

- *Automatic Client Upgrade*: Use this option to set up and standardize the installation process. During installation, ACU automatically configures each workstation's client settings, thus virtually eliminating the need to configure individual workstations.

- *User-Initiated Installation*: Use this option to set up an installation procedure with little or no user intervention. Once users are notified of the installation procedure, they can begin installing whenever it is convenient. For more information, see the online documentation.

Basic Functionality

Resource Management

NDS, Novell's directory services software, is a distributed, replicated naming service that maintains information about and provides access to every resource on the network. (It's a sort of yellow pages or road atlas for the network.)

During the installation of a Novell server, a minimal NDS framework is set up. The minimal framework consists of an NDS tree, a container object, a NetWare server object, and an Admin user object.

After installation, you can create additional NDS objects using the QuickStart utility, the NEAT utility, or the NetWare Administrator utility. NDS allows users with the proper access rights to log in to the network and view and access network resources.

NDS TREES

The *NDS tree* represents the entire network. Network resources such as servers and printers are presented hierarchically in the NDS tree. Users log in to the NDS tree with a single login name and password instead of logging in to individual servers.

TREE NAME

The NDS tree is given a name during the first NetWare server installation. The name of the tree should represent your entire organization. It can be up to 64 characters long and can contain underscores and dashes. Although other special characters are permitted, Novell does not recommend using special characters in the NDS tree name.

OBJECTS

NDS objects are used to represent network divisions or network resources such as an organization or a NetWare server. See Figure 6-5(a). Objects have properties that define their characteristics. You can create two types of objects: container objects and leaf objects.

Container Objects

Container objects are used to organize the structure of the NDS tree. A container object can hold another container object, a leaf object, or both. See Figure 6-5(b). The two main kinds of container objects are Organization and Organizational Unit. However, all of the following container objects are available:

- [*Root*] is the highest-level container object in the NDS tree. [Root] is created whenever a new NDS tree is created. [Root] cannot be renamed. All NDS objects exist in [Root]. A user with rights to the [Root] object has rights to the entire NDS tree. Only Country and Organization objects can be placed under [Root].

183

■ An *Organization* (O) object is a container object that represents the first level of grouping for most networks. Depending on the scope of your network, this level could represent a company, division, or department. At least one Organization object is required in an NDS tree. An Organization object can contain Organizational Unit (OU) objects or other NDS objects.

■ *Organizational Unit* (OU) objects are container objects that can be used to organize other objects in the NDS tree into subsets. For example, Organizational Unit objects might be departments or project groups. Organizational Unit objects are optional, but must exist below an Organization (O) object or another Organizational Unit (OU) object.

FIGURE 6-5(a)
Different objects

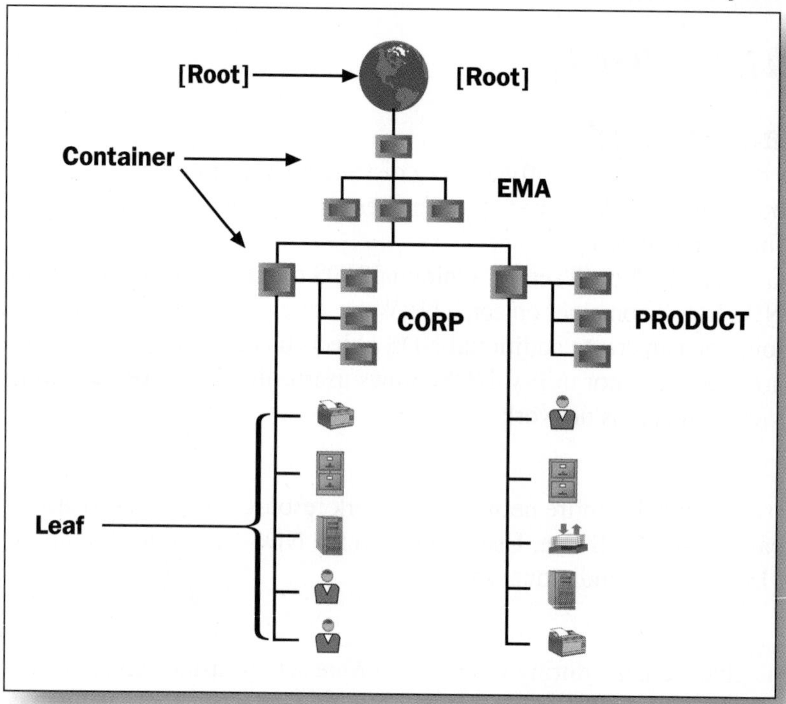

■ *Country* (C) objects are container objects that can be placed only directly off the [Root]. Although you can have as many Country objects as desired, they add a level of complexity to your NDS tree that might not be necessary. The Country container object is provided to comply with X.500 global naming specifications.

■ The *Locality* (L) container object is provided to distinguish the geographical location of an object.

When you create a new NDS tree, the container objects, such as Organization or Organizational Unit object, that will contain the NetWare Server object must be created immediately. The installation program for this product automatically creates the needed Organization object for you.

Leaf Objects

Leaf objects represent information about network resources such as servers or printers. Unlike container objects, leaf objects cannot contain other NDS objects. Many types of leaf objects exist, such as Application, Computer, Printer, User, and NetWare Server objects. At least two leaf objects are created during the server installation.

- The *NetWare Server* object is a leaf object that represents any server running any version of the NetWare operating system. The NetWare Server object is automatically created and placed into the NDS tree during server installation.

- When a new NDS tree is created, an *ADMIN user* is automatically created. ADMIN has Supervisor rights to the entire NDS tree. Supervisor rights allow a user to create and manage all objects in the tree. For security reasons, you can rename user ADMIN after the installation using the NetWare Administrator utility, or the SETPASS command-line utility.

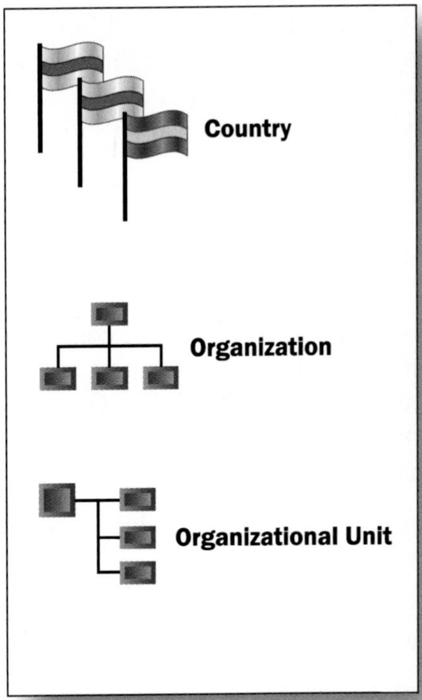

Other users can be assigned Supervisor rights to container objects and all their leaf objects. Having Supervisor rights to a container object allows the user to create and manage all objects in the container.

When installing a new server into an existing tree, you must have Supervisor rights in the container in which you are installing the new server.

FIGURE 6-5(b)
Different container objects

NDS CONTEXT

NDS allows you to refer to objects according to their positions within a tree. The NDS context describes the full path (including container objects) of an object in the NDS tree structure. This is similar to giving a friend directions to your house.

The notation to describe the NDS context is the list of container objects, separated by periods, between the leaf object and [Root]. For example, the context of the NetWare Server object SERVER1 to be placed in the Organizational Unit (OU) container SALES in the Organization (O) container ACME would be noted as: SALES.ACME. The full NDS context name for this server would be SERVER1.SALES.ACME.

NDS context can also be noted using typeful names. Typeful names include the object abbreviation types. For example, the NDS context described above written in typeful notation would be CN=SERVER1.OU=SALES.O=ACME.

When reading a typeful name, the leftmost object is assumed to be a leaf object. Leaf objects have common names (CN) which are described in typeful notation with a CN= preceding the object name.

Unique Features of NetWare

Setting Up Printers Attached to Windows 95 Workstations

Use NPRINTER Manager (NPTWIN95.EXE) to allow network users to share a printer attached to a Windows 95 workstation.

When you run NPRINTER Manager after the initial setup, the program checks which printers need to be loaded. If the print server is running and the printer specified is free, that printer is loaded, and its information window is displayed in the NetWare Nprinter Manager window. Normally this function is set up by the system administrators and not the users.

SHARING A PRINTER ATTACHED TO A WINDOWS 95 WORKSTATION

NPRINTER Manager allows network users to share a printer attached to a machine that has Windows 95 and is running Novell Client. NPTWIN95.EXE is the executable file for NPRINTER Manager. Running NPRINTER Manager and adding a local printer makes the local printer available to network users. Any printer you add will remain available to the network during that session of Windows 95. You can also specify that the printer will be activated whenever NPRINTER Manager starts.

Before you begin:

- The printer must be cabled to the workstation as if ready for local printing.

- The initial print setup must be completed, which includes creating and associating a Print Server object, Printer object and Print Queue object (see "Setting Up Queue-Based Print Services" in the online documentation).

- PSERVER.NLM should be loaded at the server console.

- Windows 95 operating system should be running on the workstation.

- Novell Client should be running on the workstation.

Note

The **PSERVER** program provided with NetWare has all of the components necessary to service print jobs in a networked environment. The components needed to accomplish this are built into **PSERVER** so no additional drivers or components need to be added for compatibility.

When the following procedure is complete, network users will capture (catch a copy of the data, make a connection to the data) a port for the shared printer, and then begin printing to the shared printer.

STEP-BY-STEP 6.5

Installing a Printer

1. Make sure the Windows 95/98/NT workstation with the attached printer is running Novell Client.

2. At the workstation, log in to the network as any user.

3. Double-click **Network Neighborhood**.

4. Navigate to the **SYS\PUBLIC** folder on your server.

5. Double-click **NPTWIN95** (the NPRINTER Manager program).

6. (Conditional) If the Add Network Printer dialog box does not display, choose **Printers** and then choose **Add**. The dialog box does not display after you have added your first printer to the program.

7. Choose an NDS printer or bindery-based print server and printer. The print servers displayed in the Print Servers and Printers window are all those which are advertising to your server. But when you choose a print server, only printers you have rights to will display.

8. (Conditional) If the Set Properties dialog box displays, set printing properties in the dialog box, and choose **OK**. The dialog box will only display if the selected printer was previously defined as Other/Unknown.

9. Choose an LPT or COM port.

10. Choose an interrupt setting or Polled mode. Polled mode is usually the default setting for interrupts. However, dedicated interrupts usually provide better printing performance. If you do not know what interrupt to set or if you are having interrupt conflicts, try using the polled mode. A polled mode printer may not be as fast as an interrupt-driven printer, but it avoids the difficulty of identifying an available interrupt and the conflicts that can arise from choosing an incorrect interrupt.

11. Choose a buffer setting from 3 KB to 60 KB of memory. Bigger is not necessarily better.
- **a.** (Conditional) If a COM port was selected, set the following to correspond with your serial printer settings.
  - **i.** Baud Rate—The speed at which the data is pumped across the serial connection.
  - **ii.** Data Bits—How long each byte is. Some systems allow different sizes to be used.
  - **iii.** Stop Bits—Either one or two bits at the end of each byte. They signal the receiver where the end of each byte is.
  - **iv.** Parity—An early form of error checking. Odd parity means that the number of ones in each byte is counted. If the total is an even number, the parity bit is set to 1, so the overall count of ones is odd. If parity is set to even and the number of ones counted in each byte is odd, the parity bit is set to one to make the count come out odd. Using this method, the receiver can count the number of ones received. If the received number is odd and parity is set to even, the receiver knows the data has been corrupted and it should be resent.
  - **v.** XON/XOFF—This is a form of hardware-driven flow control. If the modem has all the data it can hold it will set the XON/XOFF line to XOFF. This signals the sender to stop sending. When the XON/XOFF line is set to XON, the modem is free to receive information again.
- **b.** (Optional) If you want NPRINTER to load this printer and the required NLM programs the next time the program is run, check Activate Printer when Nprinter Manager loads. If the box is unchecked, the printer being added will remain active only for this Windows 95 session, and the printer must be added again to the program before it will be available as a shared printer to network users.

12. Click **OK**.

13. Verify that the printer was successfully set up by ensuring the printer's status window displays and the settings are correct.

14. If this is the only printer added to NPRINTER Manager, choose **Clear** from the Printers menu, and then choose **Add** and add the printer again.

15. If there are other printers added to NPRINTER Manager, choose **Properties** from the **Printers** menu, and uncheck **Activate Printer**. When Nprinter Manager loads, choose **Remove**, and add the printer again.

   a. (Optional) Close the NetWare NPRINTER Manager window by choosing **Printers** and then choosing **Exit**. By closing the window, you exit the program but leave the NLM programs required for printing loaded. Network users will still be able to print to the printers that have been added to the window.

   b. (Optional) To automatically run NPTWIN95 when you start the workstation, add NPTWIN95 to the workstation STARTUP folder.

16. From the Windows 95 desktop, choose **Start**, and then point to **Settings**.

17. Choose **Taskbar**, and then choose the **Start Menu Programs** tab.

18. Choose **Add**, and then choose **Browse**.

19. Navigate to the **NPTWIN95** file, and then double-click it.

20. Choose **Next**, and then double-click **Startup**.

21. Type the name that you want to see on the StartUp menu (like NPRINTER), and then choose **Finish**.

   a. (Conditional) If Windows 95 prompts you to choose an icon, choose one, and then choose **Finish**.

The attached printer should now be available as a shared network printer. Network users can now capture a port for the printer and begin printing to it.

Summary

In this lesson, you learned:

■ In 1983, Novell realized the potential of connecting a company's desktop computing resources and sharing them. This was the beginning of the local area network (LAN).

■ Simply stated, a network is a group of computers (workstations, sometimes called hosts) that can communicate with each other, share hardware resources (such as hard disks or printers), and access remote computers or other networks. Novell software requires a server, although peer-to-peer networks do not.

■ Novell NetWare networks are used in many of the major corporations around the world.

■ If your installation involves new client software installation or an upgrade from older client software, the software is installed or upgraded when users log in. The new software is copied to the client machines. The workstation must be restarted to make the changes active. Users might see system messages set up by the administrator as their workstations are upgraded, depending on how you set up the installation.

■ NDS, Novell's directory services software, is a distributed, replicated naming service that maintains information about and provides access to every resource on the network. Use NPRINTER Manager (NPTWIN95.EXE) to allow network users to share a printer attached to a Windows 95/98/NT workstation.

VOCABULARY REVIEW

Define the following terms.

container objects	leaf objects	NDS tree
LAN	NDS	WAN

MULTIPLE CHOICE

Circle the answer that best applies.

1. NIC stands for:
   A. Network InterChange.
   B. the network administrator's title.
   C. Network Interface Console.
   D. Network Interface Card.

2. When speaking strictly about networking, media refers to:
   A. the wiring used to connect the machines.
   B. the hard drives and floppy drives used to store information.
   C. the manuals or other documentation.
   D. sounds, images and text distributed across shared computers.

3. Online documentation refers to:
   A. the manuals that are digitally stored on the installation CD(s).
   B. documentation kept on the Internet.
   C. calling tech support to help resolve your issue.
   D. documentation available as an automated phone service.

4. IPX stands for:
   A. Internet Protocol Extension.
   B. Interconnected Printer Exchange.
   C. Independent Protocol Extension.
   D. Internet Protocol Exchange.

5. NetWare can be run across what cabling?
   A. Coaxial
   B. Ethernet,"ThinNet"
   C. ThickNet
   D. Fiber Distributed Data Interface, FDDI
   E. Token ring
   F. All of the above

TRUE/FALSE

Circle T if the statement is true or F if it is false.

T F 1. NetWare uses the IPX protocol.

T F 2. NetWare does not require the use of a server.

T F 3. Using NetWare it is possible to create groups of networks called WANs.

T F   4. NetWare is based on the IP protocol used by the Internet.

T F   5. NetWare does not allow for the sharing of resources between machines.

WRITTEN QUESTIONS

Write a brief answer to the following questions.

1. How is IPX is related to IP?

2. What does the system administrator change to restrict a user's access?

3. What tool does the NetWare administrator use to perform system administration?

4. What tool is used to administer the printers on the network?

5. What does "NIC" stand for and what is its function?

MATCHING

In the blank space match the following terms to their correct definitions.

____ 1. rights

____ 2. LAN

____ 3. client

____ 4. print server

____ 5. server

A. Permissions assigned to each user that determine to what he or she has access.

B. A computer connected to a network and used by an ordinary user.

C. A computer connected to a network and used by the system administrator.

D. A computer, connected to a network, that manages printer requests.

E. Local Area Network

CRITICAL THINKING

1. Novell has entered the open source market with a developer kit in which the code will be available to all, as opposed to the usual proprietary software that cannot be changed by anyone but Novell programmers. This will allow free distribution of the operating system and the ability to make user-specific changes to the operating system. Which practice do you think will benefit the customer more: open source code or proprietary software?

2. Novell, like Windows NT, has a variety of certifications available for its operating system. What are some of these certifications and what benefits do they provide?

LINUX

OBJECTIVES

Upon completion of this lesson you will be able to:

- Install the Linux operating system properly.

- Understand the basic functionalities of the Linux operating system.

- Work within the GNOME user environment.

- Work in a terminal emulation program using some of the more common shell commands.

- Describe the Linux file system.

- Describe the unique features that make Linux different from other operating systems.

- Obtain help through either the Red Hat Help Browser, the man pages, or the info pages.

- Properly shut down the Linux operating system either through an XTerm window or through the GNOME interface.

⏱ **Estimated Time: 6 hours**

VOCABULARY

daemons

Disk Druid

EXT2

GNOME

GNOME Panel

info pages

man pages

mount point

open source code

virtual display

Virtual File System

XTerm

Introduction

If you have experience with the popular Microsoft Windows operating system, the first thing you are likely to notice about Linux (pronounced len-ix) is that it is very different from Windows. Linux is primarily a command-line operating system that requires the user to type commands on the keyboard. This gives Linux the performance and flexibility that many power users require. However, Linux also has a graphical interface called *X Window*, which operates similarly to Microsoft Windows. This makes Linux more accessible to the average user. Nonetheless, Linux may intimidate many potential users because it does require that you understand a little more about how the computer operates. All in all, Linux is not for the timid. But if you want an operating system that allows you more control over your computer performance, then Linux is right for you.

As we enter the new millennium, many users want their computers to be appliances, which they can turn on and use, rather than instruments that require some degree of knowledge to use effectively. Yet there are other users who primarily want high performance and system flexibility—and they are willing to invest the time and energy required to achieve these results. This latter group of users are the ones attracted to Linux.

Some of today's operating systems, such as Windows and MacOS, are relatively mature consumer products. Linux, however, is less a product for the general consumer and more a system designed for more technical, hands-on computer users. The difference between the two types of users can be best understood through the following analogy. Using a prepackaged, ready-to-use operating system is like buying a Matchbox car at a toy store. When you take the car out of the package, it's ready to use. But what happens when you get tired of the car's color or you want to modify it for off-road use? You can't. Linux and its parent, Unix, are different. Imagine that instead you went to the toy store and bought a box of Legos. When you get home you cannot play with a car right away—first you have to build it from the parts. Then you can play with the car you just built. The box contains wheels and other things to make the building easier, but you still have to put some effort into it. The advantage here, however, is that when you get tired of it, you can take it apart and modify it. Which do you think is more fun? A Matchbox car or a box of Legos? Some people don't want the "hassle" of putting together Legos and would prefer the ease of a Matchbox car. Others would prefer the flexibility and customization available with Legos.

 Did You Know?

As operating systems have evolved, their performance has advanced to match the capabilities of newer computing chips. The initial microprocessors could handle 8 bits at a time, the next generation 16. Windows 95/NT was the first 32-bit operating system, although these systems continued to use many of the 16-bit files of earlier systems. In 2000, chipmakers such as AMD and Intel are introducing the first 64-bit chips, and the new operating systems and programs for these chips are being developed. A 64-bit system can process four times the information that a 16-bit system can.

Origins of Unix/Linux

In 1969, while working at AT&T's Bell Labs, Ken Thompson and Dennis Ritchie wrote Unix, a compact, time-sharing, multiuser operating system that ran on a Digital Equipment Corporation (DEC) computer. This initial version was written in assembly language. Although this operating system ran very quickly and efficiently, it was extremely difficult to modify. To increase the ease of modifying it, as well as to increase the number of mainframe and minicomputers that could run Unix, programmers rewrote it in the C programming language. Starting in 1974, Bell Labs licensed Unix to interested universities as a development tool. Later, Bell Labs continued to develop and market Unix itself.

Students at the colleges and universities that were licensed users of Unix quickly began to write utility programs—programs to perform small but important tasks. These were shared among all users and many of them are still part of the Unix kernel. (A *kernel* is the part of the operating system code that is closest to the machine and activates the hardware components, directly or through another software layer.)

Some licensed universities continued to develop Unix itself. The University of California at Berkeley is one such university. It developed the Berkeley System Distribution (BSD) version of Unix, and it continues to refine this version to meet the needs of the school and fully utilize the ever-changing hardware technology.

In addition to using Unix as a development tool, many of the universities began to use the operating system to share research data with other universities and with industries, using telephone lines. Through trial and error, they established a set of rules for conducting these transmissions. That method of communication is part of what we now call the Internet, and those rules that were established years ago are today referred to as Internet Protocol (IP). Today, more than 70% of the computers networked

193

with the World Wide Web (WWW) use either Unix or a Unix-like operating system. This number increases each year. Whether you are familiar with Unix or not, you will probably be using it soon—although, in most cases, you will be unaware of it.

Over the years, a great number of Unix "clones" have been developed. Many of these were modified operating systems that attempted to make Unix accessible to the desktop user. In 1991, Linus Torvalds, a student at the University of Helsinki, was frustrated with the poor performance of the DOS/Windows operating system on his desktop computer. He saw a need for a Unix-like operating system designed for desktop computers. Torvalds logged on to the Internet and broadcast his desire to create a new operating system, based on Unix but robust enough to operate on a variety of microprocessor platforms—many of which were not supported by Unix. Additionally, the code needed to be true 32-bit, and scalable (able to upgrade to new technology with ease). Torvalds' request that the Unix community help with this endeavor received an overwhelming response. The new operating system quickly grew and was named Linux to reflect the name of its originator (Linus) and its Unix foundation.

Like Unix, the Linux source code is written in the C computer language, and is supported by most compilers on the market. In fact, Linux comes with several very good C compilers that were used to build it. As the user, you have exactly the same tools and resources as the people who originally wrote it.

The primary difference between Linux and the versions of Unix developed earlier is that Linux is based upon an open source code. **Open source code** means that the operating system code has no proprietary restrictions. Anyone may alter the code to meet his or her own needs without having to seek permission from the "owner." Additionally, Linux is available to everyone free of cost. If you make any changes or additions to the code, then you must make that available to everyone free of charge as well. (However, you can charge for the media, instruction manuals, or technical support.)

Did You Know?

A *compiler* is a program used to build other programs. It converts human-language instructions (C code, for example) into machine language—the actual ones and zeros that computer chips can understand. The C computer language is extremely powerful and flexible. It is almost an industry standard for most applications. It is based on earlier languages, such as Fortran and Pascal.

Linux Today

For the past thirty years, mostly programmers and computer enthusiasts used the Unix operating system. Today, Linux is becoming more popular with businesses and individuals alike. As a result of the open source code and the sharing of information, Linux is continually changing and improving. Problems are resolved almost as quickly as they are reported—and the fixes are also free of change.

There are now more than 40 different distributions of Linux—all based on Torvalds' original code. In addition to free distribution via the Internet, Linux is also available in commercially packaged distributions. These versions of Linux are bundled on a CD, along with the company's own software, to make it easier for the average user to install and use the software—more like traditional operating systems.

Important

There are some companies that actually charge for the Linux code. These distributions (versions) are "non-standard" and aren't as well supported. Be careful if you use them.

Some of the commercial sources of Linux include Caldera, Red Hat, InfoMagic, Slackware, and Walnut Grove. While there is a charge for these "packages," the costs are usually minimal.

For this chapter, the authors choose to use the Red Hat Linux distribution. This distribution is very easy to install and Red Hat provides a good deal of technical support as well as a good set of manuals. Once, installed, however, the Red Hat Linux package still resembles the other Linux distributions in many ways. You will easily be able to apply the knowledge gained in this chapter to any of the other Linux distributions—even if you retrieve the entire operating system from the Internet.

Installing Linux

The first step in using Linux is installing it. We will use the Red Hat 6.2 distribution for this example. If you don't have that particular distribution or version, don't worry. Most of the Linux distributions use this or a similar installation.

Linux can be installed on a hard drive that contains up to three other bootable operating systems. For this installation, we will assume that the installation will be on a hard drive that is not being used for any other operating systems. Those interested in setting up multiple-boot systems should read more about *LILO*, the LInux LOader program, in the documentation provided with the Linux distribution. This program is responsible for running all operating systems and programs. You can also find information in the **man pages** (short for manual pages, the Linux help system) which will be on your hard drive after the base installation.

We will be following a "standard" installation example using Red Hat Linux 6.2. If you are using a different distribution or if your installation varies in other ways, you should refer to the documentation that you received with your software.

If Linux is already installed on your system or if you do not have permission from your instructor or computer lab personnel to install Linux, then read but do not key in the steps outlined in this section.

Beginning the Installation

There are four main ways to install Linux: from NFS (network file server), via FTP (file transfer protocol), from a second hard drive, or from a CD-ROM. The first two, NFS and FTP, require installation across a network or a PCMCIA boot disk. Since these installations can vary from system to system, we will not attempt to step through this kind of installation. Installing from a second hard drive or a CD-ROM assumes that you have some sort of local media source available from which to install. We will perform the installation using the CD-ROM and a boot diskette. If you encounter any problems during the installation, don't despair. There are a number of ways to install— one of which will work on your machine. You can read about the various installation methods on the Red Hat Documentation CD or in the Installation Guide.

TIP

In a Unix-like environment, all commands and aliases are lowercase. Linux supports case-sensitivity. This means that Red, red, REd, RED, rED, reD, and rEd are all different to Linux. In DOS they would appear to be the same thing. So be careful how you type a password or filename. If you change the case of a letter without realizing it, you could get unexpected results.

Installing Linux

1. With your computer turned off, insert your Linux installation boot diskette into the floppy drive.

2. Turn on your computer. After a few moments, a screen containing the "boot:" prompt should appear. This screen also contains information on a variety of boot options and describes the function keys used to get help with those options. This initial screen will automatically start the installation program if you do nothing for one minute. (Or you can press **Enter** to continue.)

3. Press the **Enter** key. Watch the boot messages to see whether the Linux kernel properly detects your hardware. If it does not, you may need to restart the installation and choose **Expert** mode at the boot prompt screen. This is not usually required.

4. Next, you will be asked to select the installation method: CD-ROM, Hard Drive, NFS Image, FTP, or HTTP. Click **CD-ROM** and then click **OK**.

5. When prompted, insert the CD into your CD-ROM drive, click **OK** and then press **Enter**. The installation program will begin by looking for an IDE CD-ROM drive, the most common CD-ROM type. If it finds the drive the installation will continue. If it does not, you will see a screen that asks what type of drive you have:

SCSI or Other. If necessary, choose one of these. Once the installation program has identified your CD-ROM drive, you will then be asked to insert the Linux CD.

6. After the initial boot-up, the installation program begins by displaying the language screen.

7. Use your mouse or the arrows on the keyboard to select the language to use during the installation process—this will also be the system default language. Then click the **Next** button.

8. Next, the installation program will display the Keyboard Configuration dialog box. It will display the model and layout that it believes are correct for the language you have chosen. If these are correct, click the **Next** button and continue. If not, use the arrow keys on your keyboard or your mouse to select the correct items, and then click the **Next** button.

9. The next dialog box allows you to choose the correct Mouse Configuration for your system. Choose the correct mouse type for your system and click **Next**.

10. The Red Hat Welcome screen appears next.

11. Click the **Next** button to continue.

TIP

The boot messages will not contain any references to network cards or SCSI cards that may be in your system. This is because these devices are supported by modules that are loaded later in the installation process.

12. From the Install Type dialog box you can choose whether you would like to perform the full installation or an upgrade. For this example, you will choose a full installation.

13. Click the button next to the **Install** option.

14. While still in the Install Type dialog box, you must also choose the class of the installation. Your options include: GNOME Workstation, KDE Workstation, Server, or Custom. These options are discussed in the next section.

Computer Concepts

If you want to partition your hard drive, you may do so using the FDISK option available through the Install Type dialog box (check box in the top-right corner). If you are not familiar with this program, you should read the help files regarding it before you make this selection. If you make this selection, the FDISK program will run during the installation process and also start the Disk Druid application to assign mount points to your partitions. If you do not make this selection, the Automatic Partitioning option will be selected as you continue the installation.

FIGURE 7-1
Language Selection dialog box

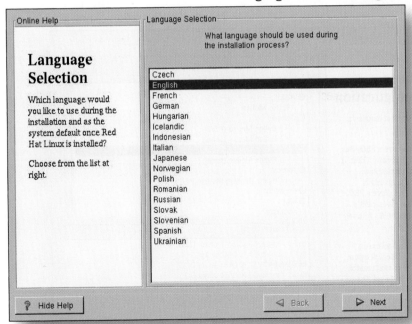

FIGURE 7-2
Keyboard Configuration dialog box

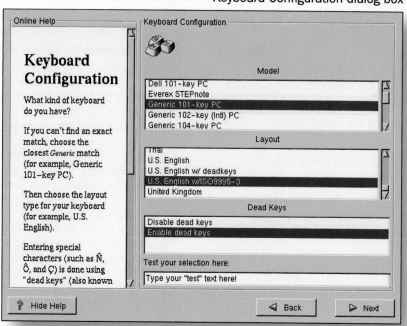

FIGURE 7-3
Mouse Configuration dialog box

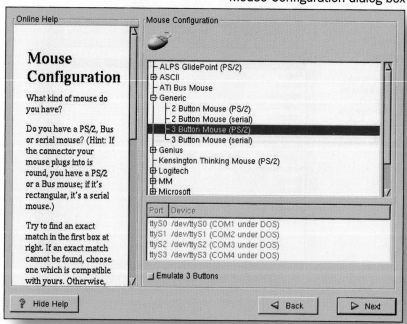

FIGURE 7-4

Welcome screen

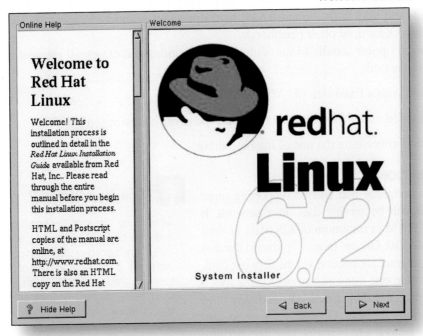

FIGURE 7-5

Install Type dialog box

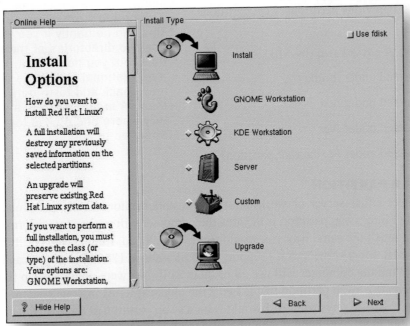

THE WORKSTATION OPTION

A *workstation* is a computer that will not be supporting more than one user at a time. It will not serve files to others and may have limited RAM, hard drive space, and CPU speed. It also may not have a modem, network card, or other peripherals.

The workstation option installs Linux with standard options and erases all previous partitions. Three partitions are created:

1. a swap partition with a fixed size (32 MB)

2. a partition mounted under /boot in your root file system of fixed size (16 MB)

3. the root partition containing the rest of the hard drive

THE SERVER OPTION

A *server* is a computer that will be supporting more than one person. It will be serving files on a network. It should have lots of RAM (a minimum of 128 MB), as well as hard drive space (10 GB or more). It should have a modem or a direct Internet connection via the network card. It may have more than one *network interface card* (NIC) used for routing between different networks and may have multiple CPUs working together. Generally the video card is of a lower quality than on a workstation machine, because users do not work directly on a server. Since all work is normally done through the network, a server may not even have a monitor, keyboard, or mouse attached.

The server option installs Linux with server options and erases all previous partitions. Five partitions are created:

1. a swap partition of a fixed size (64 MB)

2. a partition mounted under /home

3. a partition mounted under /usr

4. a partition mounted under /var

5. a partition mounted under /< (the root partition)

Did You Know?

Mounting means pretending that a directory on another disk or even on another computer is actually part of the directory system on your disk. This means that files stored in lots of different places can appear to be nicely organized into one tree-structure directory. You can mount local directories (*local* means on your own machine); this is useful if you want them to appear connected. You can also mount remote directories (on a disk or some other computer). This can be handy if you want to use two directories at the same time, but you don't want to have a navigational nightmare as you move back and forth between them. A ***mount point*** is a directory where one disk is logically attached to another.

SIZING THE SWAP PARTITION

When you select either server or workstation, the installer automatically partitions the hard drive as needed. The Linux swap partition is the area the computer will use to store information temporarily. It uses it in much the same way you would use a scratch pad. Linux swap partitions should never go above 128 MB. Most kernels won't support swap files above 128 MB, but you can have multiple swap partitions and the computer will use all of them as if they were one big swap file. A good rule of thumb is to create a swap partition that is twice the physical RAM in your system. For example, a machine with 32 MB of physical RAM would want a swap partition of 64 MB. You could make it 70 MB or 90 MB but in all likelihood it won't be used, so it is a waste of hard drive resources. You could also make a smaller swap partition but you would probably find the machine running slower than it should be.

You'll use the custom install so you can pick the components to be included. You won't find this difficult, and most of the defaults won't change. Any confusing terminology will be explained along the way.

FDISK

FDISK is included with every Linux distribution and is comparable to using FDISK with any other operating system. If you know FDISK, you will always know at least one way to modify the partitions on the drive. FDISK is a command-line driven program. To see a menu of options, you press the "M" key and then press Enter. To see pre-existing partitions, you would press the "P" key and then press Enter.

Since it is likely that you will be in a situation where you want to add Linux to a system with a pre-existing Windows 95/98 installation, it may be useful for you to learn more about this process. If you are installing on a "fresh" system the screens may appear slightly different, but the basic process remains the same.

If you add partitions using the free space on your hard drive, then you can set up a multiple boot menu so you can boot your machine into Windows or Linux at any time. Once up and running, you will be able to access the Windows partition from Linux, but not the other way around. It is fine to reuse a pre-existing Linux partition if you are reinstalling. Please note that, due to the design of Windows, if you corrupt Windows and need to reinstall you will have to archive everything on the Linux installation. This is because the Windows installation will not recognize the Linux partition; Windows will just install on top of it as if it weren't there. You will lose all Linux data in the process.

If you need to delete partitions, do so using the "d" option in FDISK. Doing this will cause the system to ask which partition number to delete. It is generally good to start with the lowest number and work up, skipping over partitions you want to keep. Please note that you will have to delete all logical drives before deleting extended partitions. The partition number is the number listed in the device name. So, /dev/hda3 is the third partition.

> **Did You Know?**
>
> Hard drives can have a maximum of four primary partitions, but any number of logical partitions. The difference is that primary partitions are bootable and, for most operating systems, logical partitions are not. Logical partitions surrender bootability to gain extra configurability. Linux does not have this problem, so you can have several different Linux installations on one drive. There are advantages to doing this. For instance, it is common to have a server and many dumb terminals or clients that boot from the network. In this scenario it is possible that not all the machines will be the same. And many may have hardware that is incompatible—such as Macs on one part of the network, PCs on another, and dumb terminals on another. It is easy and efficient to create a partition for each set. This keeps the files separate, ensuring that a change for one set of machines doesn't affect the other sets. It also means that the machines can all communicate using the same network.

DISK DRUID

Disk Druid has a slightly friendlier interface than FDISK, although it is not a true graphical user interface (GUI): you don't use the mouse, just the keyboard. As you may have noticed, Linux has a particular convention for naming disks. Each IDE device has the name /dev/hdx. Each SCSI device has the name /dev/sdx. The valid name for the third IDE hard drive in the system is /dev/hdc. Each partition is accessed by appending the partition number to the device's name. (For example, the second partition of the third IDE device is /dev/hdc2.) Using this nomenclature, you can locate the existing windows partition: its device name should be /dev/hda1.

Continuing the Installation

As you will see, the Linux installation gives you many opportunities to customize your system to exactly meet your needs. We will discuss these options so that you can see what is available to you. If you are already comfortable with computer hardware and software and consider yourself an advanced user, you may want to take advantage of these opportunities for customization. If, on the other hand, you are a novice user, then you will want to avoid attempting to make these sorts of changes until you have more experience and knowledge.

 Did You Know?

Heads, *cylinders*, and *sectors* are the units that describe where data is located on your hard drive. The hard drive is composed of *platters*, which, just like old-fashioned LP records, have two sides. There is one head for each side. Each side is divided into concentric rings called cylinders. Then each cylinder is divided into identical sectors.

STEP-BY-STEP 7.2

Workstation Configuration

1. In the Install Type dialog box, select the **GNOME Workstation** option, make sure that FDISK is not selected, and then click the **Next** button.

2. Automatic partitioning enables you to perform an installation without having to partition the hard drive(s) yourself. This is the recommended procedure if you are not familiar with drive partitioning. Note that with automatic partitioning, all data on the hard drive will be removed. (If you do not want to perform this sort of installation, then you could use the **Back** button to choose **Use FDISK** from the Install Type window or choose the **Manually partition** option from the Install Window.) Select the **Remove data** option and then press **Next**.

3. If you have a network card, the next screen allows you the opportunity to configure your networking. If this is required for your installation, ask your instructor or computer lab technician for the information to be filled in on this screen. Even if your computer is not part of a network, you can still enter a "hostname" for your system. If you do not, the default hostname "localhost" will be applied.

4. In the Network Configuration dialog box, click the **Next** button. The Time Zone Selection dialog box appears next.

5. There are two tabs on this display. The first allows you to configure your time zone, based on the physical location of the computer. On this tab, you can select by pointing and clicking on a specific location on the map or by selecting the appropriate text in the list box. Alternatively, you can choose your time zone as an offset from the Universal Coordinated Time (UTC) by selecting the UTC Offset tab. Make your time zone selection and then click the **Next** button.

FIGURE 7-6

Install Window with Automatic Partitioning options

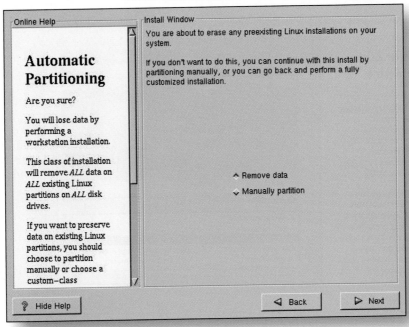

FIGURE 7-7

Network Configuration dialog box

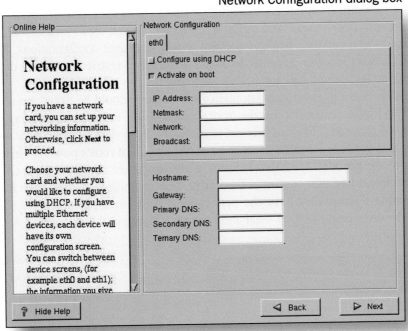

FIGURE 7-8

Time Zone Selection dialog box

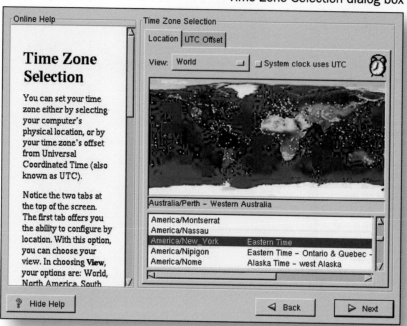

Creating Users

Much like other operating systems, Linux requires you to create users and passwords. The first users will be general unprivileged users. You might want to call the first user "joeuser" and give him the password of "tester." You can then use this account to test your user configurations. Sometimes things work for root, but not for a user, because the user's permissions restrict them from doing something. It is always best to test a configuration before assigning it.

As a rule, a root account is generated automatically and you should be asked for a root password. If you are new to Linux, remember that the /root account is able to access everything and therefore can be dangerous if misused. The /root account is generally the system administrator and usually the installer as well. It is possible for other users to have some or all of root's powers. This comes by adding permissions to the account. Be careful: Some permissions are restricted to keep you from doing something accidental like unmounting a hard drive, thus making it inaccessible. It is easy to remount, but impossible if you don't have the permissions. And since resources are shared, this means unmounting the drive could destroy what another user is doing with the drive.

S TEP-BY-STEP ⟹ 7.3

Account Configuration

1. After you have established your time zone and pressed the **Next** button, the Account Configuration dialog box displays.

2. The Account Configuration dialog box allows you to set your root password. You can also set up other user accounts to be used after

you complete the installation. In the appropriate text box, key your root password and then key it again in the **Confirm** text box.

The root password must be at least six characters long. You should avoid using your name, your birthdate, or other obvious words or numbers. The best passwords (the ones hardest to guess) are those that combine words and numbers. Also remember that the password is case-sensitive. Once you establish your password, you should write it down and keep it in a secure location.

3. Set up other user accounts following the guidelines given above—using the **Add** and **Edit** keys as appropriate.

4. When finished, click the **Next** button.

FIGURE 7-9
Account Configuration dialog box

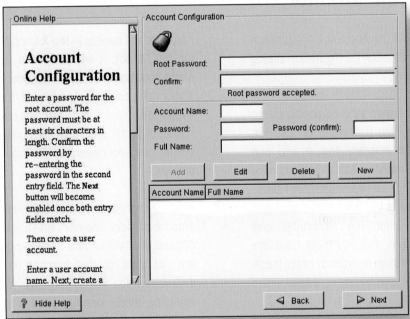

Setting Up the Monitor

Once you have completed the account configuration, Xconfigurator (the X Window System configuration tool) will run to test and set up your video card. Monitor setup is typically done by someone with computer experience because it requires some knowledge of exactly what video card you have, how much RAM it has, and the sync rates of your video monitor. (If you are not knowledgeable about these items, then you should *not* attempt to perform the monitor setup.) If your video card is shown in the list of video cards, just enter the required

Hot Tip

If you don't know the sync frequencies of your monitor you can ask your instructor or lab assistant, but don't guess. It is very easy to exceed the ratings of your monitor and cause permanent damage. If you have any doubts about this procedure, do not perform it.

information. If you aren't comfortable with this part of the installation or can't manage to get a working card, then just skip it at this time.

Once the relevant card has been set up, the correct server for X Window will be installed on your hard disk. Then you will need to identify your monitor type, which you can select from the list. If you can't find yours, then you can choose Custom and supply your own setting. The program will need to know the vertical and horizontal sync rates.

Once the monitor is configured, it is very easy to switch display resolutions. This is done with the Ctrl-Alt and "+" or "-" keys. The plus key takes you to the next higher display resolution. If you are already at the highest, then it loops back to the lowest and continues. The reverse is true of the minus key.

STEP-BY-STEP ▷ 7.4

Configuring the Monitor

1. After you complete the Account Configuration dialog box, the Monitor Configuration dialog box appears.

2. Xconfigurator generated a list of monitors from which to choose. You can either choose the monitor that was autodetected or you can choose another monitor. Make your monitor selection, heeding the warnings given previously. (You can select a "Generic" model and then manually enter the Horizontal and Vertical Sync values, but you must have the monitor documentation in order to enter these values correctly.)

3. If necessary, change the Horizontal and Vertical Sync values. However, this should not be necessary if your monitor model is correctly detected and selected from the list.

4. Click the **Next** button.

5. Xconfigurator will then probe your system for any video hardware. If you have hardware that is recognized by Linux, then the defaults for this hardware will appear in the X Configuration dialog box. If not, it will present a list of video cards and monitors from which you can select. If your video card is not in this list, it may not be supported. If this is the case, you could choose "Unlisted Card" and manually configure it, but this is only recommended for the knowledgeable user.

6. Next, Xconfigurator will ask you for the amount of video memory on your video card. Consult your video card documentation if you are not sure of this number (or ask your instructor). You will not damage your card by selecting more memory than what is available, but it may not start correctly.

7. Once you have selected all the appropriate settings for your video hardware, it is recommended that you test the configuration settings. Click the **Test this configuration** button and confirm that the colors and resolution are accurate.

FIGURE 7-10
X Configuration dialog box

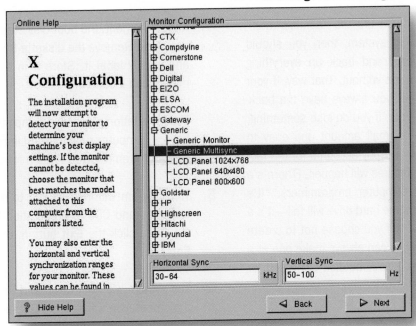

FIGURE 7-10
X Configuration dialog box

Completing the Installation

The final step is where the actual installation begins. Up until now, no permanent changes have been made to your computer. If you do not want to perform the installation you may reboot your system to return to whatever operating system and software you had already established on your machine. Once you click the Next button from the About to Install dialog box, partitions will be written and packages will be installed.

S TEP-BY-STEP ▷ 7.5

Complete the Installation

1. From the X Configuration dialog box, click the **Next** button. The About to Install dialog box appears.

2. If you are ready to install, click the **Next** button.

   At this point the installation process begins. How long it takes depends upon the number of operations that the installation has to complete and your computer's speed.

The next input required from you will be to indicate if you want to create a **boot disk**. This is a bootable floppy you can use to reboot the system in the event of a failure. It enables you to access the system when it isn't working. Since this is your first time performing an installation, it is in your best interest to make a boot disk. But bear in mind that the ultimate goal is to configure the system so that if it crashes it is easier and faster to just reinstall from scratch. If you are the "administrator" for this computer system, then you should take responsibility and back up everything that you cannot live without. That way, if your system does fail, you always have the back-ups to rebuild from. If you do lose something, it will only be a small amount and easy to replace. This philosophy accounts for the fact that hard drive failures will happen. (There's a saying among computer programmers: "It's not a matter of *if* the hard drive will fail—it's a matter of *when*.") If you choose not to create the boot floppy you can always make one at a later time using themkbootdisk command, or create it from the installation CD.

During the installation, you will take advantage of the opportunity to create a boot disk.

3. Insert a blank, formatted diskette into your floppy drive. Click the **Next** button.

4. After a moment, the boot disk creation will be complete. Remove the diskette from the drive and clearly label it. Store it in a safe, well-maintained location.

The installation process is complete. You now have a computer running the Linux operating system (often referred to as a "Linux box").

5. The program will instruct you to remove any diskettes and CDs in preparation for reboot-ing. Then click the **Exit** button (or press the **Enter** key).

6. The system will shut down and restart. After a moment, you will see the GUI login screen, where you can enter your user name and password.

FIGURE 7-11
About to Install dialog box

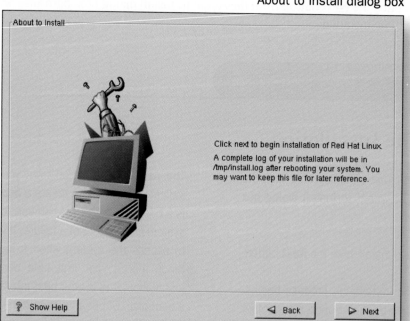

208

FIGURE 7-12
Boot Disk Creation dialog box

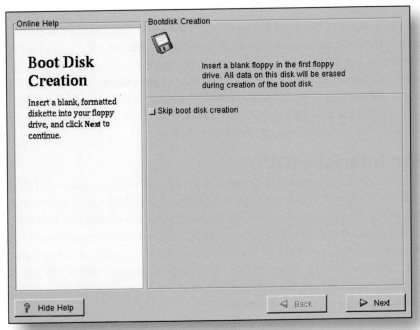

FIGURE 7-13
Congratulations dialog box

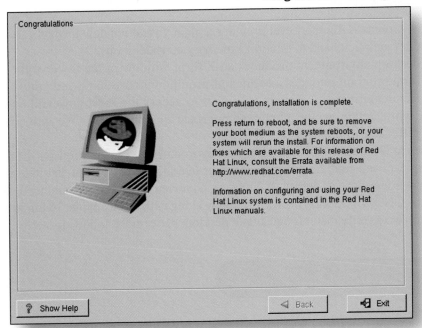

Basic Functionalities

There are two basic ways to work with Linux—or two basic "user environments." The older environment is working from the command (or shell) prompt where the user must know particular commands to accomplish a given task. In this environment, there are no clues regarding what you need to enter to accomplish these tasks. The command prompt is considered a "user-unfriendly" environment. The newer environment is X Window System. X Window, often called simply X, establishes a graphical interface between the user and the set of Unix/Linux tasks that makes navigation simple and user-friendly. We will discuss these two environments below.

Graphical User Interface (GUI)

The X Window environment mentioned above is a *graphical user interface (GUI)*. This environment is much like the Microsoft Windows, Apple Macintosh, or IBM OS/2 environments where you can choose a task using the pointing device. Unlike these other environments, however, X allows you to select one of four desktop configurations, commonly called *desktop environments*. Depending on how your system was installed, you may or may not have all the desktop environment choices. A desktop environment includes, among other things, graphical elements visible on the screen and mechanisms allowing the user to launch various applications. An X server allows the user to manage the elements of the window using a window manager.

GNOME is an acronym for GNU Network object model environment and is available in many languages for worldwide use. GNOME is a desktop environment, written in X, that allows you to use and configure your computer more easily. The GNOME Desktop environment is highly customizable and allows you to open multiple desktop areas.

The KDE (K development environment) is considered to be more familiar than GNOME to Windows users.

The desktop environment AnotherLevel provides a plain virtual window manager (fvwm). The fvwm was designed for simplicity and to minimize memory considerations.

The failsafe desktop environment produces an XTerm window in the lower-right corner of the screen. The XTerm program provides a command-prompt window that is integrated fully into the X Window System environment, allowing the user to access the most powerful and flexible features of Linux while retaining the graphical interface on the screen. We will discuss the XTerm window a little later in this chapter.

We have chosen to illustrate the GNOME Desktop environment because it provides the new Linux user with an easy-to-learn and configurable graphical user interface. The Red Hat distribution uses the GNOME Desktop environment as its default. If, however, a previous user selected another desktop, you will need to select the GNOME Desktop in order to follow along with this example. To log in and select the GNOME Desktop or to verify that it is the default desktop, perform the following steps.

STEP-BY-STEP 7.6

Log in to the GNOME Desktop Environment

1. After you have installed Red Hat Linux, your system will automatically take you to the Login screen whenever it starts. If necessary, start (or reboot) your system.

2. On the login screen, position the mouse pointer (shaped like the letter X) over the word **Session** on the menu bar and then click the left mouse button once.

3. Position the mouse pointer over the **GNOME** command on the **Session** menu and then click the left mouse button once. The GNOME session manager is selected. The line beneath the Login text box reads "GNOME session selected."

4. Type your login name in the Login text box and then press the **Enter** key. (If you did not perform the installation or you do not know what the login name is, ask your instructor.)

5. Enter your password in the Password text box and then press the **Enter** key. If you have properly entered your password, the GNOME Desktop displays as shown in Figure 7-14. If you incorrectly entered your password, the password screen will be redisplayed and you can enter the correct password. You do not need to select the desktop environment again.

FIGURE 7-14
The GNOME Desktop

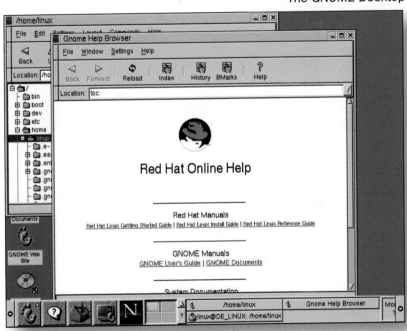

GNOME DESKTOP BASICS

The coordination of hardware and software including desktop icons, the keyboard, and the mouse are referred to as a graphical user interface or GUI. In computer terminology, an icon is a pictorial representation of a program or an action to be performed. Icons display on the desktop (the computer screen) and you select them by clicking them with the mouse. When you double-click an icon, a window opens on the screen and the selected program runs in that window. The GNOME Desktop consists of icons, foreground and background windows, and the GNOME Panel.

ACTIVE AND INACTIVE WINDOWS

When you first log in to Linux, two windows display—one in the foreground and the other in the background (see Figure 7-14). The GNOME Help Browser displays in the foreground window. The

GNOME Help Browser assists you in obtaining help about Red Hat Linux, the GNOME Desktop environment, or using the Help system itself. The second window, the File Manager window, displays in the background. You can use the File Manager to locate files and directories within each of the Linux file systems. The File Manager has two main windows (see Figure 7-15). On the left is the tree view, which represents all of the directories on your system by their hierarchical positions. On the right is the directory window, which shows the contents of the directory selected in the tree view. A plus sign to the left of the directory name in tree view indicates that the directory contains subdirectories.

FIGURE 7-15
File Manager window

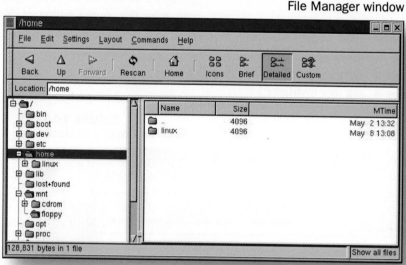

These windows, and any others that are open on the desktop, can be moved from a background position to a foreground position by clicking anywhere in the window. When you click in a background window, the window that was in the foreground moves to a background position and the chosen window moves to the foreground. You also can choose the foreground window through the GNOME Panel, as explained in the following section. Also, whenever a new program (and hence a new window) is opened, it automatically becomes the foreground window.

THE GNOME PANEL
At the bottom of the desktop you will see something that should remind you of the taskbar in Windows. It performs the same functions as the taskbar and more. This is the *GNOME Panel*, a configurable display (see Figure 7-16).

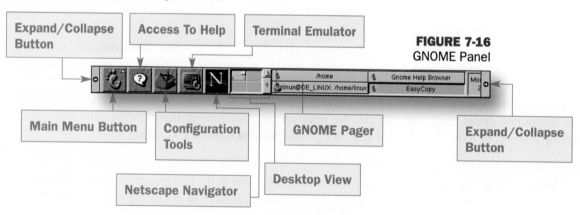

FIGURE 7-16
GNOME Panel

In the lower-left corner of the panel is a stylized GNOME footprint that serves as the Main Menu button, which provides access to program menus. This is comparable to the Start button in Microsoft Windows. Four program launchers display to the right of the Main Menu button, including the Integrated Help System, the GNOME Configuration Tool (it looks like a toolbox), a terminal emulation program (the computer monitor with a footprint), and Netscape Communicator. To the right of the program launchers is the GNOME Pager that contains two main areas—desktop views and program views. In the desktop views, each of your desktops is represented as a small rectangle, or pane. If there are any programs on the desktops, they display as small outlines according to their positions on the desktop. The program views, or tasklist, display the programs on your active desktop in a list view. The programs display as buttons. If the program window is open and in the foreground, then there will be a light, or yellow lines, behind the GNOME footprint icon and the button will display as recessed. If the program window is open but in the background, the GNOME footprint icon will not have a light behind it and the button will not be recessed. If the window has been minimized (if it is not on the desktop), then the icon changes from the GNOME footprint to a package icon.

Between the desktop views and program views is the Sticky indicator button and the GNOME Pager Settings button—both used to assist with arranging open windows and desktop areas. A sticky window is one that stays in the same location on the desktop in each of the other desktop areas. Collectively, the desktop views, the active and minimized tasks, the Sticky indicator button, and the GNOME Pager Settings button are known as the GNOME Pager.

Another interesting feature of the GNOME Panel is that it can be collapsed and expanded— much like windows can be minimized and maximized. By using the small arrows on either side of the Panel, you can collapse the Panel so that it is out of the way and so that you have use of more of your desktop area. When you need to use the Panel, you simply click the arrows again and the GNOME Panel expands to its original size. You can also customize the panel to meet your specific needs or create additional panels if required.

VIRTUAL CONSOLES

Red Hat provides you with five virtual consoles available during any Linux session. A *console* is an area within the operating system that recognizes only commands entered from the keyboard. Instead of displaying icons on a desktop, you must respond to a command (shell) prompt. Each virtual (meaning that it appears limitless) console works independently of the next. In effect, on one Linux workstation you can have X running on your desktop, and also operate each of five virtual consoles—simultaneously. A virtual console may be used by a Linux user to run diagnostic programs if X does not load correctly, or to perform an administrative task not available as an icon on the X desktop. Table 7-1 illustrates the keyboard shortcuts that enables you to enter various virtual consoles or to return to the X Window System environment if X loads correctly.

TABLE 7-1

Keyboard Shortcuts	Virtual Console
Alt + CTRL + F1	Virtual console #1
Alt + CTRL + F2	Virtual console #2
Alt + CTRL + F3	Virtual console #3
Alt + CTRL + F4	Virtual console #4
Alt + CTRL + F5	Virtual console #5
Alt + CTRL + F7	Return to X Window System

MANAGING THE GNOME DESKTOP

When activated, the GNOME Desktop occupies the entire screen. On the desktop there are the windows already discussed, any other windows you may open, and a number of icons. You may find that the desktop is not arranged exactly the way that you would like. Problems could develop, such as:

■ The window or icon you want to use is behind another window.

■ The window where you currently are working needs to be larger.

■ When you have finished working with a program, you would like to close its window.

■ You find that looking at several windows at one time is proving difficult.

All of these problems can be resolved by learning to manage your desktop areas and the respective windows.

For the most part, the operations on the GNOME Desktop are the same as what you are probably already familiar with from working with Microsoft Windows or other operating systems. Minimizing, maximizing, restoring, dragging, sizing, opening, and closing are all performed in essentially the same manner. One feature that is different, however, is the ability to open other desktop areas. The GNOME Desktop allows the user to access different desktops in the computer's memory. By default, there are four desktop areas, or desktop views, available to you; they are all accessible from the GNOME Pager. Each of these four desktop areas is represented as a pane in the desktop's view on the GNOME Pager. To open the File Manager window in a different desktop area, complete the following steps.

S TEP-BY-STEP ⬜⟹ 7.7

Using Different Desktop Areas

1. Move the mouse pointer to the upper-right pane (#2) in the desktop view on the GNOME Pager.

2. Click the upper-right pane. That pane now displays with hash marks, indicating it is selected, and it shows the current desktop (Figure 7-18). The newly selected blank GNOME Desktop is visible.

3. Click the **Main Menu** button (the footprint at the left end) on the GNOME Panel. The window manager opens the System menus.

4. Point to the **File Manager** command. The File Manager command is highlighted (see Figure 7-19).

5. Click the **File Manager** command to open the File Manager window (see Figure 7-20). A small rectangle displays in pane #2 in the desktop view on the GNOME Pager. (Note that this rectangle displays in the same relative location on the pane as the File Manager window displays on the desktop.)

6. Close the File Manager by clicking the **X** button in the upper-right corner of the window.

FIGURE 7-17
Desktop view on the GNOME Pager

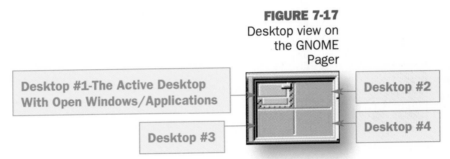

FIGURE 7-18
Active GNOME Desktop

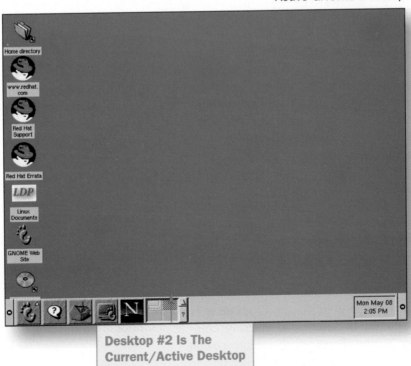

FIGURE 7-19
File Manager on the
Systems menu

FIGURE 7-20
GNOME Pager
desktop views

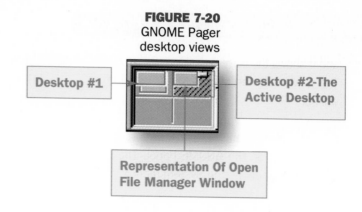

You can see how these different desktops can come in very handy when you are working with a number of files or programs and need to have several things open and visible at the same time. You may also be interested to note that you can drag open program windows from one desktop to the other simply by dragging them to the edge of the screen in the direction of the desktop to which you want to move them.

Obviously, there is a good deal more that can be said (and learned) about the GNOME user environment as well as the other GUI environments available with Linux. This was only a brief introduction. However, much of this can be learned through exploration and by reading the online help and documentation that comes with the software. Since a GUI interface is inherently intuitive, we will not devote any more time to explaining the use of these environments. Instead, we will turn our attention to the features that are less intuitive, but certainly very important if you want full use of your Linux system.

XTerm Program

In the early years of Unix the typical input/output device was a dumb terminal. A dumb terminal was a CRT combined with a keyboard that had no processing capabilities of its own. Today, a terminal emulator makes your computer behave like a dumb terminal. *XTerm* (short for x terminal) is one of these emulators. When working under X, the XTerm program allows the Linux user to execute shell commands. In addition to entering commands interactively, XTerm allows you to execute a batch script in the background that you created earlier during an XTerm session.

 Did You Know?

Regardless of which Linux distribution you have installed, once you enter a terminal session (i.e., XTerm—also referred to as a virtual console or a shell) the commands used are the same.

You can open a terminal emulator (through the GNOME or KDE interface) and use it to access all of the powerful shell commands available to Linux, while still maintaining the convenience of a GUI interface.

S TEP-BY-STEP ▷ 7.8

Beginning an XTerm Session

1. Point to the **GNOME footprint** on the GNOME Panel.

2. Move the mouse pointer up the System menus and point to the **Utilities** command.

3. Move the mouse pointer to the right and point to the **Regular XTerm** command. The Utilities menu appears with Regular XTerm highlighted.

4. Click the **Regular XTerm** command on the Utilities menu. The XTerm screen appears on the desktop.

FIGURE 7-21
Utilities menu

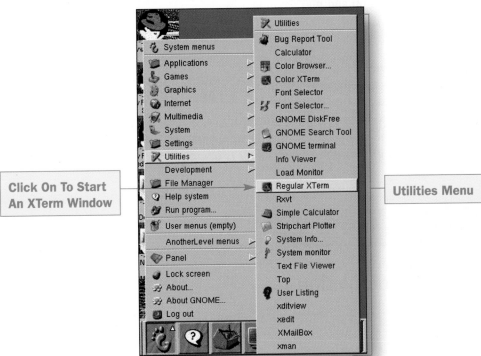

Click On To Start
An XTerm Window

Utilities Menu

Since the some of the most powerful features of Linux are the ones that are accessible from the command prompt, the rest of this section describes the use of the command prompt window. While this program is less "friendly" than the GUI, it is important if you want to gain a full understanding of the Linux system's advantages over another operating system.

FIGURE 7-22
XTerm Window

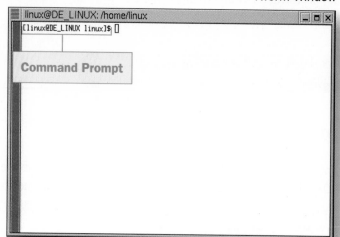

Command Prompt

Using the Keyboard to Maneuver in Linux

Since Linux was originally designed to be used without a mouse, you can do most things by typing—especially when you are not using one of the GUI interfaces available with Linux. Many users aren't very good typists. So, certain tools have been included to speed things up and make typing easier.

COMMAND COMPLETION

One of the most helpful features available when working with the command line is the command completion. Command completion enables the computer to match the command or program to what you are typing. You just press the Tab key, and the computer finishes the command for you. You just need to make sure you enter enough characters of the command so that it is obvious that you could mean no other command.

Did You Know?

You can also start the XTerm window by clicking the terminal emulation program launcher icon (the monitor with a footprint on it) on the GNOME Panel.

S TEP-BY-STEP ⟹ 7.9

Using Command Completion

1. At the command prompt, key **cd /e**.

2. Press the **Tab** key. The computer will finish the line with "tc/". (The whole line should read cd /etc/.)

If you were to press Enter you would go to the /etc directory. Of course, this particular example didn't save you many keystrokes. But many of the files you work with will have long filenames (Linux allows up to 255 characters). In order to make the filename more descriptive, many filenames contain not only the program name, but the version or boot as well. This lets you have several versions of a file in one spot. For instance, the dmesg file contains most of the boot information. You want to inspect it at least once after an install or hardware upgrade because this file provides important feedback for problem resolution. You know to start looking for dmesg in the /var directory but forget the rest of the path from there.

3. Press the **Backspace** key repeatedly to erase the text entered above.

4. Key **cd /v** and press the **Tab** key. (Remember that V and v are different.) Linux will finish the line with "ar/" because there isn't another subdirectory that begins with "v".

5. Now you think that the dmesg file is in the log directory. Key the letter **l** and press **Tab**. The computer should beep at you this time and appear to do nothing. This is because there are several subdirectories in /var that begin with "l".

6. Press **Tab** twice in quick succession and you will get a listing of all subdirectories that match what you have keyed so far.

This procedure is very useful for trying to remember long filenames that are automatically generated. It also works with finding commands. If you don't remember the spelling of a command, enter the first couple of characters (or whatever you know) at the command prompt and press **Tab** twice. This brings up a listing of all known commands that match the pattern. In some cases the list will be several pages long and the system will ask you if it should display all the listings. Say Yes (**Y**). Then use **Ctrl-Alt** and the **PgUp** key to scan upwards in the list or use **Ctrl-Alt** and **PgDn** to scan down the display.

7. Press the **Backspace** key repeatedly to erase the text that has been entered thus far.

8. Key **x** and press the **Tab** key twice. You will be asked if you want to display several hundred commands.

9. Key **Y**. The list of commands should fill the screen.

10. Press the **Ctrl-Alt** and **PgUp** keys to scan up the list. On most systems you will get to go back about five screens. The actual number may be more or less, depending on your installation.

COMMAND HISTORY

Another timesaving feature is the *command history*, which allows you to retrieve a previously entered command from the history file. This is accomplished by pressing the up arrow key. Pressing this key causes the most recent command to be taken from the top of the previously stored commands. This command then appears at the command prompt. If you continue to press the up arrow, you will cycle through all of the previously stored commands in the history file. If you go back too far, you can use the down arrow key to step forward through the command history file.

File Management

Each file in a file system is a collection of data. A file system not only holds the data that is contained within the files, but also the structure of the file system itself. It holds all of the information that Linux users and processes see as files, directory soft links, file protection information, and so on. Moreover, it must hold that information safely and securely; the basic integrity of the operating system depends upon its file systems. Nobody would use an operating system that randomly lost data and files.

One of the most important features of Linux is its support for many different file systems. This makes it very flexible and able to coexist with many other operating systems. At the time of writing, Linux supported 15 file systems: ext, ext2, xia, minix, umsdos, msdos, vfat, proc, smb, ncp, iso9660, sysv, hpfs, affs, and ufs. Over time, no doubt, more will be added. These file systems are from different operating systems.

In Linux, as in Unix, the separate file systems your computer may use are not accessed by device identifiers (such as a drive number or a drive name) but instead they are combined into a single hierarchical tree structure that represents the file system as a single entity. Linux adds each new file system into this single file system tree as the file system is mounted. As mentioned earlier, mounting is the act of connecting a device or file system to the operating system. In this way you are creating the links that allow communication to occur. All file systems, of whatever type, are mounted onto a directory. This directory is known as the *mount directory* or *mount point*. Think of the mount point as the location where you can find the device or file system. The files of the mounted file system cover up the existing contents of the mount directory.

When disks are initialized (say, using FDISK or Disk Druid) they have a partition structure imposed on them that divides the physical disk into a number of logical partitions. Each partition may hold a single file system—for example, an EXT2 file system (see details below, under Linux File System History). File systems organize files into logical hierarchical structures with directories. Devices that can contain file systems are known as *block devices*. The Linux file system regards these block devices as linear collections of blocks; they do not know or care about the geometry of the underlying physical disk. An IDE drive is treated the same as a SCSI drive, even though they operate differently. Moreover, using Linux's file systems, it does not matter (at least to the systems user) that these different file systems are on various physical media controlled by separate hardware controllers. The file system might not even be on the local system; it could just as well be a disk remotely mounted over a network link halfway around the world. Neither the users nor the programs that operate on the files themselves need know that /C is, in fact, a mounted VFAT (Windows-compatible) file system that is on the first IDE disk in the system. It does not matter either that the first IDE controller is a PCI controller and that the second is an ISA controller, which also controls the IDE CD-ROM. The long and short of all this is that Linux makes any device attached to it look exactly like any other device. By way of comparison, Windows will restrict what you can do if a drive is connected through a network. It even restricts what you can do if the device is connected locally—such as a CD-ROM drive and a hard drive. Both store data, but they work differently. Windows shows you those differences, while Linux does not. Linux lets you access the two drives exactly the same way, thanks to the virtual file system (VFS).

LINUX FILE SYSTEM HISTORY

Minix, the first file system used by Linux, was rather restrictive and lacking in performance. In this file system, filenames cannot be longer than 14 characters (which is still three characters longer than the old DOS limit). The first file system designed specifically for Linux, the extended file system, or EXT, was introduced in April, 1992 and cured many of the problems—but designers still felt it lacked performance.

The second *extended file system* (*EXT2*) was devised by Rèmy Card as an extensible and powerful file system for Linux. It is the most successful file system so far in the Linux community and is the basis for all Linux distributions that are currently shipping. The EXT2 file system, like a lot of the file systems, is built on the premise that the data held in files is kept in data blocks. The size of every file is rounded up to an integral number of blocks. If the block size is 1024 bytes, then a file of 1025 bytes will occupy two 1024-byte blocks. This means that 1023 bytes go wasted. Of course, you don't usually waste that much; on average you waste half a block per file. As always in computing, you trade off CPU usage for memory and disk space utilization.

VIRTUAL FILE SYSTEM

The *Virtual File System (VFS)* allows Linux to support many file systems—each presenting a common software interface to the VFS. All of the details of the Linux file systems are translated by software, so that all file systems appear identical to the rest of the Linux kernel and to programs running in the system. Linux's VFS layer allows you to transparently mount the many different file systems at the same time. The Linux VFS is implemented so that access to its files is as fast and efficient as possible.

To speed up access to commonly used directories, the VFS maintains a cache of directory entries. As the real file systems look up directories, the details of the directory are added to the directory cache. The next time the same directory is looked up—for example, to list it or open a file within it—it will be found in the directory cache. Only short directory entries (up to 15 characters long) are cached; this is reasonable, as the shorter directory names are the most commonly used ones.

The "/proc file system" really shows the power of the Linux VFS. Neither the /proc directory nor its subdirectories and files actually exist. The /proc file system, like a real file system, registers itself with the VFS. However, when the VFS makes calls to it, requesting inodes as its files and directories are opened, the /proc file system creates those files and directories from information within the kernel. For example, the kernel's /proc/devices file is generated from the kernel's data structures that describe its devices. The /proc file system presents a user-readable window into the kernel's inner workings. Several Linux subsystems create entries in the /proc file system.

MOUNTING A FILE SYSTEM

As mentioned earlier, the mount command allows a physical device (such as a hard drive, a disk partition, a floppy disk, or a CD-ROM) to be addressed by the Linux software. In order to do so this, you must be the root (or superuser). Normal users don't have this capability. (If you didn't log in as root, then key "su root" and press Enter. You will be asked for the root password. If you followed the example given earlier for logging in, it should be "rootbeer." If not, you will have to supply the password that you keyed in. This will make you root and allow you to mount a drive.)

Once a device is mounted it can be read, written to, or called upon to perform its functions. Each particular device is, of course, limited by the file system table (i.e., you can't write to a standard CD-ROM drive).

To mount a file system, two things must be in place. First, a physical device must exist that you want to mount to the system. An example might be an IDE Zip drive or CD-ROM. Second, a point where this device is to be mounted must exist or be created in the existing file system tree. Examples of the command format to mount a floppy drive are shown in Table 7-2.

TABLE 7-2

Command	File System Type	Device Driver	Mount Point
mount	[-t ext2]	/dev/fd0	/mnt/floppy
mount	-t msdos	/dev/fd0	/mnt/msfloppy
mount	-t vfat	/dev/fd0	/mnt/winfloppy
mount	-t iso9660	/dev/cdrom	/mnt/cdrom

If we look at the last example, the CD-ROM, the -t option (known as the type or type switch) tells the mount command that you are specifying what type of file system is encoded on the CD-ROM. There could be several. The most common are iso9660, rockridge, and joliet. The -t is required if a file system type follows. The "/dev/cdrom" tells the mount command to take the phys-

ical device of /dev/cdrom and connect it in the file system tree and the point /mnt/cdrom. This way you know where it is and from what type of file system to pull information. You could have just as easily told the mount command to connect the CD-ROM drive any other place we wanted. The only stipulation is that the mount point directory already exists and it is not already being used by something else. The name /mnt/cdrom is not set in stone. It is just as easy to call the mount point for the CD-ROM "/home/ftp/henry." Linux doesn't care what we call it—the name is purely for our reference. It is best, however, to keep it as simple and descriptive as possible. The "/mnt" directory is the mount directory.

Let's use the CD-ROM as an example because you will be required to mount it each time you change the disk. For the CD-ROM there should already be a mount point in the /mnt directory. It should be called /cdrom.

S TEP-BY-STEP ⟹ 7.10

Mounting the CD-ROM

1. First, you need to make sure that the /mnt directory already has a mount point for the CD-ROM. Key **cd /mnt** and press **Enter**. The cd command means to change directory. This will take you to the /mnt directory.

2. List the directory by keying **ls** and press **Enter**. If the directory already exists, you should see CD-ROM listed. If not then create the directory, by keying the command **mkdir cdrom** (make directory) and pressing **Enter**.

3. Now, to mount the CD-ROM drive, key **mount -t iso9660 /dev/cdrom /mnt/cdrom**.

If this worked, you should get the command prompt back without an error message. If you get an error message, make sure that there is a CD-ROM in the drive. If there is, try typing the command again. If it still doesn't work, ask your instructor for assistance or work with a classmate for the rest of this exercise.

4. To verify that the disk is actually mounted simply key **cd /mnt/cdrom** and press **Enter**. This will take you to the CD-ROM drive.

5. Now, key **ls** and look at the directory.

To see what other devices are mounted, all you need to do is key the mount command and press Enter. This will show all devices currently mounted and where they reside. Don't worry if you have difficulty discerning this information. It will become easier as you become familiar with the system. You will also notice that you can't eject the CD-ROM as you used to. This is because the file system has locked the drive. Remember that it is assumed that all devices and resources in the computer will be shared. The system locks the CD-ROM so that the media can't be ejected just in case someone is using it. To eject the disk, you must make sure nothing is using the drive and thus, that you have the right to unmount it.

UNMOUNTING A FILE SYSTEM

The umount command is used to deselect, then remove a file system. Unmounting a file system is more or less the reverse of mounting it. A file system cannot be unmounted if any part of the system is using one of its files. So, for example, you cannot unmount /mnt/cdrom if a process is using that directory or any of its children. Notice the command to unmount the device is "umount" *not* "unmount."

STEP-BY-STEP ▷ 7.11

Unmounting a CD-ROM

1. Make sure you are not in the /cdrom directory.

2. To unmount the drive key **umount /dev/cdrom**

If nothing is using the CD-ROM, then it should unmount without errors and give you the command prompt.

THE FAT TABLE

The *FAT* table is kind of like a phonebook for files. If everyone in your life had a number instead of name, it would be very hard to remember everyone's number. But numbers are much more useful to a computer than alphabetical names. So, engineers had a problem: how to bridge the gap between what is easy for humans and what can be done with a machine. The answer is the FAT table (short for file allocation table). If you give it a name like quake or WordPerfect, the computer looks up the corresponding numeric code on the FAT table. Then it knows how to load the program.

Operating systems take great care that nothing corrupts the information in the FAT table. Most of this is to ensure that all information is kept to the correct format when writing to the FAT. This includes filenames, which must be less than 255 characters. Names can include spaces, hyphens, punctuation marks, and numbers. Subdirectories are just a special type of file capable of holding other files. Files are divided into executable and nonexecutable.

Linux Shell Commands

Many of the commands that you can enter at the command prompt of the Linux terminal are commands used for file creation and system maintenance. You've already used a couple of these in the exercises above: **cd** and **ls**. In addition, there are several others that are used commonly and that would be useful to know.

PRINT WORKING DIRECTORY COMMAND

The print working directory command (**pwd**) shows your location in the directory tree. The working directory is the location where any files created will reside, unless you intentionally place them elsewhere. The working directory is sometimes called the *default directory*.

Determining the Working Directory

1. At the command prompt, key **pwd**.

2. Press the **Enter** key. The working directory (the default directory) is displayed on the line below your pwd command. Notice that the command prompt has also returned.

CHANGE DIRECTORY COMMAND

The change directory (**cd**) command is one of the most frequently used commands in Linux. The command is the same for Linux as it is for DOS. This command establishes a path to the new working directory. By typing the command cd and a subdirectory (i.e., cd /etc) you will be transferred to that subdirectory if it exists. By starting the name of the subdirectory with "/" you are implying the name is absolutely referenced from the root directory. If "/" isn't leading the directory name then the path is relative to your current position. For instance, /etc and etc are not the same thing. /etc means start at the root directory, which is indicated in Linux by the forward slash (/). Then, continuing from there, transfer to the subdirectory etc. If "/" is not included, it is assumed you mean to look at the sub-directories in the directory you are in, find the subdirectory called etc, and transfer to it. Table 7-3 shows some different uses of the change directory command.

TABLE 7-3

Command	Parameter	Result
cd	[/] directoryname	Switches to the directory specified
cd	/	Returns to the root directory
cd	..	Returns to the parent directory
cd	-	Returns to your last directory
cd		Returns to your home directory

LIST COMMAND

The list command (**ls**) lists the contents of a directory. This command can be used with or without a parameter following it and with or without an argument. The argument is just the name of the directory that you want to list. If the ls command is issued alone, the screen displays the current contents of the current directory. If an argument follows the ls command, the contents of the specified directory are listed, as in ls /etc/rc.d/init.d. As Table 7-4 shows, the ls command has several parameters that enable you to view your file list in different ways, which allows you to see precisely what you want to see.

Parameter	Function
pathname	Lists the files in that path
-a	Lists all files and directories (including hidden files)
-l	Lists the details on the file (i.e., size, date, owner, etc.)
-p	Puts the forward slash (/) after each directory name
-r	Lists files and directories in reverse order
-R	Lists filenames by subdirectory
-t	Lists files ordered by their last modification date
-x	Lists files using the full width of the display

STEP-BY-STEP ▷ 7.13

Using the cd and ls Commands

1. Key **cd /** and press **Enter**. This will take you to the top of the directory tree.

2. At the command prompt, to display a directory list, key **ls** and press **Enter**. You should see one directory called etc.

3. Key **cd etc** to transfer to that directory.

4. Key **ls** and press **Enter** to list the etc directory. You will notice it is different than the list you saw before. This is the contents of the subdirectory /etc.

5. Key **cd rc.d/init.d** to change to that directory.

6. Key **ls** to list the contents of the directory to which you just changed.

7. Key **cd etc**. (Intentionally omit the leading /.) You will get the following message "*bash: etc: no such file or directory*". This means that the subdirectory does not exist. Generally this means that you need to check the spelling of the directory or its location relative to your current position.

8. Key **cd/etc**. This will let you jump up two directory levels.

MAKE DIRECTORY COMMAND

The make directory command (**mkdir**) is used to create directories. A valid filename must be used for the directory name.

Making a Directory

1. At the command prompt, key **mkdir/ tmp/quake**.

2. Press the **Enter** key. You have just created a directory called quake beneath the tmp directory.

REMOVE DIRECTORY COMMAND

The remove directory command (**rmdir**) deletes the directory from the file system. Before you can remove a directory, it has to be empty of all files and you cannot be inside of that directory (i.e., it cannot be the current working directory). You should remove directories when they are obsolete or no longer used.

REMOVE FILE/DIRECTORY COMMAND

The remove file/directory (**rm.**) command is a relative of rmdir, which is used only to delete empty directories. Like rmdir, this command requires that a filename be specified. If the -rf parameter is used, this command will delete files and subdirectories recursively and will not ask you if it is OK to do so. This is called *forced mode*.

Removing a Directory

1. At the command prompt, key **cd /tmp** and press **Enter**. This will change your location to the tmp directory.

2. Type **ls** and press **Enter**. You should see the name of the directory you created in the previous exercise (quake). Since you are not in that directory and since you have added no files to it, it can be deleted.

3. Type **rmdir -rf /quake**. The directory quake will be removed. Because you added the parameter -rf, the removal was "forced"— there was no confirmation to verify that you wanted to remove that directory.

MOVE COMMAND

The move command (**mv**) moves a file or directory to another position in your file system tree or renames a file. It does so by rewriting the path to each file. The mv command is extremely useful. After the command is completed, the file resides only in its new location (or under its new name). The syntax for use is mv oldposition/and_files newposition/. Notice that if you omit the files at the new position, the old filenames will be used. You may also use the command to rename a file. The syntax for renaming is mv oldname newname.

COPY COMMAND

The copy command (**cp**) takes the contents of one or more files and copies them to a secondary location. The syntax is cp source_files destination_files. This command is useful when you want to modify an original file or use it for a second time. As Table 7-5 shows, there are two possible parameters for the copy command.

TABLE 7-5

Parameter	Function
-i	Inquiry copy. This will instruct the system to ask before overwriting a file.
-r	Recursive copy. Copies the files in the directory and subdirectory.

WILD CARDS

Wild cards (* and ?) are special characters used to specify whole groups instead of individual items. The * means to take any grouping of characters and substitute here. If you want to copy several files with different names, but all of them end with ".re", you could used the wild card to specify which files you wanted to copy. The command would be **cp *.re**. The asterisk is used find any file that has any filename for a beginning, but only "re" as an extension. The opposite would be true for **re***, which means find all files that begin with "re," no matter what the extension. It is easy to mix and match. You can use the wild cards with the other shell commands as well. To list all the files in your current directory that begin with "s", key **ls s***. This will list only files that begin with "s". To limit the list a bit, try using **ls se***. This will only list files beginning with "se". Remember that the asterisk can stand for one or more characters. Adding more asterisks to the list does nothing. Therefore, **ls se*** is the same as **ls se*****.

The "?" works much like the asterisk, except it stands for only one character. Here **ls se?** and **ls se??** mean different things. If "??" is used, the computer will try to find any name that has two or fewer characters after se. The single "?" means to only find names with one character after the "?". This can be used to find a group of names while excluding others.

MTOOLS

If you are a user who is already familiar with MSDOS and the commands used within a DOS window, you may find the mtools useful. *mtools* is a set of commands that allows you to access and manipulate DOS on a Linux machine. Most Linux distributions automatically install the mtools package on your computer. The mtools commands are identical to DOS commands except that in each case the letter "m" is placed in front of the command. Some examples are given in Table 7-6.

TABLE 7-6

DOS Command	mtool	Function
cd	mcd	Change directory
copy	mcopy	Copies a file
md	mmd	Makes a new directory
rd	mrd	Removes a directory
del	mdel	Deletes a file

Special Linux Files

DEVICES

Linux, like all versions of Unix, presents its hardware devices as special files. So, for example, /dev/null is the null device. Consider this device a black hole. Anything that is dropped into it disappears forever. A device file does not use any data space in the file system; it is only an access point to the device driver. The EXT2 file system and the Linux VFS both implement device files as special types of inodes. There are two types of device files: character and block special files. Within the kernel itself, the device drivers implement file semantics: You can open them, close them and so on. Character devices allow I/O operations in character mode and block devices require that all I/O is via the buffer cache. When an I/O request is made to a device file, it is forwarded to the appropriate device driver within the system. Often this is not a real device driver but a pretend device driver for some subsystem, such as the SCSI device driver layer.

S TEP-BY-STEP ⟹ 7.16

Viewing the Device Files

1. At the command prompt, key **cd /dev**.

2. Press the **Enter** key. This will change your location to the devices directory.

3. Type **ls** to list all of the files within that directory.

4. Press the **Enter** key. You will see several pages of devices scroll by. You can use the **Ctrl-Alt-PgUp** keys to page up through the list. Remember that this does not represent everything that is actually connected to your computer. Instead it shows you all the things

that can be connected to your machine. Try guessing what some of the devices are by looking at their names. Don't worry if they seem cryptic. It will become clearer as you use the system.

5. Look for the "zero device." It is a special device that only produces zeros. It doesn't actually exist. It is a virtual device. This device is useful for generating test files that contain only zeros. You would use this file because it is often unimportant what the data is, just that a program can read the file or move it from place to place.

DAEMONS

Daemons are a key part of the Linux operating system. A daemon is a very special program. There are many of them running on your system. Learning to use them can be extremely helpful in getting the most use out of your Linux system. Most are actually part of a much bigger program or suite of programs. A daemon is a process that runs all the time in the background looking for certain events to happen. When those events happen, the daemon is triggered into action. Daemons make your life easier and convenient—and they are easy to recognize. The Linux standard for naming them is to use the name of the program and tack a "d" on the end. The "atd" is the daemon for the "at" program. The "crond" is the daemon for "cron."

To understand why daemons are needed and why they work, let's take a common example, the printing spooler. The spooler is a daemon associated with printing. Or more precisely, the printing process has a daemon called lpd. The printing process is not just one thing or application generating the hard copy. It is produced by several programs working in conjunction. It takes the lpd daemon, the spooler, any filters and the operating system (for the I/O) to work.

- **lpd**—A small program or daemon that runs in the background looking in the spooler queues for jobs to print. When a user submits a job to these queues, the daemon finds the file, starts the spooler program and tells it to take the file/print job and serve it to the appropriate printer for that queue.

- **Spooler**—A program that takes a file from a specific directory and oversees the transmission of the file. This program does not require a daemon to work correctly. It must be considered one way when the daemon is running and considered another way when it isn't. This gives the program a sort of dual personality. Either way, if this program is not installed or working, then your print jobs will not make it to the printer—even if everything else is OK.

- **Filter**—A filter is a set of instructions used to make sure the print job is correctly structured for the printer. In general, filters make it possible to convert from one printer type to another, including language changes, or to remove unwanted information and add needed information. This is not limited to converting from one printer language to another or simply image scaling so multiple pages will fit on one sheet. Filters are also conversion tools.

- **Spooler queue**—A set of directories kept in a common spot, usually /var/spool/lpd/xxx, where xxx is the name of the printer. When users want to print a file, they print to a file at this directory. When the lpd daemon next passes the directory it will see there is a file and automatically try to spool it to the printer. If there are multiple files, the daemon will try to spool them each in turn. If there is a job that can't be printed, the system administrator will receive mail reporting that it failed.

On the surface, this may seem overly complicated. If you were just setting up the printer for one user you may be right. But remember that Linux is a network operating system. That means it expects to be connected to a network. And in a network setting all users don't have their own printers. The machine the printer is connected to is called a *print server*. Sending a print job across the network is called submitting the print job. When the job is finally printed, it is said that the print job has been served. If the printer goes down for any reason, the print spooler will continue to collect jobs until the printer comes back online or it runs out of drive space. For this reason alone, this method is far more reliable than just keeping the job in memory until it is printed. For instance, if power is lost, you just need to reboot and the print spooler will pick up where it left off. All the unprinted jobs are still on the hard drive as files. Even if the print server goes down, print jobs will collect on your local machine until you run out of drive space or the server comes back up and printing resumes.

All that is needed to print across a Linux/Unix network is the IP address of the machine with the printer, the local directory on the printer machine for the spooler, usually /var/spool/lpd/xxx, and the name of the printer, xxx. The lpd daemon will take the print job generated by your machine and pass it along the network to the print server. From there the local printer daemon will see that the job gets printed.

Each Linux daemon should have its own suite of utilities or command-line options to control how it behaves. The following daemons are part of **lpd**:

- *lpr*—Offline print; the actual print command issued from the command prompt. This printer facility is very flexible and fast. As a result, many applications just redirect their output to this function and let the system manage the print job.

- *lpc*—Line printer control program. This small utility shows what printers and queues are enabled, allows rearrangement of jobs, and reports printer status.

- *lpq*—Spool queue examination program. This utility is used to manage, delete, and view the printer queues.

- *Queue*—An example of a queue is the line at the bank for a teller. Everyone lines up in a queue and waits their turn—whether they are human customers or computer processes.

Unique Features

Some of the unique features of Linux are the things you don't see or know about unless you become a "power user" as discussed in the introduction to this chapter. The GUI (whether it be GNOME, KDE, or some other) makes Linux appear much like other operating systems that are currently available, and it also makes Linux much more accessible to the "average" user. However, we have not spent much time discussing the interfaces; although they do have some options and features that are not available in other operating systems (such as MacOs or Microsoft Windows), they are relatively intuitive. And they are not really what makes Linux special.

In the previous sections, we have described a few of the things that give Linux its special power. And we have scratched the surface of what can be achieved through the command-line interface. In this last section, we will explore a few more features that are unique to Linux.

Modules

Linux is a monolithic kernel—in other words, it is a single, large program where all the functional components of the kernel have access to all of its internal data structures and routines. Because of this, Linux allows you to dynamically load and unload components of the operating system as you need them. Linux modules are lumps of code that can be dynamically linked into the kernel at any point after the system has booted. They can be unlinked from the kernel and removed when they are no longer needed. Most Linux kernel modules are device drivers, pseudo-device drivers such as network drivers, or file systems.

You can either load and unload Linux kernel modules explicitly using the insmod (install module) and rmmod (remove module) commands, or the kernel itself can demand that the kernel daemon (kerneld) load and unload the modules as they are needed.

This process of dynamically loading code as it is needed is attractive, because it keeps the kernel size to a minimum and makes the kernel very flexible. Modules can also be useful for trying out new kernel code without having to rebuild and reboot the kernel every time you try it out. However, nothing is for free and there is a slight performance and memory penalty associated with kernel modules. A loadable module must provide a little more code; this and the extra data structures take a little more memory. This process also introduces a level of indirection, which gives modules a slightly less efficient access to kernel resources.

Once a Linux module has been loaded, it is as much a part of the kernel as any normal kernel code. It has the same rights and responsibilities as any kernel code; in other words, Linux kernel modules can use the kernel just like all kernel code or device drivers can.

Modules must be able to find the kernel resources in order to use them. The kernel keeps a list of all of the kernel's resources in the kernel symbol table so that it can resolve references to those resources from the modules as they are loaded. Linux also allows module stacking, where one module requires the services of another module. One module requiring services or resources from another module is very similar to the situation where a module requires services and resources from the kernel itself. However, in this case, the required services are in a previously loaded module. As each module is loaded, the kernel modifies the kernel symbol table, adding to it all of the resources or symbols exported by the newly loaded module. This means that when the next module is loaded, it has access to the services of the modules loaded previously.

When an attempt is made to unload a module, the kernel needs to know that the module is unused and it also needs some way of notifying the module that it is about to be unloaded. That will enable the module to free up any system resources that it has allocated (for example, kernel memory or interrupts) before the module is removed from the kernel. When the module is unloaded, the kernel removes any symbols that the module exported into the kernel symbol table.

Virtual Consoles and Displays

When you boot your computer, you are brought to a console. This is where the computer asks for your login name and password. Think of the console as a physical computer. You have six consoles. Each behaves like a separate computer: It's as if you have six computers in one. The consoles, which are numbered 0 to 5, can be accessed from X Window by pressing the Ctrl and Alt keys and the appropriate function key, Vex. If you are already at a console, you switch consoles by pressing Alt and the appropriate function key, Fx. One major difference is that you must start the *virtual display* (X Window) using a console. You can't start a console from X Window. However, you can start the virtual display by starting a virtual terminal, which behaves exactly like a console.

Your computer has six virtual consoles and as many virtual displays as you want. The two are slightly different. In hardware terms, the *display* is the actual monitor. In operating system terms, it is what you see on the screen. The display can have several virtual terminals. You start a virtual terminal by clicking on the icon of a monitor on your desktop. Each one acts like a console, as if it were a completely separate machine. The virtual display can hold as many of these as you like. Remember that each time you open another virtual terminal, you are creating another job for the computer. It will run slightly slower for each one you open. The display is virtual in terms that it may be logically larger than the physical size of your monitor. This means that the computer will only be able to display part of the desktop. There will always be a part of the desktop it can't display. You end up with a window that floats across the desktop. To see different parts of the desktop, you move the frame using your mouse.

CRON

CRON is a powerful daemon that loads at boot time. From then on it is always running until you, as the superuser, disable it. It works like this: The CRON daemon loads and periodically checks the /etc/crontab file. In it is a listing of all the files it is supposed to run and when. Part of the listing are five special directories: /etc/cron.d, /etc/cron.hourly, /etc/cron.daily /etc/cron.weekly, /etc/cron.monthly. CRON treats each of these slightly differently. Whatever files it finds in these directories it tries to run. Every program that CRON tries to run is called a *job*. If it can't run a job, it will generate an email message and try to send it using whatever mail service daemon is loaded to the root directory. (If a mail server isn't loaded, the message disappears into NULL.) The significance of the five directories is that you can just copy a program into the directory and it will run. There isn't any special configuration.

The only stipulation is that the directories are run at different times. For instance, the cron.monthly directory is run only once a month. The cron.weekly is run only once a week.

All the files placed in the cron.hourly directory will be run once every hour. All the files placed in the cron.daily will be run once a day. All the files placed in the cron.weekly will be run once a week, and so on. The /etc/crontab file contains the settings that tell when these events are supposed to take place.

The crontab file lists data by columns. The leftmost column represents at what minute to start each job. Next is what hour to run, then on what week to run, then on what month to run. Next is on what day of the week to run. Days are numbered 0–6 for Sunday through Saturday, respectively. The last column is the description. On the surface this may seem very complicated—having to write one file and put it in spot A, then editing a different file in spot B—which, in turn is run by program C. Remember, though, that Linux was developed specifically as an open-ended system. That means it takes a building-block approach to things. There are a million little "widgets" that don't do much by themselves. But if you arrange them properly they are very powerful and act as a whole.

The different directories allow you to quickly save a job file to a different directory without doing any configuration specific to that file. Most people don't care what part of the day their daily jobs are run as long as they get done. And for most things this works fine. But for important things you can adjust the /etc/crontab for specific times and dates.

Processes

Processes perform tasks within the operating system. A computer program is a set of machine code instructions and data stored in an executable image on disk and is, as such, a passive entity; a process can be thought of as a computer program in action. Pretty much any command you run is a process.

A process is a dynamic entity, constantly changing as the machine code instructions are executed by the processor. The process also includes the program counter and all of the CPU's registers, as well as the process stacks containing temporary data such as routine parameters, return addresses, and saved variables. The currently executing program, or process, includes all of the current activity in the microprocessor. Linux is a *multiprocessing* operating system. Processes are separate tasks— each with its own rights and responsibilities.

If one process crashes, it will not cause another process in the system to crash. Each individual process runs in its own virtual address space and is not capable of interacting with another process except through secure, kernel-managed mechanisms.

A process uses many system resources during its lifetime. It uses the CPUs in the system to run its instructions, and it uses the system's physical memory to hold the process and its data. It opens and uses files within the file systems, and it may directly or indirectly use the physical devices in the system. Linux must keep track of the process itself and of the system resources that it is using, so that it can manage it and the other processes in the system fairly. It would not be fair to the other processes in the system if one process monopolized most of the system's physical memory or its CPUs.

The CPU is the most precious resource in the system; most workstations contain only one CPU. Linux is a multiprocessing operating system, whose objective is to have a process running on each CPU in the system at all times, to maximize CPU utilization. If there are more processes than CPUs (and there almost always are), the rest of the processes must wait until a CPU becomes free so that they can be run. Multiprocessing is a simple idea: A process is executed until it must wait, usually for some system resource; when it has this resource, it may run again. In a uniprocessing system (such as DOS) the CPU would simply sit idle and waste time while waiting. In a multiprocessing system, many processes are kept in memory at the same time. Whenever a process has to wait, the operating system takes the CPU away from that process and gives it to another, more deserving process. It is the scheduler that chooses which is the most appropriate process to run next. Linux uses a number of scheduling strategies to ensure fairness.

As a process executes it changes state according to its circumstances. Linux processes have the following states:

- *Running*—The process is either running (it is the current process in the system) or it is ready to run (it is waiting to be assigned to one of the system's CPUs).

- *Waiting*—The process is waiting for an event or a resource. Linux differentiates between two types of waiting process: interruptible and uninterruptible. Interruptible waiting processes can be interrupted by signals, whereas uninterruptible waiting processes are waiting directly on hardware conditions and cannot be interrupted under any circumstances.

- *Stopped*—The process has been stopped, usually by receiving a signal. A process that is being debugged can be in a stopped state.

- *Zombie*—This is a halted process, which, for some reason, still has a task_struct data structure in the task vector. It is what it sounds like, a dead process.

- *Scheduling Information*—The scheduler needs this information in order to fairly decide which process in the system most deserves to run,

- *Identifiers*—Every process in the system has a process identifier. The process identifier is not an index into the task vector, it is simply a number. Each process also has user and group identifiers; these are used to control this processes access to the files and devices in the system,

- *Inter-Process Communication (IPC)*—Linux supports the classic Unix IPC mechanisms of signals, pipes, and semaphores and also the System V IPC mechanisms of shared memory, semaphores, and message queues.

Identifiers

Linux, like classic Unix, asks user and group identifiers to check for access rights to files and images in the system. All of the files in a Linux system have ownerships and permissions; these permissions describe what access the system's users have to that file or directory. Basic permissions are read, write, and execute. They are assigned to three classes of user: The owner of the file, processes belonging to a particular group, and all of the processes in the system. Each class of user can have different permissions. For example, a file could have permissions that allow its owner to read and write it, the file's group to read it, and all other processes in the system to have no access at all.

Groups are Linux's way of assigning privileges to files and directories for a group of users rather than to a single user or to all processes in the system. You might, for example, create a group for all of the users in a software project and arrange it so that only they could read and write the source code for the project. A process can belong to several groups (a maximum of 32 is the default) and these are held in the groups vector in the task_struct for each process. As long as a file has access rights for one of the groups that a process belongs to, that process will have appropriate group access rights to that file.

User Manual

Most of the documentation you will need is contained right on your hard drive. There are manual pages and information pages that are part of Linux. Most distributions (Red Hat included) have their own documentation as well. When you start your GNOME session, for instance, the Help Browser automatically starts. You can use this to access the Red Hat documentation, then you can "page" through the manual or perform a search to find information on the topic you seek.

MAN PAGES

The man pages are accessible through the command line prompt. The manual is a simple program used to view the operating system manual pages. Each program or set of programs has a man page associated with it. When you install the program, the man pages are installed with it and your system is updated.

To use the man pages from the command prompt, you enter the word "man" and then the topic on which you want information. There is a catch, however. If your spelling does not match known topics, man will return "No manual entry for ____." Many new users are discouraged by this idea because it can take several guesses to get the information you are seeking. But even in Windows, you have to look through the table of contents to find what you want.

The secret to using man effectively is to treat it like a search engine on the Internet. Try searching for several different variations on a single topic. The *man*[ual] *pages* will provide you with a complete online description of each command, followed by all of the command options.

STEP-BY-STEP 7.17

Using Linux Man Pages

1. If necessary, open an xterm window. At the XTerm prompt, key **man lpr**. The man command will display the man page that contains further information about the lpr (print command).

2. Press the **Enter** key. Output of the man page is shown in Figure 7-23. You should notice the colon in the lower-left corner of the

screen. This is the prompt for the man pages. You can scroll around the page by pressing the four arrow keys on your keyboard.

3. To close the Linux Man Page, key the letter **q**. The context-sensitive window immediately returns to the XTerm command prompt (although you still see the last section of the help page that you were viewing.)

FIGURE 7-23
Man page for lpr command

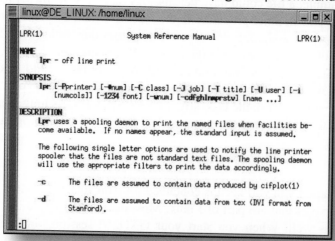

INFO PAGES

Another program that is also popular is called info. The ***info page*** provides a list of the most frequently used commands in Linux/Unix. You use it in much the same way as the man command. Just key "info" and the topic of interest and it will display the relevant topic. If no matching topics are found, it will list any that are available.

STEP-BY-STEP ▷ 7.18

Using Info Pages

1. If necessary, start the XTerm window. At the XTerm prompt, key **info grep**.

2. Press the **Enter** key. The first info page on the grep command is shown in Figure 7-24.

   Use the commands shown in Table 7-7 to navigate the info pages.

3. To close Linux info pages, key the letter **q**. The context-sensitive window immediately returns to the xterm command prompt.

4. Key **exit** and press the **Enter key** to close the XTerm session.

FIGURE 7-24

Info page for grep command

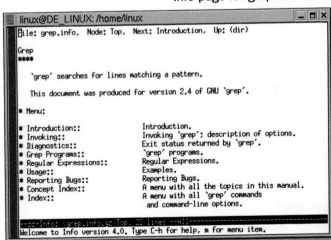

TABLE 7-7

Command	Result
q	Quits
d	Directory of commands
h	Help tutorial
n	Next screen
p	Previous screen

grep

Grep is the global regular expression parser. Given a source, it finds patterns of words that match what you supply. Grep will use any source that has been redirected to it. This could be any thing from a text file to a microwave data stream. The pattern to match can be as simple as a single letter or as complex as a Shakespeare sonnet.

For example, if you are a crossword enthusiast you could use it to help you find a word you don't know. Let's say the word is 16 letters long and means to sneeze. You could tell grep to look for all 16-letter words using the American Heritage Dictionary as a source. You would specify the number of letters by using the "?" wildcard. If there were any hits, they would be sent back to you for your inspection. If none were found you could always try another source. If you did know some of the letters, such as hy_ _ _ _ _ _ _ _ _ _ _ _ _ n, you could narrow the search. (The answer, by the way, is *hystoblogination*.) You can also use numbers in a grep search.

pico

In Unix and Linux, pico is a small, simple-to-use text editor. It is useful in creating and changing text-based files. You can also use it when you need a quick-and-dirty edit (something like Notepad in Windows) Commands are listed across the bottom of the pico screen. They are the usual two-key shortcuts found in many programs. Ctrl-x exits the program. Usage is:

pico/path/filename

Package Management

A *package* is just another term for a Linux installation program. The package manager will install all the files in the proper places for the program you want to install. Using the package manager is not the only way to install a program—but it is the easiest.

It works this way: All packages have filenames that end in rpm, or rpms. (Generally you will only see rpm.) Download the package on your hard drive. Then install it using this command:

rpm -Uhv packagename.rpm

The "U" must be capitalized and the "hv" must be lowercase. (If you want to try a few yourself, insert the Red Hat CD and mount the drive. Remember that you use the command: mount -t iso9660 /dev/cdrom /mnt/cdrom to mount the drive.) Then, change into the /mnt/cdrom/Redhat/RPMS directory. This directory contains all the packages that come with Red Hat. Try a few if you wish. Most will already be installed on your computer, so don't worry if you get a message that they are already installed.

Shut Down the Linux System

When using Linux, it is important (just as it is with Windows or any operating system) that you shut the machine down in an orderly fashion. Don't turn it off without doing a formal shutdown. Your files are kept in cache (temporary) memory. The act of shutting down writes any file changes to your hard drive. If you turn off the computer without shutting down properly, you'll lose these changes. You could also lose part of your operating system—a situation you definitely want to avoid.

You can shut down Linux either through the command prompt or the more familiar GNOME Panel.

If you shut down through the command prompt, there are two possible parameters: The -r switch that causes Linux to shut down and reboot (returning to the login prompt); and the -h switch which causes Linux to shut down and halt (telling you to turn off the computer). You can also add a time-frame parameter after the switch, which specifies the number of minutes to wait before the switch takes effect. If you want the command to go into effect immediately, you enter "now" instead of a number.

We will instead use the shutdown method accessible through the GNOME Panel.

STEP-BY-STEP 7.19

Shutting Down Your Linux System

1. Click the **Main Menu** button on the GNOME Panel (the footprint). The System menus display (Figure 7-25).

2. Point to the **Log out** command in order to highlight it.

3. Click **Log out**. A confirmation dialog box asks you to select the desired action (Figure 7-26). The Logout action logs out the current user and presents you with a new login screen. The Halt option proceeds to stops all processes and dismounts all file systems. The Reboot action performs a shut down, then loads a clean version of the kernel.

4. Click **Halt** and then click the **Yes** button. A password dialog box asks you to enter your password and then click **OK** or cancel. (If you click the No button by accident, you would return to the GNOME Desktop.) **Note:** If you have not been given permission by your system administrator to halt your computer, the Halt option may only perform a logout.

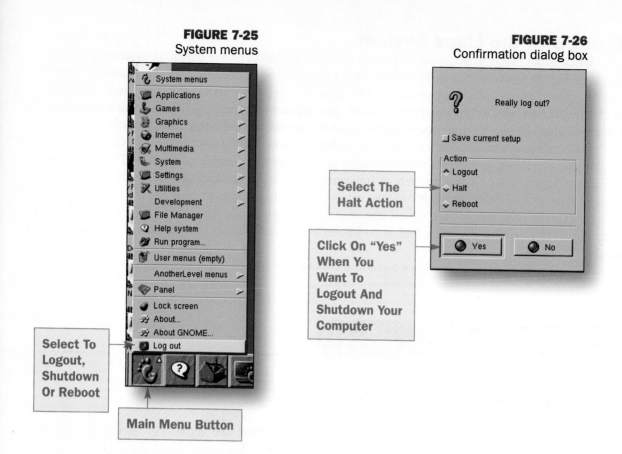

FIGURE 7-25
System menus

FIGURE 7-26
Confirmation dialog box

Select To
Logout,
Shutdown
Or Reboot

Main Menu Button

Select The
Halt Action

Click On "Yes"
When You
Want To
Logout And
Shutdown Your
Computer

After you have halted your computer, you can turn off the power to the system.

While this brief chapter cannot tell you all there is to know about a Linux operating system, it should give you a basic understanding of it and help you appreciate what makes it different from other operating systems. If you want to learn more, please read the documentation provided with Linux, or want visit one of the many web sites devoted to Linux or sponsored by one of the Linux distributors.

Summary

In this lesson, you learned:

- The installation used the Red Hat 6.2 distribution. If you don't have it available don't worry. Most distributions (there are more than 40 of them) use the same or similar installation. You can modify the base installation to fit your needs and you can tweak the installation to improve performance and add neat features. Linux can be installed on a hard drive that also contains other operating systems.

- You can work with your Linux system through the user-friendly GNOME interface or one of the other GUI environments available. Working in these environments is much the same as working in the environments with which you are already familiar—with some added benefits.

- Linux was originally designed to be used without a mouse. You can still easily access this command-line environment, in which you do most things by typing. Since many users aren't very good typists, certain tools have been included to speed things up and make it easier for the typist.

- The Linux kernel is the core of the operating system. It maintains the files in the file systems that it supports.

- Linux, like all versions of Unix presents its hardware devices as special files. The EXT2 file system and the Linux VFS (virtual file system) both implement device files as special types of inode. There are two types of device files: Character and block special files. The device drivers implement file semantics within the kernel itself: You can open them, close them and so on.

- When using Linux it is most important that you always shut the machine down properly. Don't turn it off without doing a shutdown. The act of shutting down writes any changes to your hard disk drive. If you turn off the computer without shutting down, you lose any changes to your files—and you might also lose part of your operating system.

VOCABULARY REVIEW

daemons	GNOME Panel	open source code
Disk Druid	info pages	virtual display
EXT2	man pages	Virtual File System
GNOME	mount point	XTerm

MULTIPLE CHOICE

Circle the answer that best applies:

1. The Linux man pages:
   A. refer the user to a specific page number in the Linux manual.
   B. provide a complete online description of each command, followed by all of the command options.
   C. were named after their creator, Humphrey Mandrake.
   D. None of the above.

2. In addition to the GNOME desktop environment, at startup the user can:
   A. select the AnotherLevel and Default desktop environments.
   B. select the Failsafe desktop environment.
   C. elect to log off the Linux system.
   D. All of the above.

3. You know that you have a second desktop area opened when:
   A. the words "a second desktop is open" appear at the top of your display.
   B. hash marks appear within a second pane in the desktop views area.
   C. circles appear in the desktop views indicators.
   D. the desktop views indicator flashes.

4. The command used to deselect and then remove a file system is:
   A. unmount
   B. dismount
   C. umount
   D. remove

5. To change the directory, key:
   A. chgdir
   B. change
   C. chdir
   D. cd

TRUE/FALSE

Circle T if the statement is true or F if it is false.

T F 1. cd root performs the same function as cd /root.

T F 2. To use Linux, you must pay royalties to Linus Torvalds.

T F 3. You can mount a hard drive wherever you want in the file system.

T F   4. Linux is considered a single-user operating system.

T F   5. A Linux distribution makes the Linux operating system available for free to anyone who wants it.

WRITTEN QUESTIONS

Write a brief answer to the following questions.

1. Explain the difference between a virtual console and a virtual desktop.

2. How do you access the Linux manual?

3. What is the kernel?

4. What does LILO stand for? What does it do?

5. What are some of the commands that you can use in an XTerm window and what can they do?

MATCHING

In the blank space match the command with its function.

___ 1. cd   **A.** list command

___ 2. md   **B.** print working directory

___ 3. pwd   **C.** copy command

___ 4. ls   **D.** make directory

___ 5. cp   **E.** change directory

CHAPTER 7 PROJECTS

PROJECT 1

1. Start the text editor "pico."

2. Create a new text file that lists the names of five of your friends and their phone numbers.

3. Save the new file as "myfile."

4. Use grep to locate one of your friends (search for the name) in "myfile."

5. Using the man pages, find out how you would send this job to print in 10 minutes using the AT utility.

6. Try using the AT utility again—this time setting the job to occur in a short amount of time.

PROJECT 2

1. From the GNOME Panel, launch the following applications—one in each of the four desktop areas.

   ■ The terminal emulation program in desktop area #1.

   ■ Netscape Communicator in desktop area #2.

   ■ The GNOME Help Browser in desktop area #3

   ■ The GNOME Configuration tool in desktop area #4.

2. Close each application.

CRITICAL THINKING

1. Name some of the major companies worldwide that now use Linux as their primary operating system. Why do you think they have switched from other commercial operating systems such as Windows NT and 98 to Linux?

2. Linux is developed under the GNU General Public License and its source code is freely available to everyone. How is it then, that companies and developers may charge money for the source code? Is this an ethical practice on their part?

GLOSSARY

A

ACU Automatic Client Update utility. This allows a network administrator to automatically ugrade software on a client computer the next time a user logs in.

ADB port Apple Desktop Bus. A serial, daisy-chainable port in older Macintosh computers used to connect keyboards, mice, and other input devices.

Administrator A person with special rights and privileges. This person has a better-than-average knowledge of computers. He or she runs, upgrades, and troubleshoots the network.

Alias A copy of the icon representing a pointer to an original file. Aliases have italicized text and a small bent arrow added to their icon.

Apple menu A menu, located in the upper-left corner of a Macintosh screen, that is always present and always contains the same items regardless of which program is running.

Application A program that does work or processes information. Different applications perform different tasks. Drawing programs create pictures, word processors create documents, and so on.

B

Booting up The initial startup procedure of a computer.

C

Cabling The physical wire used to carry the networking electrical impulses. It includes twisted-pair, coaxial, ThickNet, ThinNet, fiber-optic, and mixed-media cable.

Cathode-ray tube An electronic device that consists of a large vacuum tube with electron guns on one end and a display screen coated with phosphorus at the other. This technology is used for televisions and computer monitors; hence, monitors are sometimes called "CRTs."

CD Changes the directory.

Central processing unit The microprocessor that is the "brain" of a microcomputer. See *microprocessor.*

Click A mouse gesture whereby the user positions the mouse cursor over an object and then presses and releases the mouse button quickly. Used to select items on the screen.

Client workstation A computer that is less powerful than the server. It is used by common users to perform their daily tasks.

Clock cycle See *CPU cycle.*

Close box A small square button at the upper-left corner of a window, in the title bar, that closes the window when clicked (reduces it to its icon).

CLS Clears the screen.

Command key A key on Macintosh keyboards, often located next to the spacebar, with an open apple and "propeller" symbol. Used to perform keyboard shortcut commands. See *control key* and *option key.*

Command-line user interface An interface in which the user types a command to get the computer to do something.

Compression The coding of data to save storage space.

Container A method of organizing computer files. Usually called folders or subdirectories, among other things.

Container objects Containers are used to organize the network. Think of a container as a drawer in a filing cabinet.

Control key A key, usually located in the bottom corner of the keyboard, that allows the typing of control characters. It is also sometimes used as a command key. See *option key* and *command key.*

Copy Copying information (text, pictures, sounds, etc.) from a document to a temporary file (called the clipboard) for "pasting" somewhere else. See *paste.*

COPY Duplicates a file.

CP/M An early microcomputer operating system.

CPU Central processing unit. The microprocessor chip or card that is the main "brain" of the computer.

CPU cycle The amount of time required for the microprocessor to perform a single operation.

CRT See *cathode-ray tube*.

Cut Cutting information (text, pictures, sounds, etc.) from a document to a temporary file (called the clipboard) for "pasting" somewhere else. See *paste*.

D

Daemon A process that runs all the time in the background looking for certain events to happen.

DEL Deletes a file.

Desktop Generally, when people refer to the desktop they mean what is on the monitor. For all practical purposes treat this just as you would your desktop in your office.

Devices Physical components attached to your computer (examples: printer, modem, scanner, mouse).

DIR Displays a directory listing.

Disk A circular piece of plastic or metal coated with magnetic material, used for storing computer data. Also, the hardware device used to read from and write to a disk.

Disk Druid Program, like FDISK, that is used to format diskettes. It has a slightly friendlier interface than FDISK.

DISKCOPY Copies the contents of a disk.

Document A type of computer file that contains information. Documents are created and read by programs. Sometimes called a data file.

DOS Acronym for disk operating system. The generic term for early microcomputer operating systems. Especially used to refer to MS-DOS from Microsoft.

Double-click A mouse gesture whereby the user positions the mouse cursor over an object, then presses and releases the mouse button twice in quick succession. Used to open items on the screen.

Drag A mouse gesture whereby the user sets the starting position by moving the mouse cursor on the screen, then holds the mouse button down while moving the mouse. Used to select multiple items or to move items from one place to another.

E

Edit Opens the text editor to create files.

Ethernet Used to describe a type of networking. It is so common that it has become a de facto standard. You may not see any other type.

EXT2 The second extended file system (EXT2) was devised by Rémy Card as an extensible and powerful file system for Linux. It is the most successful file system so far in the Linux community and is the basis for all of the Linux distributions that are currently shipping.

Extended partition The partition that usually does not contain an operating system, but instead is divided into logical drives that you can name letters d–z. You can have up to 23 extended partitions.

Extensions Plug-ins or add-ons to the operating system to provide some new capability not originally intended. Often used to provide drivers for hardware added later.

F

FAT File allocation table.

FDDI Fiber Distributed Data Interface. This fiber-optic technology is a high-speed method of networking. It is composed of two concentric rings of fiber-optic cable. The transmission distance is measured in kilometers, as opposed to meters for other technologies. It is very expensive and therefore only used to connect large offices together, or in locations where high traffic necessitates it.

Finder The actual name of the user interface portion of MacOS.

Floppy disk 3.5-inch disk used to store data.

Folder An icon that looks like a folder. In actuality, it is a subdirectory on your hard drive. It is capable of holding other folders, icons, documents, programs, and files.

G

Gateway A computer used as a portal to everything outside of the network. All traffic is passed through this point on the network. Think of it as the only road off an island.

GNOME An acronym for GNU Network object model environment and is available in many languages for worldwide use. GNOME is a desktop environment written in X, which allows you to use and configure your computer easily.

GNOME Panel A configurable display at the bottom of the desktop in Linux that should remind you of the taskbar in Windows. It performs the same functions as the taskbar and more.

Graphical user interface An interface in which the user interacts with the computer through a screen pointing device (usually a mouse), with graphical representations of the files on the computer screen.

GUI Acronym for graphical user interface

H

Hard boot The powering down of your system by turning the power off and then back on.

Hard drive Also called "hard disk." It is the physical storage device for all data on your computer.

Hardware The physical parts of a computer, usually consisting of a box that contains the microprocessor, memory, and other components, a monitor, and attached devices.

Hardware compatibility list (HCL) A list available from Microsoft that shows which hardware devices are compatible with Windows NT Workstation.

HELP Displays help information on commands.

I

Icon Small picture that represents a file, disk, menu, option, or program.

Info pages Short for information pages. Part of the Linux help system.

IP Internet Protocol. The common language spoken by every machine on the Internet.

IPX Internet Protocol Extension. This is the language spoken by NetWare. It is the IP language with a few bits added. Think of IP as English and IPX as English with added slang.

K

Kernel The heart of an operating system. Usually used in reference to Unix, it is the part of the OS code that does not change between different kinds of hardware.

Keyboard A standard input device consisting of several rows of spring-loaded switches, each representing a letter of the alphabet, a number, or symbol

and so on, which users can press sequentially to input text into a computer. Modern keyboards are usually arranged in a QWERTY arrangement. See *QWERTY*.

L

Leaf objects Leaf objects contain information about the different components/computers on the network. Think of these as the file folders you put in a filing cabinet drawer.

Left-click The act of pressing the left mouse button once. The left mouse button is the default button for selecting an item or making an item active.

Left-drag The act of positioning the mouse pointer over an icon or option, pressing and holding down the left mouse button, and then moving the mouse to a new position. The icon will follow the mouse pointer. When the button is released, the icon is released and dropped to its new position.

Linux A version of Unix created by Linus Torvalds. Linux is unique because it is an "open source," which means that it is available for change by any programmer.

M

Macintosh A PC from Apple Computer. The first company to make a commercially viable GUI.

MacOS The Macintosh operating system from Apple Computer. See *Macintosh*.

Mainframe computer A large computer, originally handmade, built on a hardware frame (hence the name).

Man pages Short for manual pages. This is the Linux help system. By typing man and then a keyword you can receive help about the keyword.

MB An abbreviation for megabyte.

MD Makes a directory.

Media See *cabling*.

Menu bar The top edge of a Macintosh screen that has all the menus in it.

Menu-based user interface A computer user interface whereby the user selects options from a menu to get the computer to do something.

Microcomputer Early name for a personal computer. Usually built around a microprocessor such as the Intel 4004, 8008, 8086, or the Motorola 68000, etc.

Microprocessor A microscopic circuit on a small chip of silicon or similar material. A typical microchip consists of hundreds and thousands of transistors. Sometimes called the CPU, or central processing unit. See *central processing unit* and *microcomputer*.

Minicomputer Manufactured computers that are more powerful than microcomputers, but less powerful than mainframe computers.

Monitor A CRT (cathode-ray tube) or other display device connected to a computer to provide principle output.

MORE Argument that will display data one screen at a time.

Mount point The location where you can find the device or file system. The files of the mounted file system cover up the existing contents of the mounted directory.

Mouse keys Using mouse gestures in combination with control, option, shift, or command keys. The most common are shift-click (used to select multiple items on the screen) and control-click (used to replicate the function of the alternate mouse key; brings up pop-up contextual menus).

Mouse A motion-sensitive device whose actions are replicated on the computer screen; usually has one or more buttons to effect actions on the computer.

Multitasking The ability of a computer to appear to do more than one thing (run more than one program) at a time by sharing the memory and CPU.

N

NDS context This is the description of where you are in the NDS tree. Think of it as your street address.

NDS tree Novell Directory Services tree. This is the representation of how all the computers, printers, and so on are attached to the network. It looks like a tree with one computer, usually the corporate office, as the root, or control of the entire network.

NDS Novell Directory Services. This is Novell's method of keeping track of all the computers and other resources on the network.

NetWare A network scheme developed by Novell, Inc. It is an extension of IP, Internet Protocol. It was one of the first non-mainframe methods of creating large networks and connecting two or more networks into a wide area network, or WAN.

Network interface card Often referred to as NIC. This device provides an interface or access to the physical network. It allows the user to send and receive information across the network.

Network The connecting of two or more computers to share files or other services (such as printers).

NIC See *network interface card*.

NTFS New Technology File System.

O

Online This term is used to describe any device or software that is accessible by the computer. A printer is considered online if it is turned on and you can print to it. If it is turned off then the printer is offline.

Open source code Open source code means that the operating system code has no proprietary restrictions. Anyone may alter the code to meet his or her own needs without having to seek permission from the "owner."

Operating system A program that acts as an intermediary between the user or programs and the computer hardware.

Option key A key, often located next to the command key, with the word "Option" or "Alt" on it. Used to type additional characters from the keyboard. It is rarely used as a command key. See *control key* and *command key*.

OS See *operating system*.

P

Partition A logical division of a disk drive.

Paste Moving information (text, pictures, sounds, etc.) from a temporary file (called the Clipboard) to the position of the cursor in a program. See *copy* and *cut*.

PC Acronym for "Personal Computer." Originally a brand name from IBM. Now used generally for all microcomputers intended for personal use.

Permissions Authorizations allowing a user to access certain files and folders on another machine in the network.

Primary partition This is the partition on which the bootable operating system will reside. The bootable operating system is the one your system will always boot to first. You can only have one primary partition.

PRINT Allows the user to print in DOS.

Print server A dedicated computer or device that interfaces the printer to the network. It allows users to print from a remote location.

Printer A device that produces a hardcopy output of information, usually on paper.

Protocol A protocol is an agreed-upon format for exchanging information. It is very easy to pass the same information using different protocols. Various protocols have different strengths. Think of protocols as being like human languages.

Q

QWERTY The name of the standard arrangement of the keys on a keyboard. Named for the first six letters of the arrangement at the top left. See *keyboard*.

R

RAM Random access memory; the native workspace memory of a computer. Found in memory chips on the computer.

Rebuilding the desktop A technique for clearing out unneeded icons and performing other housekeeping duties for the operating system. It is done by holding the option and command keys down while the Macintosh is booting.

Registry A system file where all configuration changes to Windows NT are recorded.

REN Renames a file.

Resize button A small button located at the bottom-right corner of a window used to change the size of a window by dragging it.

Right-click The act of pressing the right mouse button. This causes a menu, which varies according to the item you clicked, to pop up. From there you can use the left mouse button to make your selection. The right mouse button also causes contextual help to appear.

Right-drag The act of positioning the mouse pointer over an icon, pressing and holding the right mouse button down, and then moving the mouse to a new position. The icon will follow the mouse pointer. Normally this causes a copy of the icon to be made at the new position. It can also create a shortcut. Depending on what item is being right-dragged, the end result may be different.

Router A device used to physically connect two or more networks together. It provides a high degree of security and traffic control. It is much more than simply twisting two wires together.

S

Scanner A device used to input graphics into a computer.

Scroll bar A graphic method for moving the contents of a window into the viewable area of the window. It usually consists of a gray bar with a small button in it that moves relative to the contents of the window. It also has arrow buttons to move the button smoothly through the gray bar (and hence, the window's contents through the viewable area of the window).

SCSI Small Computer System Interface. A way to connect high-speed devices to a computer.

Server A powerful computer that is not used directly by users on the network. It controls the network and holds common programs/data that need to be accessed by everyone. It also manages printer requests, mail, chat, and other functions of the network.

Soft boot Using Ctrl+Alt+Del to restart your system or using the reset button on the front of your computer system to do so.

Start button This button is in the lower-left corner of your monitor and is used to access all features of Windows NT and Windows 98. Using the mouse, you click on it. This causes a series of menus to be displayed. From there you can select any program or utility installed on your computer.

Start menu The menu used to access your favorites folder, documents, programs, files, and utilities and to shut down your computer.

Startup disk A floppy disk used to recover your system in the event of operating system failure.

System Folder The folder containing all the files (control panels, extensions, etc.) used by the operating system to function.

T

Tape A lengthy strip of plastic, usually coiled onto a spool and often inside a plastic case. The strip is coated with magnetic material. Tape is then used as a storage medium for computer data.

Taskbar A gray rectangular bar at the bottom of your desktop used to give quick access to programs, application windows, and system tools.

Terminal An early device for communicating with a mainframe or minicomputer. It usually consists of a keyboard and monitor, but has no CPU. Sometimes called a "dumb terminal" because of its lack of a CPU.

TIME Displays the current time.

Title bar The bar across the top of the window that displays the name of the program you are using.

Token ring The predecessor to FDDI. This older and slower technology is slowly fading away because of its high price tag. It consists of a ring of computers that communicate by passing a token around the ring. Only the computer with the token is allowed to speak. This is a similar idea to raising your hand in class before speaking. It has a high effiency rate, usually around 86%. The downside is that if one machine malfunctions, then the whole network stops working.

Trash An icon representing the delete function. Files can be deleted by dragging them to the Trash icon.

TYPE Allows the user to view the contents of a file without opening the file itself.

U

Unix An operating system that was initially used for larger minicomputers. See *Linux*.

USB port Universal System Bus; a high-speed, serial, daisy-chainable port in newer Macintosh computers, used to connect keyboards, mice, printers, and other input and output devices.

User Manager A system utility for creating and managing user accounts.

User A user is the ordinary person who uses a computer.

V

Virtual display Your computer has six different virtual consoles and as many virtual displays as you want. The two are slightly different. In hardware terms, the display is the actual monitor. In operating system terms, it is what you see on the screen. The display can have several virtual terminals. You start a virtual terminal by clicking on the icon of a monitor on your desktop. Each one acts like a console—as if it were a completely separate machine.

Virtual File System The Virtual File System (VFS) allows Linux to support many, often very different, file systems—each presenting a common software interface to the VFS. All of the details of the Linux file systems are translated by the software, so that all file systems appear identical to the rest of the Linux kernel and to programs running in the system. Linux's VFS layer allows you to transparently mount the different file systems at the same time. The Linux VFS is implemented so that access to its files is as fast and as efficient as possible.

Virtual memory A method that uses disk space to substitute for RAM when the latter is unavailable.

VLM Virtual Loadable Modules. These are software that is loadable on demand. They provide services and act as devices, but don't physically exist. VLMs are used primarily to translate information.

W

WAN Wide Area Network; two or more local area networks connected together. An example of this is connecting all the regional offices in a company to the main office. Each office has its own network, but all of them connected together form a WAN.

Windowshade A small square button in the upper-right corner of a window used to roll the window up into its title bar, or pull it down again.

Windows The brand name for several GUI operating systems from Microsoft.

Window The main functional object on the screen. A window contains icons that represent files, and has a title bar, close box, zoom box, and other controls to change its look and function.

X

XTerm (short for x terminal) is a terminal emulator, which makes your computer behave like a dumb terminal (a CRT combined with a keyboard that has no processing capabilities of its own). When working under X, the XTerm program allows the Linux user to execute shell commands. In addition to entering commands interactively, XTerm allows you to execute a batch script in the background that you created during an earlier XTerm session.

Z

Zoom box A small square button in the upper-right corner of a window used to toggle the size of the window.

Option (Alt) key combinations, 66 to 67, 246
organization (O) object, 184, 185
organizational unit (OU) object, 184, 185
output devices, 5, 6 to 7

P

package manager (Linux), 236
packet, 173
Paint accessory (Windows 95/98), 108
Palo Alto Research Center (PARC), 18
PARC. *See* Palo Alto Research Center.
parentdirectory (..), 43
parity, 187
partition, 25, 49, 99, 144, 165, 200, 203, 246
    logical, 201
    primary, 201, 246
password, 160
    changing, 147
    forgetting, 146
paste, 246
patch. *See* cabling.
pathname, 31
PC, 18, 246
PC-DOS, 24
PCI controller, 220
permissions, setting, 161, 162, 165, 246
PgDn key, 115
PgUp key, 115
pico text editor, 236
pipes, 157
pixel, 7
plain virtual window manager (pvwm), 210
plasma display, 7
platter, 10, 202
Plug and Play, 98, 144
point and click, 98, 104
polled mode, 187
Power PC chip, 55
power user group, 158, 165
PowerBook, 57
PRAM (permanent random access memory), resetting 89
Preferences file, deleting (MacOS), 89
Preferences folder, 86, 92
primary partition, 27, 28, 99
PRINT command (DOS), 39, 247
print server, 173, 229, 247
Print wizard, 136
printer, 7, 59, 247
    installing, 136, to 137, 186 to 188
    setting up in network, 185 to 188, 189
process, 232 to 233

program, 1, 7, 91
    icon for, 150
    adding and removing, 134 to 135
Programs menu (Windows 95/98), customizing, 128
prompt. *See* command prompt.
protocol, 172, 247
PSERVER program (NetWare), 186
Publish and Subscribe (MacOS), 84, 92
pwd command, 223

Q

queue, 230
Quick Launch toolbar (Windows 95/98), 99
QuickStart utility, 183
QuickTime, 75, 91
QWERTY keyboard, 247

R

RAM. *See* random access memory.
random access memory (RAM), 5, 9, 20, 55, 247
Read Me files, 91
Read permission, 161, 165
read-only memory (ROM), 5, 20
Recycle Bin, 122 to 123
Red Hat Linux, 195, 196, 199, 210, 239
reduced instruction set computing (RISC), 55
registry. *See* Windows registry.
remote access sessions, 143
REN (rename) command (DOS), 42, 247
resize button, 247
resource fork (MacOS), 87
resource management, 7 to 10, 20
restarting, 88
    from a CD-ROM, 89
    to Extension Manager, 89
Restore button (Windows 95/98), 108
Return key, 67
right-click, 70, 85, 92, 104, 115, 117, 119, 247
right-drag, 247
rights, assigning, 180
RISC. *See* reduced instruction set computing.
Ritchie, Dennis, 193
rm (remove file/directory) command, 226
rmdir (remove directory) command, 226
ROM. *See* read-only memory.
ROM disc, 55

root (directory), 31, 35, 37, 40, 115
    account, 204
    object, 183
    password, 204
router, 172, 173, 247
running state, 233

S

Sad Mac, 91
SAM database, 161, 165
ScanDisk, 45, 46, 129 to 130
SCANDISK command (DOS), 46
scanner, 6, 247
scheduling information state, 233
scheme (Windows 95/98), saving, 132
screen saver, changing (Windows 95/98), 131
screen settings (Windows 95/98), 132 to 133
ScreenTip, 149
scroll bars, 72, 108, 247
SCSI (small computer system interface), 55, 60, 220, 247
search, 11, 123 to 126
sector, 202
security, 160 to 162. *See also* Windows NT security.
security ID, 159
Security Reference Monitor, 162, 165
serial port, 59
server, 143, 157, 172, 173, 200, 247
services (drivers), choosing (MacOS), 75
sessions, 157
setup utility, 145 to 146, 165. *See also* installation.
share, 157
shared resource. *See* share.
Shares button, 157
shell, 2, 210
shell commands (Linux), 223 to 228
shift-click (MacOS), 64
shortcut, 70, 126 to 128, 150 to 151
    icon, 150
    keys, 74
    link, repairing, 127
    menus, 103
shutdown screen, 79
shutting down, 8, 107 , 155
SimpleText (MacOS), 91
SKY computer game, 16
Slackware Linux, 195
soft boot, 28, 101, 247
source, 39
speaker icon, 58
Special menu (MacOS), 79
speech recognition, 6